Refactoring
in Large
Software Projects

Refactoring in Large Software Projects

Martin Lippert

and

Stephen Roock

John Wiley & Sons, Ltd

3 1257 01750 2732

Copyright © 2006   John Wiley & Sons Ltd, The Atrium, Southern Gate, Chichester,
West Sussex PO19 8SQ, England

Telephone   (+44) 1243 779777

Email (for orders and customer service enquiries): cs-books@wiley.co.uk

Visit our Home Page on www.wiley.com

Other Wiley Editorial Offices

John Wiley & Sons Inc., 111 River Street, Hoboken, NJ 07030, USA

Jossey-Bass, 989 Market Street, San Francisco, CA 94103-1741, USA

Wiley-VCH Verlag GmbH, Boschstr. 12, D-69469 Weinheim, Germany

John Wiley & Sons Australia Ltd, 42 McDougall Street, Milton, Queensland 4064, Australia

John Wiley & Sons (Asia) Pte Ltd, 2 Clementi Loop #02-01, Jin Xing Distripark, Singapore 129809

John Wiley & Sons Canada Ltd, 22 Worcester Road, Etobicoke, Ontario, Canada M9W 1L1

Wiley also publishes its books in a variety of electronic formats. Some content that appears in print may not be available in electronic books.

Library of Congress Cataloging-in-Publication Data

Lippert, Martin.
   Refactoring in large software projects : performing complex restructurings successfully / Martin Lippert and Stephen Roock.
      p. cm.
   Includes bibliographical references and index.
   ISBN-13: 978-0-470-85892-9 (pbk. : alk. paper)
   ISBN-10: 0-470-85892-3 (pbk : alk. paper)
 1. Software refactoring. 2. Computer software--Development. I. Roock, Stephen. II. Title.
   QA76.76.R42L56 2005

                              2005028993

British Library Cataloguing in Publication Data

A catalogue record for this book is available from the British Library

ISBN-13 978-0-470-85892-9 (PB)
ISBN-10 0-470-85892-3 (PB)

Typeset in 10pt Sabon Roman by Laserwords Private Limited, Chennai, India
Printed and bound in Great Britain by Bell & Bain, Glasgow
This book is printed on acid-free paper responsibly manufactured from sustainable forestry in which at least two trees are planted for each one used for paper production.

Contents

1
Introduction

Once, software developers believed it was possible to create the technical software design for a comprehensive system completely, correctly and free of contradictions right at the beginning of a project. Many projects proved though that this ideal approach can hardly be realized. More often it causes significant problems.

Big Upfront Design

A typical example of this fact are those requirements that were either unknown or not taken into consideration at the beginning of a project and thus were not integrated into the original system design. Later on, integration of these disregarded requirements into the project is much more difficult. If the developers are lucky, the requirements will fit seamlessly into the existing system. However, this is rarely the case. So-called 'work-arounds' are needed. These enable developers to meet the requirements within the system, even though the actual software design is not suitable for such an approach.

One problem of these work-arounds is that they cause a gradual degeneration of the system design that leads to a *loss of structure*. The more work-arounds are built into the system, the more difficult it becomes to recognize and apply the original software design. Often developers describe such a system as 'historically grown.'

Loss of Structure

Today, many development methods have a different approach to software design. Especially agile development methods – most prominently *extreme programming* – no longer treat software design as a clearly and rigidly defined constant that is defined at the beginning of a development project. Instead, they assume that a software design emerges step by step during the development process. If it is continuously adapted and improved to meet present requirements, it is called *emergent design*. Design improvements become established as an important and independent activity during development and evolve into an integral part of this process. This activity is called *refactoring*.

Refactoring   First of all, refactoring means changing the internal structure of software to make it easier to read and modify without altering its observable behavior. Besides acknowledging this rather technical definition, many developers also associate a process-related aspect and a certain attitude with the refactoring term. In the context of extreme programming, refactoring means first and foremost an ongoing and repeated reflection about the software's structure and improving it in small increments.

Refactoring Catalogues   In his book on refactoring (Fowler, 1999), Martin Fowler gives much advice on how refactorings can be accomplished. In this book he refers to very basic modifications of an object-oriented system, like, for example, 'Rename Method' or 'Encapsulate Field.' For each of these very small refactorings he describes – besides other aspects – the 'mechanics' of a refactoring. The mechanics of a refactoring describe an exact sequence of very small steps necessary to perform the refactoring. Small increments ensure that the system remains operable at any given time. This procedure reduces the risk of introducing errors, created by unwanted side-effects, into the software during refactoring. In addition to the book, Martin Fowler's refactoring homepage provides a comprehensive list of refactorings.

Based on the refactorings depicted by Martin Fowler, Joshua Kerievsky (Kerievsky, 2004) identified further refactorings focusing on design patterns. These show how design patterns can be introduced into an existing system (or separated and removed from it), e.g. 'Introduce Observer' or 'Replace Constructor with Factory.' Kerievsky provides depictions of 'mechanics' similar to those of Fowler.

The descriptions of concrete refactorings, such as 'Rename Method' or 'Introduce Observer,' are very valuable for developers, because they demonstrate when and how such a refactoring can be accomplished. Today, many development environments support developers quite efficiently during those small refactorings.

1.1   Architecture Smells

Refactorings are often executed in response to code smells. A certain portion of the source code 'smells like a problem.' This is, for example, the case if the same code section occurs more than once in the system.

Besides smells on the code level, smells can also be identified on a higher level, e.g. if the defined interface of a subsystem has been circumvented. Since most people call this higher design level the architecture of a system, we call these smells *architecture smells*. Both kinds of smell refer to the design of the software, but on different levels. We will provide a catalogue of *architecture smells*; some of which call for larger restructuring measures.

1.2 Large Refactorings

Theoretically, we could continuously provide an optimal system structure via small refactorings, but in practice, when dealing with complex projects, this is not realistic. Even projects involving skilled developers with a lot of know-how occasionally require larger restructuring measures of the system – large refactorings. Ron Jeffries' experiences confirm this observation:

Our feeling is that if we could stick to our XP rules, we wouldn't need special taxes or special times to clean things up. But realistically, can you play our best game day in and day out?[1]

In his book, Fowler also explains the necessity of large refactorings, called *big refactorings* by him and Kent Beck. Various examples of such big refactorings can be found in his book, as well as on his refactoring website (http://www.refactoring.com/rejectedExample.pdf, Chapter 15: A Longer Example). In many object-oriented development projects it poses a big challenge to handle these large refactorings.

Large refactorings often take longer than a day and change significant parts of a system. These properties of large refactorings create a number of problems that the developers will have to deal with. Among others, we observed the following problems:

- Developers 'lose track' of large refactorings, because they are created over a long period, and this process is frequently interrupted. They remain incomplete. As a consequence, the software's structure is in worse shape than before the refactoring.
- If a refactoring influences large parts of the system, a high demand for merges is often the result. This situation occurs when a refactoring is supported by an IDE and many parts of the system are altered at once; or when a big refactoring is not broken down into smaller increments. Such high demand for merges quickly discourages the developers' use of large refactorings. Thus, much-needed design modifications will not be made.
- In many cases it is very difficult to foresee the consequences of single steps of large refactorings. Frequently during the execution of a large refactoring, developers realize that the separate increments cannot be carried out as planned. There is still no easy-to-handle means for dealing with such necessary changes of procedure.

---

[1] http://c2.com/cgi/wiki?TechnicalDebt.

■ Because of the previously described difficulties, large refactorings will often not take place parallel to the normal system development. Instead, the team puts the system's development process on hold for a certain period to focus solely on the large refactoring. This method of handling large refactorings does actually have more in common with re-engineering than with refactoring. Also, many projects do not allow for temporary interruptions of development processes.

These are the problems we wish to discuss in Chapter 4. Our attention will center on the following questions:

■ How can large refactorings be broken down into smaller increments? Can large refactorings be assembled from small refactorings?
■ How can large refactorings be planned? How can existing refactoring plans be adapted when it becomes clear that they cannot be realized as planned? How can one obtain undo-functionality for large refactorings during the actual refactoring process?[2]
■ How long can/may large refactorings take? How can I further proceed to develop (add functionalities to) the system during the execution of a large refactoring? How can one make sure that the development process does not counteract the refactorings?
■ How can plans for large refactorings be integrated into the development process? What type of development process is suitable here? Which prerequisites must the development process meet? How can/must/should I document/communicate the present stage of a large refactoring?

1.3   Refactoring and Databases

Today, there is hardly an application system in existence that works without a (most common: relational) database to store the objects of an application. If the storage structure of a class, or the interaction of classes within the system is changed, this often means the database structures as well as data present in the database need to be accommodated too. Modifications of the database structure and the stored data have the reputation of being a complex and tedious task.

Many small or large refactorings can lead to frequent modifications of the system's classes. Since we do not expect the design to be

---

[2]   Specialized support for undo and redo might become important if larger refactorings are performed in parallel to normal system development. A more detailed discussion of this can be found in Chapter 4.

established at the beginning of development, the database schema cannot be laid out at the project start. On the one hand this means that refactorings of the program code can affect the database structures. The structures need to be refactored together with the code. On the other hand it may be necessary to additionally enhance the database schemata themselves and thus refactor them.

In this book we will show how refactorings affect a system's connection with a database.

1.4 Refactoring and Published APIs

Refactorings do not alter the observable behavior of software. The software is always treated as a whole. If, for example, we rename a method in a Java system, all occurrences of the original name in that system must be changed too.

Normally it is no problem to identify all references to a method name in a system and adjust them accordingly. Many development environments will do this automatically. The simple renaming of a method will become difficult though if a system cannot be considered as a whole. Typically this is the case when a system provides an API that is also used by other systems. Such an API is also called a 'published API' as opposed to a 'public API.'

If a method, which is externally visible through a system's published API, is renamed, the IDE or the developer cannot adapt all existing references for this method, because a number of these references will lie within those systems that build on the published API.

As we can see, published APIs constitute a problem for an aggressive refactoring approach. In many cases this means that a modification of published APIs will be completely prohibited (or only be allowed to a very limited extent). As a result, not all refactorings of a system can be carried out, since some of them would alter the published API.

In this book we will address these problems and describe methods that will allow developers to integrate published APIs into their refactorings. At the same time we will aim to permit *merciless refactoring*, even if this affects published APIs.

1.5 Recommended Reading

Chapter 2 provides a brief introduction to the refactoring topic. Those readers who already have some practical experience with refactorings can skip this chapter.

Chapters 3 and 4 should be considered and read as a unit. They constitute the book's core.

Chapters 5, 6 and 7 can be read independently from each other. Developers who have experience working on large refactorings in projects will understand Chapters 5 and 6 without having read Chapters 2 to 4.

It is recommended that you read Chapter 3 before you start reading Chapter 7.

1.6   For Whom Was this Book Written?

This book primarily targets developers who have had some first experiences with refactorings and are familiar with the concepts Martin Fowler presents in his book. For all others there is a brief introduction to the topic at the opening of the book.

1.7   The Background of this Book

The book conveys experiences with specific refactoring situations and offers readers a variety of tips as well as assistance for how to use these refactorings in their own development projects.

The book is in part based on our own development project experiences, but also to a large extent on discussions with other developers, which took place on mailing lists, but also at conferences or workshops.

Acknowledgments

Repeatedly we discussed our problems and insights with other people and tested them in projects. Therefore we would like to thank all those who supported us, who participated in discussions and provided valuable ideas and suggestions. Our special thanks go to:

- The employees and partners of it-wps GmbH (now C1-WPS GmbH) for their committed collaboration on a number of projects.
- Walter Bischofberger and Henning Wolf, whose work with the *Sotograph* generated important input for Chapter 3. They also read early texts for this book and gave us much appreciated feedback.
- Marcel Bennicke has analyzed Eclipse with the Sotograph and allowed us to publish the results. You will find them in Chapter 3.
- The participants of the Workshop on Large Refactorings at the OT 2003 Conference. During our discussion, they relayed important and very interesting experiences, which further motivated us to research this topic.

A number of authors have contributed their own articles to this book: Walter Bischofberger, Sven Gorts, Berrin Ileri, Dierk König, Klaus Marquardt, Jens Uwe Pipka, Markus Völter and Henning Wolf.

We would like to thank the following persons (in alphabetical order) for their input regarding earlier drafts of this book as well as for their constructive criticism: Walter Bischofberger, Christoph Kögl, Claus Lewerentz, Klaus Marquardt, Torsten Mumme, Jens Uwe Pipka, Joachim Sauer, Bruno Schaeffer, Axel Schmolitzky, Kurt Schneider, Marco Schulz and Robert Wenner. Special thanks go to Sven Gorts who provided a huge amount of feedback for the translated version of the book.

References and Further Reading

Brant, J. & Roberts, D. *Smalltalk Refactoring Browser.* http://st-www.cs.uiuc.edu/~brant/RefactoringBrowser. The first tool to support refactorings. It enabled developers to realize many automated refactorings in Smalltalk and served as a blueprint for many integrated development environments where refactoring-support was pivotal.

Fowler, M. 1999. *Refactoring – Improving the Design of Existing Code.* Addison-Wesley. The standard work in refactoring. It covers the fundamental refactoring methods and is a standard tool for every developer.

Kerievsky, J. 2004. *Refactoring to Patterns.* Addison-Wesley Signature Series. In this book Joshua Kerievsky addresses the question of how patterns can be inserted into an OO system step by step. The book is a consequent continuation of Fowler (1999).

Opdyke, W.F. 1992. *Refactoring Object-Oriented Frameworks* Ph.D. thesis, University of Illinois at Urbana-Champaign. The first comprehensive work dealing with refactoring. It focuses on refactoring to push the development of frameworks.

Roberts, D.B. 1999. *Practical Analysis for Refactoring*, Ph.D. thesis, University of Illinois at Urbana-Champaign. This work is about the practical application of refactorings and analyzes how refactorings can be automated through the use of appropriate development tools. The implementation of the Smalltalk Refactoring Browser constitutes the basis of this work.

Wake, W.C. 2003. *Refactoring Workbook.* Addison-Wesley. This book contains many practical tips on how refactorings can be handled. It can also be used as a workbook for simple refactoring.

http://www.refactoring.com, 2004. A site created by Martin Fowler that offers a collection of refactorings. Here, you will also find the refactorings from Fowler (1999).

2
Refactoring – An Overview

This chapter provides an overview of the refactoring topic. To this end, we will first address the basic idea behind agile development methods, the idea that software is designed in a stepwise process (*Emergent Design*). This view is in opposition to the classic demand to create the entire software design prior to programming (*Big Design Upfront*).

Refactoring is the main instrument used in a step-by-step design process. A brief introduction of the basics will deal with the questions of when and how refactorings should be carried out. Then we will proceed to look at the relationship between refactorings and tests and discuss how modern refactoring tools are changing the present refactoring practice.

2.1   Emergent Design

The classic approach to software design is to come up with a complete design at the beginning of a project. There follows a mostly exact implementation of this design. People think of design as something static throughout the project. However, in recent years it has become clear that this procedure is rarely feasible. To keep the design of software in a healthy state over a longer period, it is necessary to continuously improve it. Otherwise, the software system will age, making it increasingly difficult to realize modifications. At some point, no developer will dare change the running system.

But if developers improve the system design to meet current software requirements, the ageing process can be stopped and even reversed. In time, the software design can be improved. People start to consider design as something dynamic rather than static. Refactoring is one important technique to help developers improve the design.

2.1.1   Developing Software Is a Learning Process

For modern, evolutionary and iterative development processes, developers assume that software development is a learning process. Whereas research results in this field strongly emphasize that it is a learning process for *all* those involved in a project, we will focus on the system's developers here.

The longer a project progresses, the more developers will learn about its requirements and the suitable software design. While some design choices made in the course of the project will prove beneficial and correct, others will turn out to be wrong or awkward. The reason being that there is no such thing as a universal or best design for software.

During recent years, new approaches in the context of object-orientation have been researched as well, and new findings made regarding how certain design problems can be solved elegantly. At the same time, a software design is always created for a specific application type; depending on both the context in which the application is set and on the tasks it shall fulfill. If these factors change in the course of a project (and for evolutionary and iterative development processes it is assumed they do), the design must inevitably be adapted.

Opinions regarding software design and design modifications have changed due to these findings: design changes are no longer considered a necessary evil or proof of mistakes; they merely document that software is able to meet the demands of changed prerequisites and will do so.

2.1.2   No Design, Simple Design, Emergent Design

If you consequently follow this train of thought, it implies that the developers don't need to present a precise idea of the design for the whole application at the beginning of a development project. Instead, they should draft a rough design for the entire system, and a detailed design for the portion of the system which is currently in development. They should always make design adjustments and thus improve it. The application's design will then evolve gradually.

One important prerequisite for an emerging design is that it is continuously adapted to the changing conditions. Developers should not ignore recognized weaknesses in the system's design, i.e. code smells. It is common knowledge that the longer a smell exists in the system, the more difficult it will eventually become to eliminate. In a worst-case scenario this could mean that the developers do not refactor at all during development, but execute a redesign of the system at the end of a release cycle instead. There are a number of reasons why ignored smells become worse over time:

▢ Code smells are duplicated over time. This can happen because developers copy and paste the smelly code parts, accidentally taking the smelly code as a blueprint for how to solve some problem or for similar reasons.

▢ Smelly code parts become more important. Because the appropriate code parts become more important over time, more and more references to this smelly code appear. Refactoring this code would mean having to adapt more and more referring code.

▢ Smelly code creates the need to implement work-arounds. The more work-arounds exist, the worse the design becomes.

With the ongoing refactoring of the source code, we choose to take the opposite route: refactoring and design will become parts of the daily development work. This does not mean that less designing takes place. The efforts are merely distributed more evenly over the whole period of the development process. This approach has an important advantage: having refactoring integrated as part of the daily work allows the team to experience the gains of these small refactoring increments immediately.

2.2   What Does Refactoring Mean?

Today refactoring is an integral part of many development projects. It is one of the tools a developer uses, just like a suitable programming language or an integrated development environment.

Agile Methods and Refactoring

Refactoring means improving the design[1] of software without altering its observable behavior. The developers do not add any new features during a refactoring, i.e. they don't do any bug fixes or change anything about the software that would be detected by the software user. Instead, only the internal structure – the technological design of the software – is changed.

Creating a design is a challenging task. Besides comprehensive experience in software systems design, the developers first of all need to know precisely the respective software system's tasks and requirements to create a good design. Often it is not feasible to determine all requirements in advance, because:

▢ Too much time passes before programming begins and the software can be utilized.

---

[1]   Design refers here exclusively to the software-technological design of software, that is, its inner structure. It does not refer to the visual design of the user interface.

- The requirements are changing in the course of the project.
- Misunderstandings arise, which will only be recognized and eliminated after the first couple of implementations.

In modern development processes, the project participants even act on the premise that the project requirements will change during each iteration, that new ones will emerge and old ones might be eradicated altogether.

Changing requirements are one reason why changing the design becomes important to keep the design up-to-date and healthy. In addition to that, the design might also be unhealthy because of forgotten refactorings in the past or simply because the team hasn't chosen a good design solution for the given problem in the past.

As a result developers are forced to adapt the software design again and again – through refactorings. This is the only way to keep the software modifiable – 'soft' indeed. One might say that the software's aging is thus prevented.

2.2.1   An Example

An example[2] will illustrate the underlying idea of the refactoring term. We developed a class Movie for a video store's rental system:

```
public class Movie {
  static final double BASE_PRICE = 2.00; // Euro
  static final double PRICE_PER_DAY = 1.75; // Euro
  static final int DAYS_DISCOUNTED = 2;

  public static double getCharge(int daysRented) {
    double result = BASE_PRICE;
    if (daysRented > DAYS_DISCOUNTED) {
      result += (daysRented - DAYS_DISCOUNTED) *
            PRICE_PER_DAY;
    }
    return result;
  }
}
```

Because there are various places in the system dealing with amounts, these shall be calculated via a class of their own, labeled Euro, from now on. The new Euro class ensures that amounts of money are correctly calculated, that they always have two decimal places, and developers will know that the amounts are calculated in the Euro currency. We introduce this new class and replace the constants of the class Movie.

---

[2]   This example is taken from Westphal (2005).

```
public class Movie {
  static final Euro BASE_PRICE = new Euro(2.00);
  static final Euro PRICE_PER_DAY = new Euro(1.75);
  static final int DAYS_DISCOUNTED = 2;

  public static double getCharge(int daysRented) {
    Euro result = BASE_PRICE;
    if (daysRented > DAYS_DISCOUNTED) {
      int additionalDays = daysRented - DAYS_DISCOUNTED;
      result = result.plus(
              PRICE_PER_DAY.times(additionalDays));
    }
    return result.getAmount();
  }
}
```

Therefore, at first, the new class Euro will only be used in the internal implementation of the class Movie. Consequently, Movie will not give out the amount as double, but directly as Euro:

```
public class Movie {
  static final Euro BASE_PRICE = new Euro(2.00);
  static final Euro PRICE_PER_DAY = new Euro(1.75);
  static final int DAYS_DISCOUNTED = 2;

  public static Euro getCharge(int daysRented) {
    Euro result = BASE_PRICE;
    if (daysRented > DAYS_DISCOUNTED) {
      int additionalDays = daysRented - DAYS_DISCOUNTED;
      result = result.plus(
              PRICE_PER_DAY.times(additionalDays));
    }
    return result;
  }
}
```

Unfortunately this modification leads to compile errors, because the clients of the Movie class for getCharge will continue to expect the return type double. Within a large system, this can create hundreds or even thousands of compile errors at once. In order to make the refactoring process as pain- and risk-free as possible, it should be realized in small increments

Thus we will make sure that our changes of the class Movie are carried out without rendering all client classes invalid. An often-used method to accomplish this is:

1. Extract the complete method body of getCharge into a new getEuroCharge method. First, this new method will receive the same signature as the old method.

2. Change the signature of the new method to return Euro instead of double and adapt the implementation of the old method to convert the result of the new method into a double return value of its own.

```java
public class Movie {
  static final Euro BASE_PRICE = new Euro(2.00);
  static final Euro PRICE_PER_DAY = new Euro(1.75);
  static final int DAYS_DISCOUNTED = 2;

  public static Euro getEuroCharge(int daysRented) {
    Euro result = BASE_PRICE;
    if (daysRented > DAYS_DISCOUNTED) {
      int additionalDays = daysRented - DAYS_DISCOUNTED;
      result = result.plus(
              PRICE_PER_DAY.times(additionalDays));
    }
    return result;
  }

  /**
   * @deprecated
   */
  public static double getCharge(int daysRented) {
    return getEuroCharge(daysRented).getAmount();
  }
}
```

Now we have two methods with different names and a different return type that serve almost the same purpose. The compiler relays warnings to all clients who use getCharge, providing us with a to-do list for the conversion of the clients. Once all clients are using getEuroCharge, getCharge can be deleted from Movie. Using automated refactoring to support the old method can also be inlined automatically. This would automatically adapt all invocations of the old method to use the new one.

If necessary, the method getEuroCharge can subsequently be renamed getCharge, either via method duplication or – much easier – with the aid of the development environment's refactoring support.

2.2.2   Refactoring Categories

Refactorings can concern various parts of a software system. In his book *Refactorings*, Fowler discriminates the following categories:

1. *Composing methods.* These refactorings serve restructurings at the method level. Examples of refactorings from this group are: *Extract Method*, *Inline Temp* or *Replace Temp with Query*.
2. *Moving features between objects.* These refactorings support the moving of methods and fields between classes. Among them,

refactorings like *Move Method*, *Extract Class* or *Remove Middle Man* can be found.

3. *Organizing data.* These refactorings restructure the data organization. Examples are: *Self-Encapsulate Field*, *Replace Type Code with Class* or *Replace Array with Object*.

4. *Simplifying conditional expressions.* These refactorings simplify conditional expressions, such as *Introduce Null Object* or *Decompose Conditional*.

5. *Making method calls simpler.* These refactorings simplify method calls, such as *Rename Method*, *Add Parameter* or *Replace Error Code with Exception*.

6. *Dealing with generalization.* These refactorings help to organize inheritance hierarchies, such as *Pull Up Field*, *Extract Interface* or *Form Template Method*.

For many refactorings, a reverse refactoring exists. For instance, a new method can be extracted if an existing method seems to be too long (*Extract Method*). On the other hand, a method can be dissolved if it has become obsolete (*Inline Method*). A similar strategy exists at the class level (*Extract Class*, *Inline Class*) or inside inheritance hierarchies (*Pull Up Field/Method*, *Push Down Field/Method*).

2.2.3   Observable Behavior

If developers carry out a refactoring and thus change the software's structure, the software's observable behavior should not change – one could also say that refactorings do alter a program's syntax, but not its semantics.

Refactorings Do Not Change Software's Observable Behavior

When developers carry out a refactoring and thus modify software's structure, its observable behavior should not change. Opinions regarding interpretation of the term 'observable' vary though. Strictly speaking, each single refactoring influences a system's dynamic behavior, but usually these changes are merely marginal. The difference would be measurable, but normally go unnoticed by the system user. A run-time change in the tenth-of-a-second range would be considered 'not observable' in most applications.

The question of what exactly observable behavior is cannot be answered independently from the system and its application context. Pragmatically, one can settle for the definition that observable behavior has changed when the system user notices it. In other words: a refactoring may change any behavior that is not explicitly required by the software.

2.2.4   When Is a Refactoring Carried Out?

Refactorings are not an end in themselves, but always aim at eliminating a weakness in design. Weaknesses are present when the existing system structure hampers or even prevents modifications. Such weaknesses are also referred to as *badsmelling code* – so-called *code smells*.

A code smell can for example be a long and complex method in a class, a cyclical uses relation between two classes, or a parallel inheritance hierarchy. For a more comprehensive listing and depiction of common *bad smells*, see Fowler (1999). Often developers will encounter code smells during their daily work – more specifically whenever the system refuses to accept a modification.

Most code smells can be cured with the appropriate refactoring. A method that is too long, for instance, can be broken down into many smaller methods with the refactoring *Extract Method*.

When developers detect a code smell, it can be eliminated with the aid of a refactoring at various stages of the project:

- Before implementing a new feature, the developers analyze the code and debate how this new feature can be realized. It is possible that the new feature will integrate badly with the existing design, or not at all. In this case, in a first step refactoring must be used to rearrange the design to fit the new feature, followed by the developers' incorporation of it in the software.
- After a new feature has painfully been implemented into the existing design, the developers notice that the design no longer meets the software's requirements. Using suitable refactorings, the developers can continue to improve the software design until it meets the required functional range.

In many cases both methods are used, so that the following programming mini-cycle is created:

1. Cleaning up the code smells that prevents implementation of the new requirements – with refactorings.
2. Implementation of the changes. If this turns out to be a complex task, refactorings will be used during implementation.
3. Cleaning up the new code – of course with refactorings.

2.2.5   How Is a Refactoring Carried Out?

Refactorings will alter executable software. This always implies a risk, because there is the chance that new errors will find their way into the software. Therefore two axioms, which should be observed for refactorings, have been established:

- Refactorings are always to be broken down into small iterations that constitute complete and testable entities.
- Refactorings must only take place after the required automated unit or acceptance tests have been conducted. With these tests developers check if the software displays the same behavior as it did prior to refactoring.

Of course tests can only inspire some level of confidence (and do not serve as a proof of correctness) that the behavior of the system hasn't changed.

While we are going to discuss the second axiom in greater detail later in this chapter, we will now deal with the first axiom, which states that refactorings should be broken down into small iterations.

Newcomers to refactorings show a tendency to bundle many small restructurings and implement them in a single, big step. Instead of dissecting only one method at a time, a superclass is created simultaneously, some parameters are complemented, a float value is packed into a value object, and two other classes are combined. Quite frequently developers get lost in the growing jungle of structural changes. The result is a system that will not be executable for a long period and which is difficult to get running again. Often new errors will sneak into the software. Due to the number of parallel introduced modifications, they are easily overlooked. As a result, the behavior of the software is broken and the refactoring has failed.

But if a refactoring is executed step by step, significantly smaller changes of the system can be committed back to the code repository, each of which contributes to a fully functional system. The risk of introducing new errors into the software will clearly be reduced, because the single alterations are straightforward and separately testable. Also, the risk of merge conflicts, because other developers have changed the same classes, is reduced.

Even a seemingly simple refactoring has the potential to influence substantial parts of a system. If, for instance, the developers rename a method, one of the consequences might be that substantial parts of the program can no longer be compiled. If the refactoring is carried out in one big step, the developers will spend a relatively long time finishing it – at least as long as they don't have a tool to support them. Also, the danger of making mistakes increases.

It is not always easy to break down a refactoring into small increments. At first sight, the renaming of a method seems to resist deconstruction. Once the method has been renamed, all references must be changed as well. In his book, Martin Fowler assigns so-called 'mechanics' to each refactoring (Fowler, 1999). They describe what steps are to be taken to execute a refactoring. For example, to rename a method, the developer could proceed as follows:[3]

1. Create a new method with a new name and copy the implementation from the old method into the new method.
2. Compile.
3. Change the old method's implementation so that it calls the new method.
4. Compile and test.
5. Find all references to the old method and step-by-step change them into the new method. Compile and test after each modification.
6. Remove the old method.
7. Compile and test the system.

These mechanics show that even the renaming of a method can be carried out in at least four separate steps (1, 3, 5, 6). After each step, the system can be compiled and tested. Even if the method is used in many places in the system, the developers can always check in modified versions of the source code into the shared repository. The step-by-step procedure as well as the tests guarantee that the system will remain functional at any given time.

Although today the renaming of a method is done automatically by many development environments, and thus is a job that a developer can finish within a few seconds (we will address this issue in a later section of this chapter), this example shows that in principle it is possible and useful to break down refactorings into many small increments.

Martin Fowler's book on refactoring provides the respective mechanics for the refactorings listed in his book. On the one hand they can serve as instructions for refactorings, on the other hand they offer ideas for how refactorings can basically be broken down into small increments. Practice has proven that all refactorings can be treated in this way, even if it seems impossible at first sight.

2.2.6   'Detours'

Breaking down refactorings into small increments is no trivial task. Let's have another look at the example from the previous section: the old method continues to exist, while the new method has already been implemented. Only when all references to the old method have been

---

[3]   This is a slightly simplified version of the mechanics used by Fowler (1999).

replaced by references to the new method, will the old method be removed. In this way the old method serves as a kind of detour. The entire system stays functional, although parts of the code have not yet been adapted for the new method.

Such detours are a typical characteristic of mechanics for refactorings. The comparison with road construction is not too far-fetched: here too, detours will be created to enable traffic to flow in spite of the ongoing construction work.

For the example above this means that the old method no longer contains implementations of its own, but calls the method with the new name instead.

During a refactoring, detours will temporarily make the system more complex. In the example above two methods for the same task exist simultaneously during the refactoring process. Only after all references to the old method have been modified, will the old method be deleted and the desired structure be realized. Therefore it is of the utmost importance to complete refactorings and conduct only a few refactorings at the same time. If these rules are not observed, the system's structure will deteriorate due to the many remaining detours.

2.2.7   Refactoring Catalogues

Like for design patterns, for refactorings an attempt was made to find and write down universal descriptions and instructions, which eventually became refactoring catalogues. These catalogues describe a number of essential refactorings, each with a brief explanation of when the respective refactoring should be used, and how it can be realized.

The standard catalogue for refactorings can be found in Fowler (1999). This catalogue describes in detail 72 refactorings for the restructuring of object-oriented constructs. Supplementing the book, Martin Fowler has put up an online catalogue with an extended list of refactorings on his refactoring website (http://www.refactoring.com/).

While all the refactorings depicted by Martin Fowler in his book focus on basic object-oriented concepts, Joshua Kerievsky has assembled a catalogue of pattern-based refactorings (Kerievsky, 2003). The refactorings in his catalogue are, for example, for adding an observer pattern (*Replace Hard-Coded Notifications with Observer*) or a composite (*Replace Implicit Tree with Composite*).

2.2.8   Practical Experience and Advice

▪ Read Martin Fowler's refactoring book completely and keep on using it as a reference. It contains many tips and ideas, a comprehensive refactoring catalogue, and it shows how refactorings can be broken down into small increments.

▪ Be open to the practice of executing refactorings in small steps. Admonish yourself again and again to follow the small steps and check those small changes regularly.

▪ Even if it appears too difficult or not feasible at all to break down each refactoring into small increments: go ahead and try it!

▪ If you fail to break down a refactoring, carry out a review afterwards. After refactoring you will know how you did it, which will quite often make you realize how you could have broken it down.

▪ Practice proves that one can always come up with small steps. One of the underlying ideas is to build a detour first and then tear up the road. This also implies that in the beginning the system will become a bit more complex. Therefore refactorings should always be completed. Never let refactorings drag on over a long period.

2.3   The Role of Tests

Automated tests play a significant role in refactoring. They serve to check again and again if the entire system works exactly as it did before single steps of a refactoring or a complete refactoring have been executed. This security measure ensures that developers run a much lower risk of introducing new errors into the software.

Of course this only works as long as the refactoring does not alter the interface of a class. As soon as the interface of a class is modified as part of a refactoring, the tests need to be adapted to the modified interface. This raises the question of how the tests can function as a safety net if we have to manipulate them ourselves.

There are two different approaches to dealing with tests during a refactoring: either the developers conduct the actual refactoring first and then customize the tests (*Code-First Refactoring*), or the tests are modified prior to the actual refactoring process (*Test-First Refactoring*).

2.3.1   Code-First Refactoring

For code-driven refactoring, the developers will carry out the refactoring and use the still unchanged tests as a safety net. In the course of the refactoring the tests are customized to fit the new code structure.

For renaming methods this means: as long as the old method still exists, old tests of this class can be carried out without requiring modifications. During the refactoring process the old test class can be fitted to the new method. This must happen before the old method is deleted from the class.

Detours are beneficial during test procedures: they ensure that one can continue to use the old test classes, but when the detours have been removed, the tests must be adapted to match the new structure as well.

2.3.2   Test-First Refactoring

Alternatively the fundamental idea behind test-driven development can also be applied to refactoring.

In test-driven development the developers first write the test, followed by implementation of the class, until the test turns out to be successful. If we apply this idea to refactoring tasks, we will arrive at test-first refactoring: the developers will first change the tests and carry out the refactoring afterwards. This will be done until the modified tests are running successfully. Here the tests serve as a kind of 'target' for the refactoring.

Whereas developers will test a new or altered functionality during 'normal' test-driven development, followed by its implementation, they will focus on the structure of the code during test-driven refactoring. If, for example, a too long method is broken down, the test for the new, extracted method will be implemented first. On this basis, the developers will modify the original method and extract the new method. The already modified test class enables them to immediately test the old as well as the new method.

Test-driven refactoring has the same advantages we can also witness during test-driven programming: the new code structure is designed and implemented with its exemplary use (for testing) in mind, while for the new structure a test is readily available, etc.

2.3.3   Practical Application: A Combination of Both Approaches

In practice, both approaches will rarely occur by themselves, i.e. isolated. In most cases, developers will combine the two procedures.

For renaming methods, for instance, first a test for the new method is implemented within the existing test. This is accomplished by copying the test for the old method and changing the method used accordingly. Afterwards, the new method can be added to the code, and one can follow the mechanics described above. Finally, the old method is deleted together with the test for the old method.

Even if a refactoring is automated completely through its development environment (e.g. *Rename Method*), both approaches will be combined. The development environment makes sure that both tests as well as tested code are modified simultaneously.

2.3.4   Dependent Classes

In both cases, the test classes of dependent classes function as an additional safety net.

Let's have a look at the example of the renamed method: the class's clients will first call the old method. The clients' test classes check indirectly if the old method is still working. Step by step, all clients are adapted to the new method. Since these modifications only affect the implementation details of the clients, the clients' test classes don't have to be changed. They can also be used as a safeguard for the clients' modified versions. Thus the developers can automatically check if they made a mistake when they manipulated the clients.

This procedure will only work as long as the dependent classes don't use any Mock, Stub or Dummy objects. In that case, integration tests must be utilized.

2.3.5   Refactoring of Tests

Test classes also need to be refactored from time to time. They are prone to the same code smells that we might 'scent' in the application's normal code. For 'normal' refactorings we used the test classes as safety nets to prevent the introduction of any new errors into the software. What can serve as our safety net though if we are going to refactor the tests themselves? After all, here too we can make mistakes.

The answer is simple: the class to be tested will serve as our safety net. We proceed on the assumption that the test class ran successfully prior to refactoring. If a test within the test class fails after the test class has been refactored, an error must have been made during refactoring (or we have found a new error in the class to be tested).

In addition, we can use test coverage tools (e.g. JCoverage, Clover) to check test coverage before and after refactoring. However, it is only possible in part to let the test coverage tools check the same functionality after refactoring as before, and it requires a lot of tweaking. This is because such testing simply isn't the primary purpose of test coverage tools.

2.4   Tools Support for Refactorings

Refactoring tasks can be supported effectively through the use of suitable refactoring tools. The first tool specifically for refactoring was the *Smalltalk Refactoring Browser*, developed by John Brant and Don Roberts at the University of Illinois at Urbana Champaign. With this tool, many fundamental refactorings can be carried out automatically.

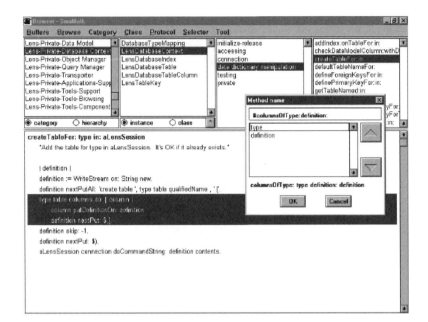

Fig. 2-1
Smalltalk Refactoring
Browser

The refactoring browser for Smalltalk (see Figure 2-1) offers the option of renaming a class, for example. If the developer assigns a new name to a class with the aid of this function, all references will be automatically updated to match the new class name. The developer no longer needs to manually update clients of the respective class. The same can be done for renaming methods. The refactoring browser also enables the extraction of a method. To achieve this, the developer only needs to highlight the code section that shall be extracted and assign a name to the extracted method. The code will then automatically be copied into a new method with the assigned name and replaced by a call in the original method. Also, the refactoring browser automatically determines which parameters and return values are required by the new method.[4]

The refactoring browser for Smalltalk has significantly changed the thinking about and work with refactorings. In the meantime, many integrated development environments have started to offer similar functionalities. Especially current Java-IDEs, like IntelliJ IDEA or Eclipse (see Figure 2-2), offer powerful refactoring support. Their implementations have long surpassed the original refactoring browser for Smalltalk.

---

[4]   The Smalltalk refactoring browser also supports a variety of other refactorings. We only introduce a few of them to illustrate the principal handling of this tool.

Fig. 2-2
The Refactoring Menu
of Eclipse

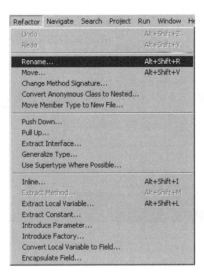

It is interesting to observe how this tool support has changed the work with refactorings. Renaming a class, an interface, or an operation in the common IDEs is a matter of a few seconds. Just by pressing a couple of keys, the old name will be replaced in the entire system. The same is true for converting an expression into local variable, for example (see Figure 2-3).

Tool support has advanced to the point of even correcting references to the respective name in source code comments or other files (such as XML files). However, this will only work with files that possess clearly defined semantics that are known to the refactoring tool. For a refactoring tool this is the only way of finding out if, for instance, a certain type is referenced or not. For JSP files (JavaServer Pages), for example, this can easily be done, because the semantics of the embedded source code are clearly defined. For an XML file it will be more difficult: here the IDE can only conduct a text search to find out if a certain type is referenced. If the type is not fully qualified (with complete package identifier), the refactoring tool will soon announce its defeat.

The number of supported refactorings in development environments grows with each new version. The current version of Eclipse for example allows developers to extract interfaces. Here the IDE not only creates the interface and lets the class implement it, moreover, all clients of the class are analyzed, and type references to the class are replaced by the interface where this is feasible. Present research is one step ahead: researchers are trying to automate design pattern-based refactorings (Cinnéide, 2000).

This shows that a growing number of, and more complex, refactoring operations are supported by IDEs, making it easy for developers to execute the desired refactorings. Refactoring is becoming a part of their daily work with source code.

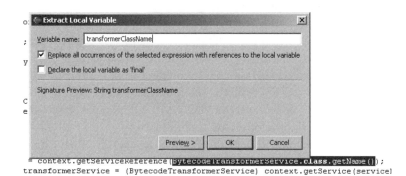

2.4.1   Incremental Refactoring vs. Tools-Supported Refactoring

A tool-based automation of refactorings seems to render the previously described mechanics and the step-by-step proceedings during refactoring obsolete. As a matter of fact, it is no longer necessary to rename a method in a series of single steps, because the IDE can accomplish this completely in a few seconds. Nevertheless, the basic idea behind incremental refactoring is not at all outdated.

There will always be refactorings that are either not supported by an IDE or that cannot be supported by an IDE (see next section). In these cases, it is still sensible to carry out refactorings step by step. Here too, the examples in Fowler's book can provide valuable advice on how one's own refactoring can be broken down.

2.4.2   Limitations of Tools Support

Unfortunately, refactoring tools have their limitations too. They cannot support all possible refactorings. In this section, we will take a brief look at some of these limitations and point to possible solutions:

- Refactoring tools can only provide automated support for such refactorings that can be generically described. This is the case with most refactorings introduced in Fowler (1999), but the developer still has to manually combine several refactorings to form a composite refactoring. Refactorings like *Extract Hierarchy* or *Separate Domain from Presentation* cannot be executed automatically by today's software tools because they require too much context information. For example, in the case of the *Separate Domain from Presentation* refactoring, developers must decide which portions of the code belong to the application's domain model and which ones to the presentation-specific part.

- Refactoring tools rely on having the complete source code at their disposal, which will potentially undergo change through the refactoring. Only then can the refactoring be executed *safely*. If, for instance, a method that redefines a method from a library shall be renamed, the redefined library method must be renamed too to guarantee the same behavior. However, all popular refactoring tools will alert developers to such situations instead of blindly modifying the code. This problem not only emerges when external libraries are used, but also when development takes place in different locations or when the system is developed in subprojects for one reason or another.

- If the application itself possesses a published interface for other systems, this interface can be changed with refactorings, but the interface clients will need to be refactored as well. We will dedicate an entire chapter labeled 'API Refactorings' to this problem.

- A regular refactoring can alter an application's source code. Persistent data will usually not be included in such an automated refactoring. Therefore it must be manually adapted to the application's new version. This problem is known for relational database connections as well as for purely object-oriented persistence mechanisms.

- If an object-oriented system uses a relational database, a mapping of object-oriented elements to the relational elements of that database is necessary. If a part of the object-oriented application is refactored, this can affect mapping to the database. This problem will also be discussed in a whole chapter.

2.5   Experiences and Recommendations

- Tests and refactorings constitute an inseparable unit. Automated tests keep the risk of overlooking newly introduced errors low.

- If the interface of a class is changed in the course of a refactoring, the corresponding test class must also be adapted. In this case it is recommended that you first modify the test class and then proceed with the refactoring step (test-first refactoring).

- A design can emerge and grow in the course of a project. A rough outline of the architecture will often suffice in the beginning.

▪ However, starting without any idea of a base architecture makes the refactoring process more challenging. You continuously need to evolve your design through refactorings to obtain a matching architecture one day. Otherwise you risk falling back on hacking.

▪ Refactorings are an essential part of software development. Only continuous refactoring will help to change and improve the software's design during development.

▪ Do not put off refactoring work. You can compare refactoring work to taking out garbage. If you don't regularly take out your garbage, you will drown in it at some point.

▪ Use the refactoring options offered by modern development environments.

References and Further Reading

Cinnéide, M. Ó. 2000. *Automated Application of Design Patterns: A Refactoring Approach*. Ph.D. thesis, Trinity College, Dublin, October. In his Ph.D. thesis, Mel Ó Cinnéide elaborates on how many of the well-known design patterns can be integrated in the code with refactoring techniques. Other than Kerievsky, Cinnéide is working on a tool-based approach that will enable the automated introduction of design patterns into the code.

Clover: http://www.thecortex.net/clover. Clover is a commercial tool for measuring the test coverage of Java programs.

FIT: http://fit.c2.com. FIT is a tool for the conduction of automated acceptance tests (also function tests). These tests are specified via HTML tables (e.g. using tables with input values and expected output values for certain system functions) executed by a test runner. Using fixtures, the test runner binds the application to be tested to the tables containing the tests. The test result documentation is then delivered in the form of HTML pages.

Fitnesse: http://www.fitnesse.org. Fitnesse is based on FIT and not only offers FIT, but also a Wiki web that allows easier test specification and organization.

Fowler, M. 1999. *Refactoring: Improving the Design of Existing Code*. Addison-Wesley. Not only does Fowler depict basic refactorings; he also introduces the distinction between public and published interfaces.

JCoverage: http://www.jcoverage.com/.

JCoverage is a tool for measuring the test coverage of Java programs. It exists in two versions: an open source and a commercial version.

Kerievsky, J. 2004. *Refactoring to Patterns*. Addison-Wesley. In his refactoring-to-pattern catalogue, Joshua Kerievsky consequently continues with Martin Fowler's work and describes how a number of popular design patterns can be treated during refactoring. The catalogue contains instructions for introducing a specific design pattern, but also a complementary refactoring for the respective pattern's removal.

NoUnit: http://sourceforge.net/projects/nounit. NoUnit is a tool for finding untested program sections.

Pipka, J.U. 2002. *Refactoring in a 'Test First' World*. XP 2002. http://www.agilealliance.com/articles/articles/JensUwePipka--RefactoringinaTestFirstWorld.pdf. This article addresses the problem that test code is often changed by refactorings too, and therefore no longer applicable as a safety net for refactorings. We suggest a refactoring procedure similar to the test-first approach, i.e. to adapt the test first and then execute the refactoring.

Roberts, D., Brant, J. & Johnson, R. *A Refactoring Tool for Smalltalk*. Published in *Theory and Practice of Object Systems,* special issue on software re-engineering. http://st-www.cs.uiuc.edu/users/droberts/. A description of the Smalltalk refactoring browser.

Westphal, F. 2005. *Testgetriebene Entwicklung mit JUnit und FIT*. dpunkt Verlag. Westphal explains test-driven procedures in software development. Of course he also touches upon the issue of refactoring (in German).

3
Architecture Smells

When experienced developers look at the code and the structure of a system, they very soon develop a feel for its weaknesses. They will say that the system *smells*; it possesses distinct smells, which point to conspicuous design in the system. Whether these designs really pose a problem or not must be decided in each individual case. If we follow a smell and actually detect a problem, we will solve it using refactorings.

In his book about refactoring (Fowler, 1999), Martin Fowler describes smells that can be cured with small refactorings. Examples of causes for these smells are long methods, long case statements, etc.

Besides these code smells, architecture smells can frequently be identified.[1] In contrast to code smells, architecture smells refer to bad smells that occur on a higher level of the system's granularity. Where code smells, for example, might refer to bad references between single classes. A similar architecture smell could reveal bad coupling between subsystems or layers. Such architecture smells often require larger refactorings.

The following sections will describe occurrences of architecture smells that we repeatedly encountered. As with code smells, an architecture smell does not always inevitably indicate there is a problem, but architecture smells point to places in the system's architecture that should be analyzed further. When we conduct architecture reviews, we refer to architecture smells for guidance.

---

[1]   The term 'architecture' is used in this context focused on the architecture of the software instead of covering the overall picture including the deployment mechanisms, hardware choices, and so on. Whereas most of the discussion that follows in this chapter makes sense for a system implemented homogeneously in one language, many of the underlying ideas should be valid for other cases, too.

Architecture smells can be found on various levels:

- In uses and inheritance relations between classes: these smells refer to the elemental relations between single classes.
- In and between packages: for many programming languages, concepts for grouping related classes exist, for example the package concept in Java. In and between such packages, architecture smells can also occur. We are going to address them here.
- In and between subsystems: packages alone do not constitute a sufficient concept for the structuring of larger systems, which is why packages are often bundled in so-called subsystems or modules. In and between such subsystems, architecture smells can occur.
- In and between layers: besides subsystems, so-called layers are often introduced into larger systems to control complexity. They also serve to structure the system. Often these layers will serve to separate the UI model from the domain model. They can also be used to separate, for example, a domain-specific platform of a system from higher-level, application-specific parts. From our experience we often find between 5 and 10 different layers in larger systems. We have identified a number of architecture smells that can emerge *in* as well as *between* layers.

The larger a system is, the more important are analyses of subsystems and layers. In small systems, the interesting aspects of their architecture express themselves in packages and classes, whereas subsystems and layers often don't exist at all. Nevertheless, smaller systems too will become more clearly defined when they are divided into subsystems.

If the system is big enough to consist of a significant number of subsystems, it is more important to ascertain that the relations between the subsystems are clean than to ensure that the subsystems possess an optimal internal structure. If a chaotic structure exists within a subsystem, it will quasi be 'quarantined' by clear structuring of the subsystems – chaos cannot spread to the remaining parts of the system. Later on, the chaotic subsystem can be isolated from the rest of the system and either be revised or completely newly developed.

Of course it is also important to select the correct size for each level. Classes, packages, subsystems and layers should not contain too many, but neither too few, elements. Figure 3-1 illustrates the resulting tension between understandability and reusability. The more components are part of a layer, the more of them can be reused by the layers above them. It should not go unmentioned though that the layer will become more difficult to understand as its number of components increases.

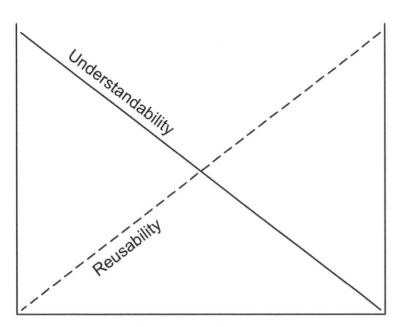

Number of Elements

Fig. 3-1
Tension between
Understandability
and Reusability

Figure 3-1 obviously simplifies the relationship between understandability and reusability. In practice, the optimum between both values does not always meet at an intersection. Instead, there is rather a large 'middle zone.' Moreover, it might happen that reusability deteriorates along with decreasing understandability, because everybody avoids using items that are complicated or even not understandable at all.

It is not possible to provide general numbers, but there is a rule of thumb that can serve as a guideline: if an element consists of more than 30 subelements, it is highly probable that there is a serious problem:[2]

(a) Methods should not have more than an average of 30 code lines (not counting line spaces and comments).
(b) A class should contain an average of less than 30 methods, resulting in up to 900 lines of code.
(c) A package should not contain more than 30 classes, thus comprising up to 27,000 code lines.

---

[2]   These numbers are drawn from personal experiences with analyzing large systems. Special thanks to Walter Bischofberger for discussing his experiences with us.

    (d) Subsystems with more than 30 packages should be avoided. Such a subsystem would count up to 900 classes with up to 810,000 lines of code.

    (e) A system with 30 subsystems would thus possess 27,000 classes and 24.3 million code lines.

    (f) If the system is divided into 3 to 10 layers, each layer comprises 3 to 10 subsystems.

These numbers cannot be used to characterize architecture smells, of course. But they can provide a meaningful hint where to find those smells.

In view of these numbers it soon becomes clear that one can carefully approach the upper limit of 30. If this is done consistently for each level though, the cumulative effect will lead to serious problems, as clarity might be impaired. Therefore, in practice the average values should stay visibly below the upper limit of 30.

The development environment Eclipse provides an apt example to demonstrate how these numbers can look like in the real world:[3]

    (a) Eclipse counts about 1.5 million lines of source code including line spaces and comments; without line spaces and comments it has about 730,000 lines of source code.

    (b) This source code is distributed over c. 460 packages, c. 12,400 classes and interfaces, plus approximately 89,500 methods.

    (c) This means that a method has an average of about 8 lines of source code – without comments and line spaces.

    (d) Classes and interfaces have an average of c. 7.2 methods.

    (e) Common packages contain about 27 classes and interfaces.

    (f) The Eclipse plugins can be viewed as subsystems. Consequently, Eclipse consists of 48 subsystems. A subsystem comprises an average of 9.6 packages plus 260 interfaces and classes.

    (g) Eclipse itself does not define layers. If one analyzes the static dependencies of subsystems, a layering consisting of 10 layers can be identified (see Figure 3-2, provided by Marcel Bennicke), with approximately five subsystems assigned to one layer. The illustration shows that extreme variances occur: from layers with only one subsystem to layers with sixteen subsystems everything will be assembled here.

---

[3]   These numbers refer to Eclipse Version 2.1 with the plugins that are part of the software's standard package. We are grateful to Marcel Bennicke, who generously provided them.

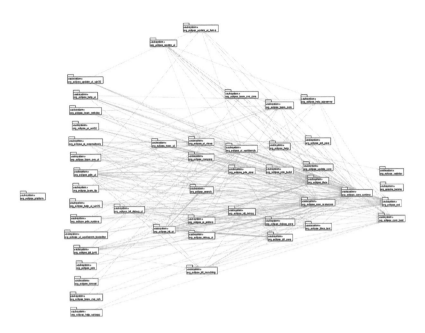

Fig. 3-2
*Eclipse Subsystems:
Vertical Layers*

Figure 3-3 gives an overview of architecture smells in this chapter.

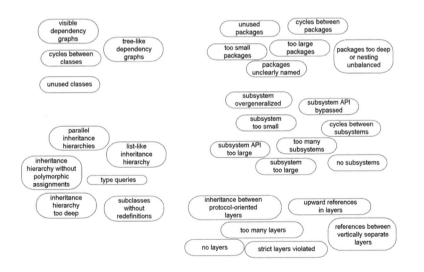

Fig. 3-3
Architecture Smells

3.1 Design Principles

Like code smells, architecture smells are caused by a violation of recognized design principles. This is the reason why design principles can provide us with valuable tips for curing architecture smells. If the violated design principle can be identified, it will give us a first idea of how a better system structure might look. Therefore, we provide an overview of today's popular design principles in Figure 3-4.

Fig. 3-4
Design Principles

Principle	Explanation
DRY - Don't Repeat Yourself	Do not write the same or similar code more than once. Also called 'Once and Only Once' principle.
SCP - Speaking Code Principle	The code should communicate its purpose. Comments in the code could indicate that the code communicates its purpose insufficiently.
OCP - Open Closed Principle	A design unit should be open to adjustments. Such adjustments shall not render existing clients invalid. Inheritance is one of the mechanisms that will let you achieve this goal: the subclass can make adjustments while the clients of the superclass remain valid.
LSP - Liskov Substitution Principle	One instance of a class must be usable for all instances where the type is the superclass. Not only is it required that the compiler translates the source code, but after the modification the system must still work correctly.
DIP - Dependency Inversion Principle	High-level concepts shall not depend on low-level concepts/implementations. The dependency should be vice versa, because high-level concepts are less liable to change than low-level concepts. One can introduce additional interfaces to adhere to the principle.
ISP - Interface Segregation Principle	Interfaces should be small. They should contain only a few methods, but those methods that are contained in an interface should be closely related.
REP: Reuse/Release Equivalency Principle	The elements that are reused are the elements that will be released.
CRP: Common Reuse Principle	The classes of a package are reused as a whole.
CCP: Common Closure Principle	The classes of a package shall be closed against the same type of changes. If a class must be changed, all classes of the package must be changed as well.
ADP: Acyclic Dependencies Principle	The dependency structure between packages shall be acyclic.
SDP: Stable Dependencies Principle	A package shall only depend on packages that are at least as stable as itself.

Principle	Explanation
SAP: Stable Abstractions Principle	The more stable a package is, the more abstract it should be. Instable packages should be concrete.
TDA: Tell, Don't Ask	Don't ask an object about an object, but tell it what to do. Similar to the 'Law of Demeter': each object shall only talk to 'friends,' i.e. only to objects that it retains as fields or receives as parameters.
SOC: Separation Of Concerns	Do not mix several concerns within one class. This is also known as the 'Single Responsibility Principle.'

Fig. 3-4 (cont.)
Design Principles

3.2 Smells in Dependency Graphs

Classes can be coupled through use and inheritance. First, we will only deal with use. If we look at the uses relations between the classes of the system, we will see the *static dependency graph*. During system runtime this will result in the *dynamic dependency graph* between objects. In this chapter, we are only interested in the static dependency graph.

3.2.1 Obsolete Classes

Classes that are no longer in use will burden the system with obviously obsolete functionality. Most of this burden results from the fact that developers spend more time searching for the right class. Build-times get longer and in general the system becomes more difficult to understand (because it is not obvious which classes are obsolete and which ones are not).

In contrast to completely obsolete classes, more often you can find classes that are partially obsolete. This often results from the fact that a class implements more than a single responsibility and one of the responsibilities becomes unused in the meantime. This situation can easily be reduced to our obsolete class smell by refactoring the separate responsibilities into separate classes.

Not only single classes can be no longer in use, but also entire class graphs[4] (see Figure 3-5).

---

[4] In our analyses, we will focus on complete applications. Naturally, 'obsolete' classes can easily emerge in frameworks and libraries if they are only provided to service the client.

Fig. 3-5
Unused Classes:
D, E, F

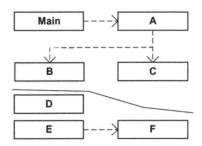

Unused classes mainly emerge for two reasons:

1. *Technology is hoarded as a supply:* a developer speculates that the class might eventually be used, although there is no evidence of a concrete demand for it.
2. *Refactorings:* a formerly required class becomes obsolete due to modifications of the system.

3.2.2   Tree-like Dependency Graphs

Tree-like dependency graphs (see Figure 3-6) indicate a functional decomposition of the system. Each class of the tree is used by exactly one other class.

Whereas functional decomposition in an object-oriented application can often be judged as a code smell by itself, a tree-like dependency structure also smells like code duplication. In the example in Figure 3-6 the protocol class seems not to be reused for other purposes, whereas the same protocol is used aside from the data storage. That part of the system might reimplement the same protocol. Reuse does not happen.

Fig. 3-6
The Tree-like
Dependency Graph

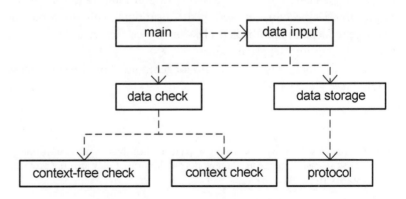

3.2.3   Static Cycles in Dependency Graphs

Two classes using each other constitute the simplest imaginable cycle in a dependency graph (see Figure 3-7). Cycles can also include various classes (see Figure 3-8).

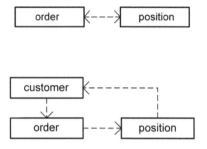

Fig. 3-7
A Cycle between Two Classes

Fig. 3-8
A Cycle Including Various Classes

The presence of many cycles in a system will lead to its *lumping*. Cycles have negative effects on:

(a) *Understandability*: the classes cannot be understood 'one after another,' because they presuppose each other to be understood. Instead, one has to alternate between classes to comprehend the graph in its entirety.

(b) *Maintainability:* cyclic dependencies can have severe and unpredictable consequences, thus making it harder to change the systems affected by them.

(c) *Planability:* cycles make it more difficult to anticipate the effects of changes. It will be more difficult to assess the effort required for, and the complexity of, a change.

(d) *Clarity in design*: often in one cycle each class can either directly or indirectly access any other class in the dependency graph. Therefore, in principle, concerns can be arbitrarily distributed among these classes. The danger of placing methods in 'wrong' classes is considerable, which in turn makes it more difficult to comprehend the design.

(e) *Reusability*: the class graph can only be (re)used as a whole. If in a given context only one class from the graph is of interest, this class cannot simply be reused.

(f) *Testability*: the classes can only be tested in their totality as a graph. This increases the demand for testing and error-searching. If one wishes to isolate classes during the test, relatively complex test patterns, such as Mock Objects (see References), must be utilized.

(g) *Exception handling*: often exceptions will accumulate in cycles. If some method in the cycle throws an exception, this event will potentially affect all other methods in that cycle.

(h) *Dependency Import Problem*: Each of the classes in a cycle is (transitively) dependent on each of the dependencies imported by either of the classes.

Obviously longer cycles have much stronger smells than short ones. Especially cycles between exactly two classes can be desired – such cycles are even conditional for some design patterns (for example iterator, see References). Besides their length, interaction of the cycles is also of interest. If several cycles share the same classes, the situation will become much more complicated and soon lead to uncontrollable chaos. An impression of this constellation is given in Figure 3-9, although here 'only' the dependencies between packages are illustrated. If one tried to understand Swing in its entirety in order to modify it, no reasonable starting point could be found. Also, modifications at any point in Swing might result in side-effects in any other location in Swing.

Fig. 3-9
Cycles in
Swing Packages

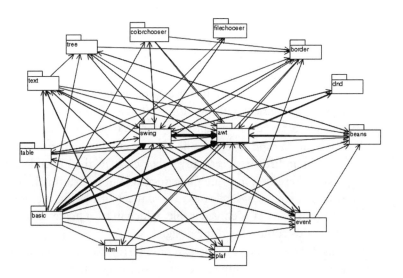

3.2.4   Visibility of Dependency Graphs

Object-orientation supports the principles of *encapsulation* and of *information hiding*: the internal implementation is hidden behind an interface.[5] The client of the class does not 'need to know' anything about the internal implementation of the API. Otherwise, the interface or the implementation of the class is flawed. Many developers believe that encapsulation and information hiding will emerge solely because fields are declared private. This is not the entire truth though: in many systems it is possible for clients of an object to receive field values from the object via accessor methods (the typical 'getters'). Based on the delivered objects, the client can continue to navigate. As a matter of fact, the dependency graph in the system is public and not at all hidden. A system with a public dependency graph will create more problems if one tries to change it, whereas changes to a private dependency graph will only have local effects.

The *Law of Demeter* (see References), as well as the *Tell, don't ask* principle (see References), are pointing in the right direction: ideally a client tells the used object what it is supposed to do. The client shall not accept another object from the used object, nor work with it.

Let us, for instance, imagine a number of orders in various states. We can especially differentiate between open or closed orders. Open orders are the ones in which the company has invested some money, but payment issues with the customer have not yet been settled. Thus it is interesting to find out how much the total value of all open orders is.

If we spot a method `calculateValueOpenOrders` somewhere in the following form, the *Tell, don't ask* principle has been ignored:

```
public float calculateValueOpenOrders
    (ListOfOrders orders) {

  float totalValue = 0.0f;
  for (int i=0; i<orders.getNumber(); i++) {
    Order a = orders.getOrder(i);
    if (a.isOpen) {
      totalValue += a.getValue();
    }
  }
  return totalValue;
}
```

The reason is that the client `Foo` asks the `Orders` directly to return information about their state instead of telling them what to do (Figure 3-10).

---

[5] In this context, 'interface' refers to the public API of a class rather than to the Java interface construct.

Fig. 3-10
A Violation of
'Tell, don't ask'

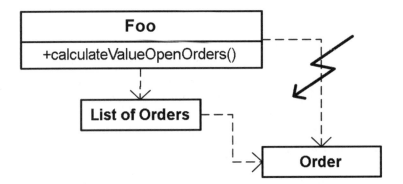

Now we move the case statement between open and not open orders into the class Order and get:

```
public class ListOfOrders {
  public float calculateValueOpenOrders() {
    float totalValue = 0.0f;
    for (int i=0; i<getNumber(); i++) {
      Order a = getOrder(i);
      totalValue += a.getOpenValue();
    }
    return totalValue;
  }
}

public class Order {
  public float getOpenValue() {
    if (isOpen()) {
      return getValue();
    }
    else {
      return 0;
    }
  }
}
```

We might be unhappy about the fact that in this example the order returns the open value. If you decided to apply the *Tell, don't ask* principle one more time, you would supplement the class Order with a method addOpenValue and remove the method getOpenValue. However, this would mean that the class Order would know that a certain number of orders exists. In this case, we would violate the

Separation of concerns principle. We should not forget that rather than blindly applying design principles, we design the system by making trade-offs. In this example we can decide whether to put the method into the class or not by asking ourselves if the method would fit into the domain-driven design of the class.

Not only is this new implementation a bit shorter, it also possesses a number of additional advantages:

- The functionality is where it belongs. It is no coincidence that in the first example the name of the class containing the method `calculateValueOpenOrders` has not been mentioned. In most cases, such methods can be located directly in UI classes (e.g. `OrderEvaluatorDialogue`) or in help classes with bizarre names (e.g. `OpenOrders Calculator`).
- The *Tell, don't ask* principle ensures that types are only used locally, plus they are no longer distributed all over the system. Thus they will simplify the realization of optimizations.

What makes this smell so unpleasant is the fact that it cannot be found by merely taking a close look at the package or class dependency graph. One must take a look at the method dependency graph or read the actual code to determine if many *get methods* exist, and if they are used in an undesirable way.

3.3   Smells in Inheritance Hierarchies

Classes are not only coupled through use, but also inheritance. Inheritance provides the advantage of polymorphism, but it comes with a price. This price is paid in part with the coupling we get through inheritance. Inheritance results in a closer coupling than a compositional relationship. Since the discussion about design patterns, we know that in case of doubt use is preferable over inheritance: the classes will be coupled less closely, and the resulting structures can be used more flexibly.

This is why inheritance hierarchy problems are quite severe: due to the close coupling of the classes in the hierarchy, problems will be passed on from superclasses to their subclasses. Due to new requirements, a subclass requires a change to the superclass, for example. Because all other subclasses also depend on the superclass, there is a possible impact on all other subclasses as well.[6]

---

[6]   We could make the same reasoning for composition. However, in the case of composition the problem is less severe because of a better encapsulation through the public API of the class. This is also why people argue towards explicit inheritance interfaces in addition to client APIs of classes.

3.3.1   Type Queries

Type queries in the system (*instanceof*) can be regarded as smells: the inheritance relation expresses itself not only in the classes of the inheritance hierarchy, but in the clients too. If alterations in the inheritance hierarchy are required, the type queries must be adapted as well (see Figure 3-11). In regard to the design principles, type queries violate the *Once and only once* principle:

Fig. 3-11
Inheritance Hierarchy
and Type Queries

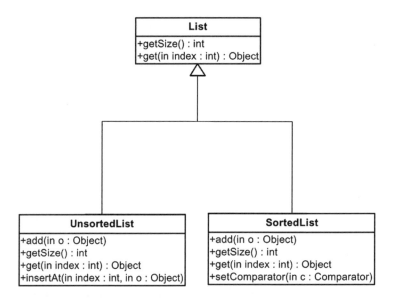

The following code snippet demonstrates how client code for this inheritance hierarchy could look:

```
public void doSomething (List l)
{
  Customer k = new Customer();
  if (l instanceof UnsortedList)
  {
    UnsortedList ul = (UnsortedList) l;
    ul.insertAt(0, k);
  }
  else
  {
    SortedList sl = (SortedList) l;
```

```
        sl.add(k);
    }
}
```

Actually, the smell is quite helpful here. The type queries are almost begging for the developer to take a closer look at the inheritance hierarchy. Indeed, the problem can be solved quite easily when the method add has already been implemented in both List and UnsortedList with the behavior depicted here.

A large system can hardly be realized without type queries. If a high number of type queries can be found in a system though, this indicates errors in an inheritance hierarchy. Maybe a subclass has been derived from another class, because the latter showed some similarity to it. As a matter of fact, a new superclass, from which both classes will inherit, should have been extracted first.

Figure 3-12 shows a popular example of a flawed inheritance hierarchy. It is plausible that a sorted list *is* a list and therefore permits the formation of subclasses, but the method insertAt has sneaked into the list class, and this method does not make sense in the subclass SortedList. Secretly it has changed all the lists to be unsorted lists. Finally, this is a violation of the *Liskov substitution principle*. The subclass SortedList now violates the contract of the superclass List because it does not allow the insertion of elements into the list in specific positions. So what happens if a client calls insertAt via the List type, but on an object created as SortedList?

Therefore a new superclass List must be created, which will combine the characteristics shared by sorted and unsorted lists alike.

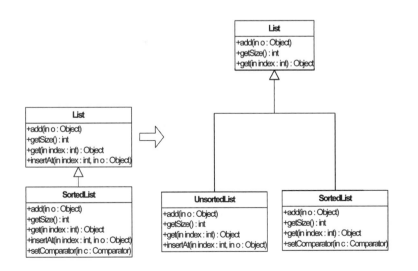

Fig. 3-12
Wrong Inheritance
Hierarchy
(on the left side)

3.3.2   List-like Inheritance Hierarchy

In a list like inheritance hierarchy (see Figure 3-13) each class possesses a maximum number of one subclass. Such inheritance hierarchies either point to speculative generalizations or to too big classes.

Fig. 3-13
List-like Inheritance
Hierarchy

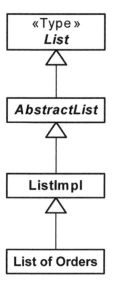

Speculative generalization means that superclasses were implemented for a definitely required class in the hope that the created abstraction might come in handy later on. This situation occurs quite often when the class hierarchy only consists of two classes.

Unfortunately, we cannot foretell the future and don't know for sure which abstractions will be needed later on. Experience has shown that speculative abstractions are not a good solution if an abstraction is actually needed. Frequently one will find that, for instance, wrong fields or methods were put in the superclass, or that the generalization is required in an altogether different place, or that the design problem can be solved much more elegantly with aggregation instead of inheritance. Usually, in such cases the speculative structures need to be rearranged.[7]

List-like inheritance hierarchies occasionally also emerge when classes become too long. Reducing the class's size through subclass

---

[7]   The fact that our observations are always based on complete applications also applies to this section, whereas in frameworks you will likely find superclasses and interfaces with possibly only one single implementation. This will particularly be the case if the framework uses the respective class or class hierarchy as API for clients.

formation is especially seductive for newcomers to object-oriented programming: some methods will stay in the original class, while other methods will be put in a newly created subclass. This procedure is so tempting because hardly anything can go awry. Besides, it doesn't require too much thought.

The close coupling of sub- and superclass will indeed reduce the size of the superclass, but the subclass will actually stay too big. Its size is not only determined by its own methods, but by those inherited from the superclass too.

A subclass formation that is implemented due to the aforementioned motives will seriously impair the system's structure: the concept of inheritance is applied in an 'alien' context, which can seriously impede the understandability of the system.

One indication of too long classes is the absence of redefined methods inside the subclass (see next section).

3.3.3 Subclasses Do Not Redefine Methods

If subclasses do not redefine the methods of their superclass, this can indicate that no abstraction is expressed through inheritance – we are facing pure implementation inheritance. Often a uses relation between classes will turn out to be more effective (see Figure 3-14).

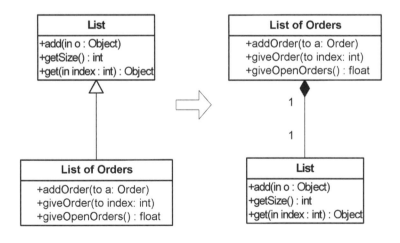

Fig. 3-14
Implementation Inheritance: No Redefinition of Methods

3.3.4 Inheritance Hierarchies Without Polymorphic Assignments

Similar to the previously mentioned smell, inheritance hierarchies without their respective polymorphic assignments point to the presence of unnecessary generalizations. The most significant advantage of inheritance as opposed to use is its flexibility, which is achieved through polymorphism. If no polymorphic assignments exist, this flexibility will not be used, and inheritance can be replaced by uses relations.

This smell is difficult to detect, because it only emerges when two situations are combined (inheritance hierarchy and assignments). A first indication of its presence is when too few assignments exist for the superclass type and too many for the subclass type, or when the superclass type is not much used in the system.

3.3.5 Parallel Inheritance Hierarchies

You can find parallel inheritance hierarchies in many systems because they are so beautifully symmetrical. For example, Figure 3-15 illustrates an existing domain-specific inheritance hierarchy between the business objects *Partner*, *Customer* and *Supplier*. Partners, customers and suppliers should be displayed on the UI level in list form. Thus, one view class exists for each of the three business object classes. These view classes inherit from each other according to the business object classes' hierarchy.

Last but not least, parallel inheritance hierarchies necessitate that one and the same design choice (namely that of the abstractions) must be expressed in two places. If a revision of this design choice needs to be made, all parallel inheritance hierarchies must be adapted.

Fig. 3-15
Parallel Inheritance
Hierarchies

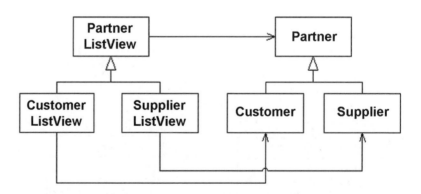

In many cases, parallel inheritance hierarchies can be resolved in such a manner that only one inheritance hierarchy is left, while the classes of other inheritance hierarchies are integrated through use.

Figure 3-16 shows a modified version of the system from Figure 3-15. The views for customers and suppliers are using the view for partners now, which no longer inherits from them.

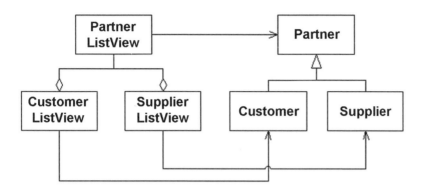

Fig. 3-16
Parallel Inheritance Hierarchies Have Been Removed

This smell is also mentioned in Martin Fowler's refactoring book (Fowler, 1999).

3.3.6   Too Deep Inheritance Hierarchy

Especially in the pioneer days of object-oriented programming, very deep inheritance hierarchies could be found in systems, because if the concept of inheritance is sound, more inheritance must be better than less inheritance.

In fact, deep inheritance hierarchies can result in extremely flexible systems. Unfortunately, at the same time the system's understandability and the adaptability of its inheritance hierarchies suffers. If inheritance takes place across 10 levels, it is almost impossible to determine which implementation of a method is called by reading the code.

If the superclass needs to be changed, this not only affects many subclasses. It is also difficult to project how this change will affect the classes at the bottom of the inheritance hierarchy (see Figure 3-17).

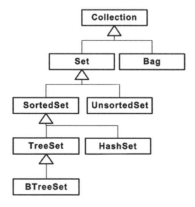

Fig. 3-17
Deep Inheritance Hierarchy

Inheritance hierarchies always demand careful planning. Deep inheritance hierarchies require a lot of attention to detail. This attention to detail will not always be delivered in a project's daily business routine. This is the reason why speculative and unnecessary generalizations are often found in deep inheritance hierarchies.

Easier to handle are shallow inheritance hierarchies, which tend to be broader or have been united in the formerly separate classes (see Figure 3-18).

Fig. 3-18
Shallow Inheritance
Hierarchy

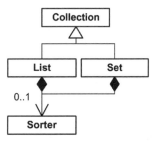

3.4   Smells in Packages

Java and other programming languages offer concepts for the grouping of classes. We will call these groupings *packages,* in keeping with Java terminology. A package can contain a number of classes.[8] The complete class name consists of the package name and the class name.

In Java, packages can be nested *syntactically.* For instance, the packages java.util and java.io are located in the package java, or respectively in packages called java. While specific visibility rules must be observed for classes within a package, this does not apply to nested packages. If one decided to rename the package java.io in jio and thus move it to the root level, this would not affect the classes – merely the imports would need to be adapted.

In programming languages without a package concept, usually file system directories will assume the role of packages. Naturally, in this case specific package visibility is no longer provided.

A few of the smells introduced here can also be found in Marquardt (2001). In addition, this article also provides solutions for some package smells discussed in this chapter.

3.4.1   Unused Packages

Packages that are not in use burden the system with clearly obsolete functionality (see Figure 3-19).

---

[8]   We will summarize interfaces in Java or comparable constructs in other programming languages under the term 'class' here because this is simpler.

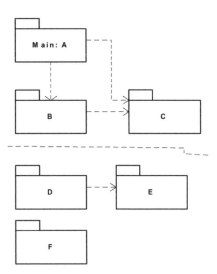

Fig. 3-19
Unused Packages

Unused packages, like unused classes, are created primarily for three reasons:

1. *Technology hoarded as a supply:* a developer speculated that the package will be required later on, although there is obviously no need for it.
2. *Refactorings:* modifications of the system rendered a formerly required package obsolete.
3. *Changed requirements:* the package contains functionalities that are obsolete due to new requirements.

3.4.2   Dependency Cycles between Packages

Cycles between packages can be created through use, inheritance, or through a combination of use and inheritance (see Figure 3-20).

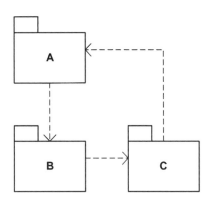

Fig. 3-20
Cycles between Packages

Apart from the fact that cyclic dependencies between packages are typically easier to resolve than cyclic dependencies between classes, they are not less important:

(a) *Understandability*: one cannot gain an understanding of packages through looking at them 'one by one,' because they presuppose each other to ensure understandability. Instead, one must skip between packages and perceive the package graph as a whole.

(b) *Clarity in design*: the dependency structure of the packages results in first restrictions for permissible dependencies between classes. If packages are cyclically dependent, the permissible relations between classes can no longer effectively be restricted. Also, the assignment of classes to packages becomes less compelling. If each package can be accessed by any other package, it would in principle be feasible to place classes in any package, but this in turn would impede the design's understandability.

(c) *Reusability*: as a rule, the package graph can only be (re)used as a whole. If actually only one package from the graph is of interest in a given context, this package cannot be simply reused.

(d) *Testability*: packages can only be tested as a complete set. This leads to a higher demand for testing and error-searching. If one wishes to isolate packages during testing, relatively complex test patterns such as Mock Objects (see References) must be utilized.

(e) *Debugging*: due to a cycle between packages, a problem might be spread over different packages rather than remain localized, which makes it more complicated to analyze and trace problems in such (cyclic) settings.

Other than in cyclical relations between classes, *exception handling* is not impaired by cycles between packages.

Often cycles between packages point to poorly arranged packages. In most cases, this problem can be solved through simple restructuring, for example by merging all packages participating in a cycle into one package, which will then be arranged based on better criteria.

Cycles between packages will frequently lead to cycles between subsystems (see below).

3.4.3   Too Small Packages

Packages with one or two classes are often not worth the effort of introducing them: the complexity created by the package is not offset by its additional structuring.

Such too small packages can easily be removed through relocation of their classes to other packages. However, one must make sure that in this process no new cycles between packages are created.

Of course packages should never be just organized by size. Instead, we mostly arrange packages around responsibilities. Nevertheless, the size of a package might be an indicator that the packaging is misleading.

3.4.4   Too Large Packages

Packages with a high number of classes indicate that they serve more than one specific responsibility. Splitting them up will lead to a better separation of concerns and especially to better understandability.

Sometimes too large packages indicate missing subsystems. The creation of a subsystem from a too large package can solve this problem – for instance, if one splits the initially too large package into an interface package and one or more implementation packages.

3.4.5   Package Hierarchies Unbalanced

If the package structure is unbalanced, understandability is also impaired. Should all of the application's business objects be located under `com.mycompany.myproject.bo`, the fact that not all UI classes can be found in a different place under `com.mycompany.myproject.ui`, but only packages containing subpackages instead, might cause confusion.

A similar problem occurs if package hierarchies are too deep to be easily understandable. The Java SDK, for example, requires just two-level packages (e.g. `java.util`), in some rare cases even three-level ones. Nevertheless, the JDK is able to usefully organize some thousands of classes. Similarly to inheritance hierarchies, shallow package hierarchies are more easily understandable than deep ones. Generally, two to three layers below the first three should suffice for a system structuring, also existing naming conventions (from *Sun* or within a project) might influence these numbers.

3.4.6   Packages Not Clearly Named

Especially packages containing classes that are not domain-oriented are often named ambiguously, and assigning of identical names occurs. If various packages with names like `util`, `base`, `framework` and `toolkit` can be found side by side in the same system and on the same level, it will be hard for developers to find the package containing the desired class right away.

Developers will face even greater difficulties when a new, not domain-oriented class is created. Its placement does not seem to matter. This uncertainty might lead to the idea of introducing another package – one that is equally vaguely named.

Ambiguously named packages frequently indicate that the developers had no real understanding of what is inside the packages, so it will come as no surprise if such packages contain classes with work-arounds or were simply miscreated.

3.5   Smells in Subsystems

Similar to packages, subsystems summarize classes. They differentiate between internal realization and public interface. The internal realization is invisible for other subsystems. The public interface is comprised of a subset of the subsystem's classes.

Packages also distinguish between public and private classes and methods. However, usually a single package will not suffice to define an entire subsystem. This requires a number of packages.

A large system should be divided into subsystems. This division will contribute to the system's learnability, maintainability, multi-project development and deployment.

(a) *Learnability*: a first, superficial understanding of the system can be acquired if one looks at the subsystems and how they relate to each other.

(b) *Maintainability*: changes of a subsystem can be carried out in relative isolation from other subsystems. If a subsystem possesses a poor internal structure, this will not affect the entire system.

(c) *Multi-project development*: the development of single subsystems can take place in teams specifically assigned to that subsystem.

(d) *Deployment*: if the system is not needed as a complete entity, single subsystems can be delivered.

(e) *Testability:* subsystems can be tested as isolated units. This also includes the option of defining and executing comprehensive and isolated test scenarios (Figure 3-21).

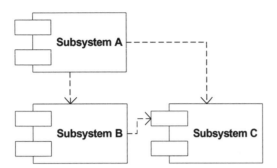

Fig. 3-21
Subsystems

In very large systems, the subsystem principle can be applied recursively, which will lead to a subsystem consisting of subsystems.

Unfortunately, the popular programming languages do not offer any options for the definition of subsystems. Often suitable runtime environments are applied to define and use subsystems. A mechanism based on the language Java can be found as part of the Eclipse platform's plugin concept. Similar runtime environments are, e.g., the DLL concepts, COM components or .NET assemblies.

If such a mechanism is not available, one must fall back on conventions, for example by using the root packages as public interfaces of the subsystems and interpreting all subpackages as internal realizations.

Some of the smells surrounding subsystems are caused by missing subsystem concepts in programming languages. This is, for instance, the case for the 'Subsystem-API Bypassed' smell.

Depending on the terminology used, subsystems are also called *components* or *plugins*.

3.5.1   No Subsystems

From a certain size on, a system's structure – if it is defined exclusively on the package level – will become increasingly incomprehensible. If the system consists of more than 100 packages, for example, it is extremely difficult to recognize and define the structure between the packages and to maintain it consistently.

3.5.2   Subsystem Too Large

The phenomenon that no subsystems are defined is a special case of too large subsystems. From the subsystems' perspective one could say that the entire system constitutes a single (too large) subsystem.

Like missing subsystems, too large subsystems run the danger of
becoming incomprehensible and containing too many concerns. In
many cases, the occurrence of very large subsystems is accompanied by
a loss of clarity: the subsystem is no longer responsible for a single
task, but it also takes on concerns in other areas.

3.5.3   Subsystem Too Small

Too small subsystems shift complexity from subsystems into the
dependencies among the subsystems themselves (see Figure 3-22). In
the most extreme case, each class represents its own subsystem. Obviously this will not lead to a reduction of complexity, instead developers are confronted with an impracticable tangle of dependencies
between subsystems (see also *Section 3.5.4*).

Usually it is possible to merge too small subsystems into larger
subsystems with little effort. However, developers must make sure that
no cycles are created between these new subsystems.

3.5.4   Too Many Subsystems

If a system consists of many more than 30 subsystems without further
grouping, the understandability of the system will be seriously impaired.
This many subsystems and their interrelations can no longer be handled (see Figure 3-22).

Fig. 3-22
Too Many Subsystems

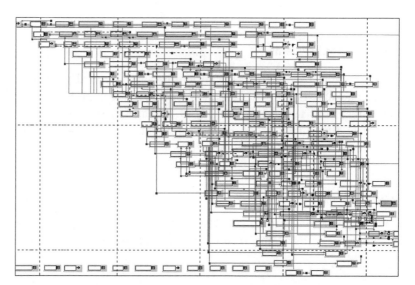

In such a case, further subsystems that encapsulate the existing subsystems should be defined.

Sometimes the subsystems were only created too small (see previous subsection). Here, merging the existing subsystems will solve the problem.

3.5.5   Subsystem-API Bypassed

Since the popular programming languages do not offer generic mechanisms for the definition of subsystems, projects must fall back on conventions. Consequently the subsystem's public interface – the API – will be defined through conventions.

Experience shows that such conventions are bypassed under pressure, e.g. lack of project time – either by mistake or on purpose. Bypassing the subsystem-API and directly accessing the internal implementation of the component is a practice that is not only common, but also potentially fatal (see Figure 3-23). The clients actually unauthorizedly expand the subsystem-API. The originally exclusively internal interface, which is now used by a client, becomes involved in the dependency relationship between subsystems. The result is the 'Subsystem-API Too Large' smell that we are going to describe in the next subsection.

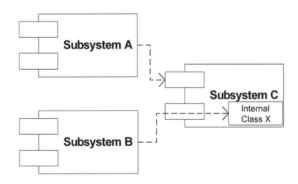

Fig. 3-23
Subsystem B
Bypasses the API of
Subsystem C

This scenario will have even more negative implications if the subsystem developers don't notice the API's expansion. Should they wish to alter or exchange the internal realization of the subsystem, this will have serious consequences for the clients that bypassed the subsystem-API.

Such violations can easily be detected or even prevented with the aid of a suitable runtime environment. For instance, the Eclipse Plugin Runtime will let you declare the visible packages (public API) of a

Suitable
Runtime Environments

plugin (subsystems). The runtime ensures that other plugins (subsystems) may exclusively use classes of those packages that have been defined as visible.[9]

3.5.6   Subsystem-API Too Large

When the API of a subsystem becomes too large in relation to the implementation, the main purpose of the subsystem is not served. A major part of the system will be visible to all other subsystems. Therefore, no significant complexity reduction has been achieved (see Figure 3-24).

Fig. 3-24
Too Large
Subsystem-API

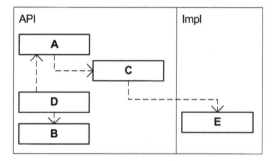

This smell can be detected by a simple means: one only needs to count the number of classes in the API and then compare the result to the total number of classes in the subsystem.

What precise kind of relation between API and implementation size is useful depends heavily on the context, so that we cannot provide any rule of thumb values here. Library-like subsystems, for example, will offer a very versatile API (e.g. a container library).

3.5.7   Cycles between Subsystems

Cycles between subsystems can be created via use, inheritance or through a combination of use and inheritance (see Figure 3-25).

---

[9] In the case of a mistake, the corresponding `ClassNotFoundException` will be automatically released because a plugin can only 'see' such classes via the class-loading mechanisms that have been declared public. In addition the Eclipse-IDE warns the developer of such API violations right within the IDE via the incremental compiler.

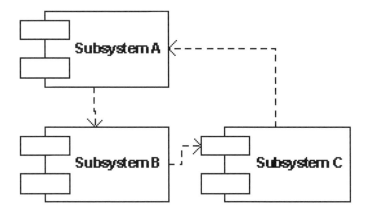

Fig. 3-25
Cycles between
Subsystems

At first sight, cycles between subsystems have less serious implications than cycles between classes:

(a) *Understandability*: subsystems cannot be understood by looking at them in a sequential order, because they presuppose each other to ensure understandability. Instead, one must skip between subsystems and perceive the subsystem graph as a whole.

(b) *Clarity of design:* often cycles between subsystems hint at unclear concerns of the subsystems. In many cases it is impossible to resolve immediately in which subsystem the wanted class is located, or where a new class could sensibly be placed.

(c) *Reusability*: the subsystem graph can only be (re)used as a whole. If, in a given context, only a single subsystem from the graph is of interest, this subsystem cannot be reused as a stand-alone, i.e. isolated from the other subsystems.

(d) *Testability:* a subsystem cannot be tested in isolation from the other subsystems.

(e) *Parallel development:* cyclic dependencies between subsystems make the parallel development of subsystems by different teams and/or as part of different projects more difficult.

Exception handling is not affected by cycles between subsystems. Although cycles between subsystems create fewer problems quantity-wise than cycles between classes, they are much more problematic in practice. The relations between subsystems are an important aspect of software architecture and – contrary to cycles between classes – they cannot be cured locally. To achieve that, the system's architecture must be modified. If we are dealing with a large system, the APIs between the subsystems must be changed. However, sometimes the subsystems are maintained by different teams. In that case, the teams must coordinate their efforts.

Often cycles between subsystems point to unfavorably arranged subsystems. The problem can be solved, for example, by merging all subsystems participating in a cycle into a single subsystem, which then can be broken down based on better criteria.

3.5.8   Overgeneralization

In order to assure that subsystems provide the greatest extent of reusability, they must be flexibly applicable. This generalization can be overdone though, which will result in the subsystem's overgeneralization. It will become more flexible than it actually needs to be. Not only does this lead to additional subsystem development work; it also makes using the subsystem more difficult. Overgeneralization occurs when the clients – in relation to the size of the used subsystems – require a large amount of code.

Another indicator of overgeneralization is violation of the *Once and only once* principle. All clients of the subsystem write very similar code to parameterize the subsystem for its purposes.

This problem can be tackled by trying to migrate the very similar code into one common piece of code, which could then be moved away from the clients into the subsystem. Afterwards, the subsystem can be refactored internally, so that overgeneralization will not become an issue. This requires that you will be able to refactor the similar client codes into a common piece of code, which might not be trivial to do.

Of course the problem of overgeneralization can also be found on the methods, classes and packages levels.

3.6   Smells in Layers

Besides the breaking down of large systems into subsystems, the ordering of subsystems in layers has proven to be efficient. Each layer is assigned a specific aspect of the system. One of the most popular generic layer models is the 3-tier model (3-tier architecture, see Figure 3-26). It emphasizes that the UI layer, domain model and persistence should be kept separate.

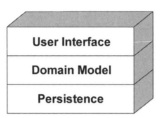

Fig. 3-26
3-tier Model

A more detailed layer model is that by Bäumer (see Figure 3-27). It distinguishes between three domain-independent layers: *system base*, *technology* and *handling & presentation*. The three domain model layers *business domain*, *business section* and *application context* build on the generic layers. In the business section layer different products are located, which may not depend on each other (see dashed line in the illustration). The stretched angles of the *technology* and *handling & presentation* layers indicate that the layering is not strict: all three domain model layers may use these two technical layers. More details regarding this layer architecture can be found in Bäumer (1998).

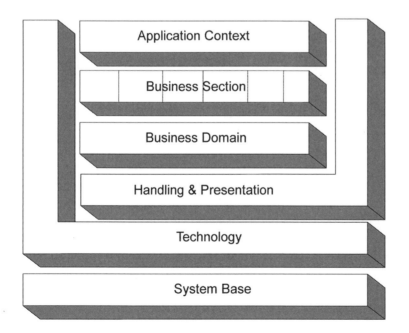

Fig. 3-27
Bäumer's Layer Model

Domain-specific layer models are the ISO-OSI model[10] for distributed systems (see Figure 3-28) or the layering of plugins in Eclipse[11] (see Figure 3-29).

Fig. 3-28
ISO-OSI Layer Model

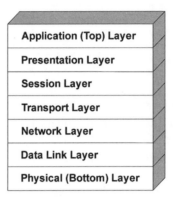

Fig. 3-29
The Layers of Eclipse

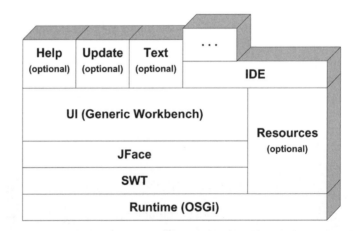

The layer models assume different perspectives of the term *layer*. Consequently, the layers of the 3-tier model as well as those of the ISO-OSI model are *strict*: each layer may only access the layer directly below it. Layers that are located farther down cannot be used. Thus the UI layer of the 3-tier model is not entitled to directly access the

---

10   Details can be found in Kerner (1989).
11   Although the documentation for the Eclipse platform does not mention any
     explicit layer architecture, the layering displayed inside the Eclipse platform
     and the projects building on it are easily recognizable.

persistence layer. Strict layers always apply the principle of information hiding: each layer conceals all layers below it.

If a layer is allowed to access other layers, accessing it through the layer directly below, it is called *non-strict*. Strict and non-strict layers can both be utilized within the same layer model: for instance, in the WAM[12] layer model the handling & presentation layer is non-strict, whereas the technology layer is strict and hides the system basis layer from other layers.

A second distinguishing criterion is the interface between the layers. For *protocol-oriented* layers, such as the ISO-OSI model, the interfaces between the layers are provided by functions. At the interface, no classes for building subclasses are offered. The APIs of *object-oriented* layers (e.g. in the Eclipse layer model) primarily include interfaces and abstract classes that either should or should not be implemented. In principle though, protocol-oriented and object-oriented layers can be mixed.

The major advantage of object-oriented layers is their flexibility, which is achieved through subclass-forming. Protocol-oriented layers, on the other hand, offer more flexibility in layer implementation and allow the use of non-object-oriented technologies for the realization of layers. This can be a huge advantage if relevant portions of the layer implementation already exist in a non-object-oriented programming language like Cobol or are built from purchased systems that do not possess an object-oriented interface. Thus, protocol-oriented layers allow a much simpler exchange of complete layer implementations.

In very large systems some layers are also separated vertically in addition to their horizontal separation, often to define a so-called *product line* or to separate between different application areas on top of a common platform. One example of this practice is the business section layer in the layer model according to Bäumer. The single products in the business section layer are not allowed to depend on each other. Typically for such product line architectures, the separation of products is not applied to all layers: the lower layers are used by all products. Otherwise one would simply have completely separate systems.

3.6.1   No Layers

Demand for change can occur in different areas. Often layers are formed based on the large areas in which modification requirements

---

[12]   The German acronym WAM stands for *Werkzeug, Automat & Material*, which translates into 'tools, machine & material'.

emerge. For example, the 3-tier model uses the areas *user interface*, *domain model* and *persistence*.

This type of layering enables easy identification of those areas of the system that will potentially be affected by a change. For instance, will a change of only the domain model not affect persistence.

If no layers exist, this kind of orientation aid is missing. Should the system consist of a large number of subsystems, it will be extremely difficult to identify potentially affected subsystems without layers.

For most systems, developers can name a layering that was intended. However, in many systems this intentional layering is violated so gravely that in the end no layers can be identified anymore.

3.6.2 Upward References between Layers (Cycles between Layers)

If a layer uses a higher located layer, the basic principle of layering has been ignored. Modifications of one layer cannot only have consequences for the higher layers, but also for those that are located further below (see Figure 3-30).

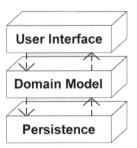

Simultaneously, upward references also create cycles between layers. They have similar effects to those created by cycles between subsystems (see section 3.5.7) and might lead to the emergence of cycles on the subsystem level. Other than subsystems, layers make it comparatively easy to identify which relation is the one that is not permitted: namely always the one from bottom to top.

3.6.3 Strict Layers Violated

Since the common programming languages do not provide concepts for the definition of layers, layers must be built based on conventions. In this scenario, one cannot reliably prevent that strict layers are violated. It can always happen that a layer skips the one directly beneath it and accesses a layer further below instead, be it accidentally or on purpose (see Figure 3-31).

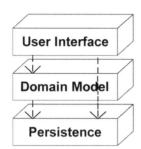

Fig. 3-31
Strict Layers Violated

If layers that are basically strict are violated, their alterability is affected. The number of a layer's potential clients will increase, and the dependency between layers will grow.

Additional techniques allow the recognition of such layer violations at the time of development. AspectJ, an aspect-oriented language extension for Java, offers mechanisms for controlling method calls between layers. One example of such an aspect can be found in Bodkin *et al.* (2004).

Recognizing Violations of Layers

3.6.4   Inheritance between Protocol-Oriented Layers

Inheritance between protocol-oriented layers is not allowed. Otherwise a stricter than desirable coupling would occur. In particular it would become impossible to reimplement the layer that inherited in a non-object-oriented programming language later on. Moreover, inheritance generally restricts the alterability of the lower layer, because changes to the superclasses can only to a certain extent be hidden from subclasses.

3.6.5   Too Many Layers

As a rule of thumb, each layer in a system has to carry its own weight. This means that each layer has a clear responsibility and that this responsibility is rich enough – in terms of functionality, features or abstractions – to justify the existence of the layer.

As a result, too many layers in a system often cause too many indirections. One indication of unnecessary indirections are dumb delegations: one method simply invokes another method without implementing any functionality of its own. Whereas the single occurrence of a delegation is not necessarily to be considered bad, extensive use of delegations between many layers can point to problems. If many delegations exist, most likely a number of negative effects will follow in their wake:

▤ A lot of effort must be invested in the programming of methods without implementing any functionality if the functionality of one layer has to be modified or extended. As a result, all delegator methods in all layers must be adapted. Specifically, modifications of parameter lists in a lower layer are painful because those changes impact all higher layers.[13]

▤ Program understandability may suffer because an unnecessarily high number of layers exists. In addition, the responsibility of each layer may not be obviously recognizable and understandable. This might not concern someone sitting on top of all layers using just their API, but for someone working on the code within one of the layers or for someone who has to take care of the overall structure, too many layers make it harder to understand the overall picture and the relationships between the layers.

3.6.6   References between Vertically Separated Layers

We already discussed that layers cannot only be arranged horizontally, but also vertically (see the introduction to this section, p. 61). This is often done to structure separate products or business sections. For example, a product line is a set of software systems that share a common basis. Besides using the same basis, no further references between these systems are allowed.

References (regardless of which kind) between vertically separated layers create dependencies between layers (see Figure 3-32). Thus the purpose of product lines can no longer be served:

▤ *Delivery*: vertical layers shall be deliverable and applicable independently from each other.

▤ *Parallel development*: for each single vertical layer one team shall be responsible, which does not have to confer with other layer teams regarding changes.

---

[13] Changing parameters across different layers might not be bad in all cases. If the right layers are in place, this allows you to introduce API changes incrementally, layer by layer. Nevertheless this would only be useful if the layering itself was chosen wisely. If too many layers existed, you would not benefit from the incremental introduction of the change. Instead you would just need to modify layer after layer without gaining benefits from each modification.

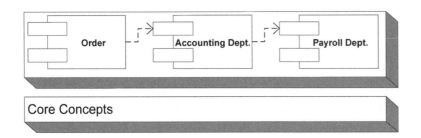

Fig. 3-32
References between
Vertical Layers

If fundamental relationships between different products in the system exist, the described vertical separation between layers cannot be made. In this case, these basic relationships (the stable domain layer model) will be located in the core concept layer as represented in Figure 3-32, on which the vertically separated layers are founded.

3.7   Locating Smells

The smells we have discussed so far can hardly be found through sim-ple code reading. After all, they usually emerge not from a single class, but from the interaction of many classes. Code reviews offer a good framework for the detection of smells, but even for code reviews a suit-able tool support is mandatory to visualize the system. Whereas simple UML tools for code reviews will at least visualize the system on the package level, more specialized tools are required for the detection of numerous architecture smells.

Reading the Code
Is Not Enough

Modern development environments (for instance Eclipse) offer powerful semantic search functions. Thus we can easily determine which classes inherit a specific class, or how many references to a method exist. In this way, hypotheses about smells can be verified. For example, if we suspect that only one subclass of class A exists, we can easily check this: we simply ask for a display of A's type hierarchy.

Unfortunately, these display options are not sufficient for the detection of architecture smells. If you don't know yet which classes are involved in a smell, you have no venturing point from which to start searching.

Besides development environments, a number of tools exist that can help detect common smells in software systems.

A brief overview of these tools is listed in the following subsections (the URLs for these tools are listed in Chapters 3–9).

More Specific Tools

3.7.1   PMD

For Java systems, the open source tool PMD alerts developers to code
smells such as empty catch blocks or unused methods. However, PMD
analyses are restricted to only one class at a time and do not consider
relations between classes. Thus PMD analyses are not sufficient for the
identification of architecture smells. PMD is available as a plugin for
the popular Java development environments.

3.7.2   JDepend

JDepend analyzes the dependencies between packages and classes and
calculates Robert Martin's metrics (Martin, 1997). JDepend possesses
an interface for the display of dependencies and couplings (see Figure
3-33), but it also offers a programming interface. The latter enables,
e.g., the formulating of JUnit tests that make sure that no unwanted
dependencies are introduced into the system.

Fig. 3-33
JDepend:
Dependencies of
Packages

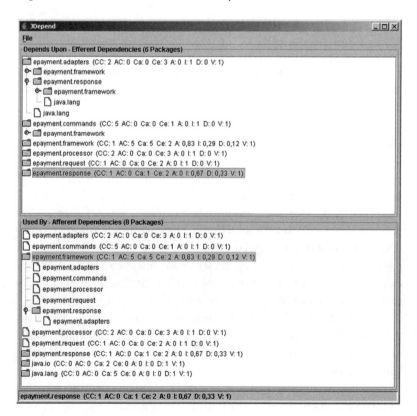

The following Java source code shows how you can test package   *Example*
dependencies in JUnit tests (source code borrowed from JDepend):

```
import java.io.*;
import java.util.*;
import junit.framework.*;

public class ConstraintTest extends TestCase {
    private JDepend jdepend;

    public ConstraintTest(String name) {
        super(name);
    }

    protected void setUp() {
        jdepend = new JDepend();
        try {
          jdepend.addDirectory
            ("/projects/util/classes");
          jdepend.addDirectory
            ("/projects/ejb/classes");
          jdepend.addDirectory
            ("/projects/web/classes");
        } catch(IOException ioe)  {
            fail(ioe.getMessage());
        }
    }

    protected void tearDown() {
        jdepend = null;
    }

    /**
      * Tests that the package dependency con-
straint
      * is met for the analyzed packages.
      */
    public void testDependencyConstraint() {
        DependencyConstraint constraint =
          new DependencyConstraint();
```

```
            JavaPackage ejb =
              constraint.addPackage("com.xyz.ejb");
            JavaPackage web =
              constraint.addPackage("com.xyz.web");
            JavaPackage util =
              constraint.addPackage("com.xyz.util");

            ejb.dependsUpon(util);
            web.dependsUpon(util);

            jdepend.analyze();

            assertEquals("Dependency mismatch",
            true,        jdepend.dependencyMatch(con-
        straint));
        }

    public static void main(String args[]) {
        junit.textui.TestRunner.
          run(ConstraintTest.class);
    }
}
```

3.7.3   ClassCycle

ClassCycle is an open source tool for the detection of cycles between classes. The detected cycles are displayed either in an XML or an HTML report (see Figure 3-34). Based on the dependencies between the classes, layers are generated and classes assigned to layers.

3.7.4   Eclipse Metrics Plugin

The Eclipse Metrics Plugin is an open source metrics tool that has been realized as a plugin for the Eclipse development environment. In a first step it supplies reference values that enable an evaluation of a software system's quality. One must keep in mind though that these values often refer to the code level (e.g. average method length) and therefore offer relatively little support for an examination of the architecture. Moreover, it often remains unclear *where* the problems are stemming from and what must be done to solve them.

At least the Eclipse Metrics Plugin is able to graphically display the relations between packages, so that one can detect one or another architecture smell, given a bit of patience and some knowledge about the targeted architecture (see Figure 3-35).

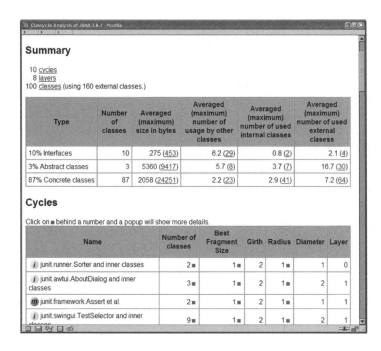

Fig. 3-34
ClassCycle: An Example of a Result Generated by JUnit

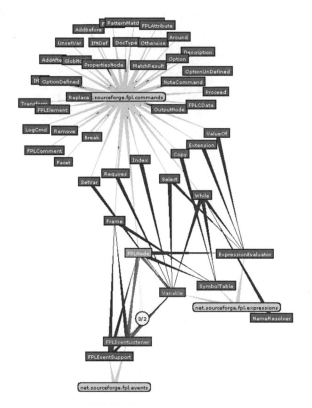

Fig. 3-35
Eclipse Metrics Plugin: Package Overview

3.7.5   RefactorIT

RefactorIT is a commercial refactoring tool that not only supports refactorings, but also the preceding step of detecting smells. To this end it provides the common metrics as well as some dependency analyses.

3.7.6   Dr. Freud

Dr. Freud visualizes dependencies between packages and classes (see Figure 3-36) and calculates Robert Martin's metrics (Martin, 1997). Currently, Dr. Freud is still being developed, but it worked quite decently in our tests.

Fig. 3-36
Dr. Freud: Package
Overview

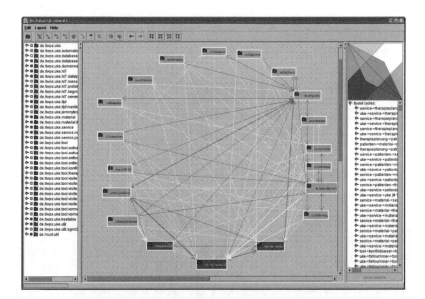

3.7.7   SA4J: Structural Analysis for Java

SA4J is a promising IBM technology preview. This tool visualizes the dependencies between packages in different ways. Particularly interesting is its highlighting of packages that are difficult to change as well as its tracking of direct and indirect dependencies, starting with a class. These functions allow developers to anticipate the consequences of changes to a class.

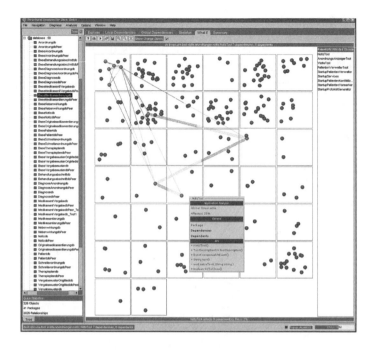

Fig. 3-37
SA4J: Dependencies

In addition, SA4J possesses an *Auto Explore* function that will run a movie clip showing dependencies between packages (see Figure 3-38). This feature provides an amazingly concise insight into the system's structure and quickly detects problematic dependencies.

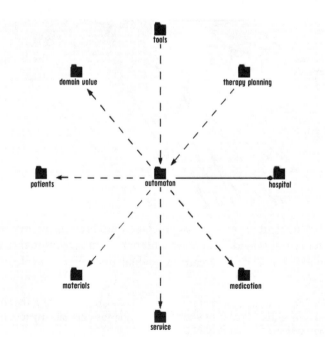

Fig. 3-38
SA4J: Dependencies of Each Single Package

3.7.8   Sotograph

The commercially available Sotograph[14] was developed specifically for the detection of architecture smells. It identifies the smells depicted here with little effort and is thus an important aid in controlling the architecture of a large software system. As far as we know, Sotograph is the only tool that can analyze relations between subsystems and layers (see Figure 3-39).

Fig. 3-39
Sotograph: A Part of a
Subsystem Graph

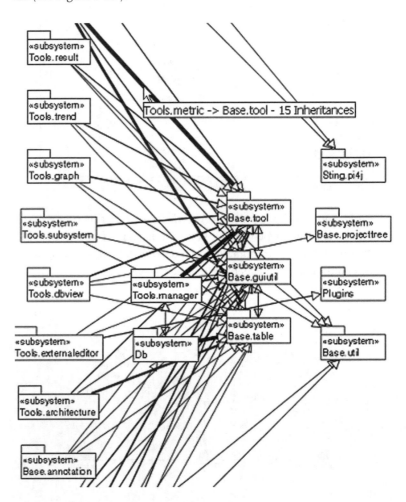

Moreover, it is an interesting fact that Sotograph manages all information obtained from a system analysis in a relational database, thus making it easy to create individual queries and evaluations in

---

14   The name is a compound of software and tomograph. In effect, the Sotograph is a tomograph capable of visually displaying the internal structure of a software system.

Sotograph. Due to its own database storage, Sotograph also allows the efficient analysis of extremely large systems (several million lines of code). Sotograph is described in detail in Chapter 7.

3.8   Preventing Smells

In practice it is extremely hard to prevent all these smells. We have analyzed a number of projects and we never(!) found a project without any of the smells discussed here. The reasons for the occurrence of smells are manifold:

- *Ignorance*: a widespread reason is the fact that many development projects that we have seen are not aware of the benefits of well-managed dependencies within systems. Therefore they just don't take care of them. As a result, the dependency structure of these systems is extremely hard to understand and changes often result in negative side-effects.
- *Invisibility*: most IDEs don't have a mechanism yet to detect dependency violations. Therefore developers tend to forget about them.
- *IDEs*: modern development environments automatically insert the imports for required classes and packages. Developers are no longer forced to encode the imports manually and must not reflect about whether the import is permitted, or if it might lead to a cyclical dependency between subsystems.[15]
- *Pressure of time*: when the upcoming release of a system shall be delivered as soon as possible, developers are frequently pressured into violating the architecture. It is the only way of meeting the deadline, they think. Due to time pressure, these violations of architecture are often not documented, and often they will not be removed after release.
- *Misunderstandings*: sometimes developers do not fully understand the scope and premise behind a system's architecture. They conform with what they did understand and unintentionally violate the architecture. This phenomenon occurs almost always during the training of new employees or project members.
- *Changes in architecture*: projects that run over a longer period usually require repeated adaptations of the software architecture. These adaptations are not always done incrementally, so that existing code violates the new architecture.
- *Technological changes*: the replacing of a technology component with a new version or with a totally different component can cause a whole series of *deprecated* warnings to occur at once.

---

[15]   This could also happen without the automatic import if developers copy & paste import code from other sources.

In spite of these problems, some of them can be constructively prevented. There exist a number of practices and tools that help to keep track of some smells directly while programming:

- *Different projects*: many IDEs offer support for organizing systems with multiple projects where the developer needs to define which project can depend on which other project. This allows the compiler to check violations due to non-visible types.
- *AspectJ*: by implementing a special aspect, the AspectJ compiler can produce compiler warnings and errors, for example if calls across layers are allowed or not. The rules (what is allowed and what is not) are then implemented within the aspect using the pointcut programming construct (see Bodkin *et al.*, 2004 for an example).
- *SonarJ*: this is a commercial tool for the detection of architectural flaws while programming. The architecture model is defined using XML. The tool plugs into IDEs (currently Eclipse) and detects violations of the defined architecture right inside the IDE. This improves the visibility of those smells while typing.
- *Eclipse Plugin Runtime and the PDE (Plugin Development Environment)*: the plugin runtime of Eclipse and the appropriate development environment for plugin-based applications allow developers to define dependencies between plugins. In addition to that, the code of a plugin can explicitly be separated into a public API part and the internal implementation. For both cases, the compiler inside the environment produces special warnings and errors if they are violated.

Excursion: You Have to Live Architectures

A contribution by Markus Völter (voelter@acm.org)

In the course of the development of an enterprise system (J2EE server, rich client) with about 20 developers, soon a classic 'dying' of the architecture set in. With 'dying architecture' I mean that the architecture smells have such a severe impact that the quality level targeted by the architecture can no longer be reached.

Alas, everything started out so well! The concepts were clear-cut. The technical prototype was a success, the customer was thrilled and Gartner Group decided that the architecture was flawless. Then real life began to take its toll: the number of developers went up, the average qualification dropped, the architect always had other things on his plate – and time pressure increased.

The consequence was that the architecture concepts were executed less and less consistently. Dependencies were in a tangle, performance dropped (too many client/server hops and too many single database queries), and originally small modifications turned into huge catastrophes. To a certain extent the architecture concepts were circumvented on purpose. For example, classes were instantiated via Reflection because the class was not accessible at compile-time.

One problem of architectures is the fact that traditional development methods do not allow an automated checking of many architectural specifications [with model-driven development and AOP (aspect-oriented programming) some betterment can be expected]. The purpose of many specifications remains in the dark anyway as long as developers can't see the whole picture. Due to typical project-related constraints, developers often have no chance to familiarize themselves well enough with the architecture.

So What Is the Morale of this Story?

- Architecture concepts are all very well, indeed they are very important. Just as important is the training and coaching of the developers to ensure a correct implementation of the architecture.
- Regular reviews of the code are essential to discover and eradicate unintentional or wilful violations of architectural specifications as early as possible.
- It is common knowledge that the correction of a mistake will become more expensive the longer you wait with it in the process. Since architectural concepts mostly define fundamental issues, it is particularly important in this context to heed this principle.

References and Further Reading

Bäumer, D. 1998. *Software-Architekturen für die rahmenwerkbasierte Konstruktion großer Anwendungssysteme*. Ph.D. thesis, University of Hamburg, Department. of Informatics, Software Engineering Group. http://www.sub.uni-hamburg.de/disse/12/Beleg.pdf. Bäumer describes the architecture principles of large software systems and presents a model architecture. We derived the distinction between protocol-oriented and object-oriented as well as that between strict and non-strict layers, which we used in this chapter from his book.

Bäumer, D., Gryczan, G., Knoll, R., Lilienthal, C., Riehle, D. & Züllighoven, H. 1997. Framework development for large systems. *Communications of the ACM*, **40** (10). The authors describe a tier architecture for large, object-oriented application systems. The tier architecture introduced here clearly ventures beyond the scope of common 3-tier models.

Bodkin, R. *et al*. Enterprise Aspect-Oriented Programming with AspectJ. Presentation material for the tutorial, http://www.new-aspects.com/. This tutorial about Enterprise Aspect-Oriented Programming with AspectJ teaches, among other topics, how AspectJ's capabilities as a language can be utilized to determine at compile-time whether there are method calls that illegally bypass layers.

ClassCycle. *http://classycle.sourceforge.net/index.html*. ClassCycle is an open source tool for the detection of cycles between classes. It generates reports about class cycles in XML or HTML.

Code-Smells. http://c2.com/cgi/wiki?CodeSmell. This page of the C2-Wiki is about code smells and contains a list of often-occurring code smells. Besides code smells, one can also find references to a couple of architecture smells.

Dr. Freud. http://www.freiheit.com/technologies/download. Dr. Freud visualizes dependencies between packages and classes and calculates Robert Martin's metrics (see Martin, 1997).

Eclipse. http://www.eclipse.org. Eclipse is an open source development environment with refactoring support for Java. Its plugin architecture allows for an easy expansion of its functionalities, so that today a great variety of open source-plug ins as well as commercial plugins for Eclipse exists.

Eclipse Metrics Plugin. http://sourceforge.net/projects/metrics. This is an open source plugin for Eclipse that provides common metrics for object-oriented systems, e.g. the average method length. The resulting values let developers – where this makes sense – directly navigate towards the source of a smell, e.g. exceptionally long methods.

Fowler, M. 1999. *Refactoring. Improving the Design of Existing Code*. Addison-Wesley. The standard work about refactorings. Besides refactorings, this book contains a list of code smells – that is, the little sisters and brothers of the architecture smells discussed here. The comprehensive code examples refer to Java, but they can relatively easily be applied to other object-oriented Programming languages.

Gamma, E., Helm, R., Johnson, R. & Vlissides, J. 1997. *Design Patterns. Elements of Reusable Object-Oriented Software*. Addison-Wesley. This standard work on design patterns also contains patterns which lead to some of the architecture smells addressed in this chapter. This is, for instance, the case for the iterator pattern, which results in cyclical relations between the container and the iterator. The cycle could be eliminated, but this will lead to some loss of clarity. This cycle is acceptable though, since only two classes are involved in it. These are closely coupled anyway and will be put in the same package.

Hunt, A. & Thomas, D. *Tell, don't ask.* http://www.pragmaticprogrammer.com/ppllc/papers/1998_05.html. A depiction of the Tell, don't ask principle.

JDepend. http://www.clarkware.com/software/JDepend.html. JDepend analyzes the dependencies between packages and classes and calculates Robert Martin's metrics (see Martin, 1997).

JDepend4Eclipse. http://andrei.gmxhome.de/jdepend4eclipse. JDepend as an Eclipse plugin.

Kerner, H. (Hrsg.) 1989. *Rechnernetze nach ISO-OSI, CCITT.* Describes the ISO-OSI layer model.

Lakos, J. 1996. *Large-Scale C++ Software Design.* Addison-Wesley. This book introduces important architecture principles of comprehensive software systems that are relevant beyond the C++ context.

Law of Demeter. http://c2.com/cgi/wiki?LawOfDemeter. This page of the C2-Wiki gives a description of the Law of Demeter, according to which an object is supposed to communicate only with its direct 'friends.' Technically this means that an object shall not invoke a method on an object that it received from another object: method calls on objects which have been the results of functions are not permitted.

Lieberherr, K. & Holland, I. 1989. *Assuring Good Style for Object-Oriented Programs.* IEEE Software. September, pp. 38–48. The article depicts the *Law of Demeter.*

Mackinnon, T., Freeman, S. & Craig, P. 2000. *Endo-Testing: Unit Testing with Mock Objects.* XP 2000 Conference. The online version of this resource can be found at: http://www.connextra.com/aboutUs/mockobjects.pdf. The original article about Mock Objects was introduced at the XP 2000 conference.

Marquardt, K. 2001. *Dependency Structures. Architectural Diagnoses and Therapies.* Proceedings of the Sixth European Conference on Pattern Languages of Programming and Computing

(EuroPLoP 2001). In this article, a number of bad smells are discussed in the form of diagnoses and therapies. The collection of diagnoses primarily focuses on architectural aspects and offers a variety of possible therapies for each smell that will help remove it.

Martin, R.C. 1997. *Stability*. C++ Report. Although this article is several years old, the content has neither collected dust, nor is it C++-specific. Martin explains important architecture principles that can also be found in this chapter's architecture smells.

Martin, R.C. 2002. *Agile Software Development. Principles, Patterns, and Practices*. Prentice-Hall. This book by Robert Martin contains, aside from the main focus on agile software development, also a more detailed description of most of the design principles that are mentioned in this chapter.

Mock Object. http://c2.com/cgi/wiki?MockObject. This page in the C2-Wiki depicts the Mock Object test pattern which allows isolated testing of interdependent parts of the system. The use of Mock Objects furthers the *Law of Demeter* and the *Tell, don't ask* principle.

PMD. http://pmd.sourceforge.net. PMD is an open source tool for the detection of code smells in Java systems, such as empty catch blocks. It can also be used to check portions of program conventions. As a plugin, PMD can be integrated in various development environments.

Produktlinien. http://www.sei.cmu.edu/plp/product_line_overview.html. This source explains the concept of product lines. According to the definition given here, a product line is a set of software systems that share a common basis.

Refactoring website. http://www.refactoring.com. On the refactoring website operated by Fowler, among other material, an online catalogue of refactorings, which has long exceeded the scope of Fowler's refactoring book, can be found. One can also find links to other websites dealing with refactoring.

RefactorIT. http://www.refactorit.com. RefactorIT is a commercial refactoring tool, which – as a plugin – can be integrated in various development environments. Not only can RefactorIT execute refactorings, but it is also able to create a number of metrics for Java systems.

SonarJ. http://www.hello2morrow.com/. SonarJ is a tool for detecting architecture violations within Java systems. It plugs into existing IDEs (currently Eclipse) and detects violations right while typing.

SA4J. http://www.alphaworks.ibm.com/tech/sa4j. SA4J (Structural Analysis for Java) is a promising IBM technology preview. This tool visualizes the dependencies between packages in various ways.

Sotograph. http://www.sotograph.com. The sotograph supports the quality assurance of large systems on the software architecture level. Besides the system to be checked, the Sotograph also reads a description of its architecture, against which it checks the system. Thus architecture smells are easily identified.

Szyperski, C. 1997. *Component Software*. Addison-Wesley. The subsystems mentioned in this chapter can also be referred to as components.

Tell, don't ask. http://c2.com/cgi/wiki?TellDontAsk. This page of the C2-Wiki gives an explanation of the *Tell, don't ask* principle, which can also be understood as a clarification of the *Law of Demeter*: objects shall not be asked for information, which will make the client act on it. Instead, the client shall tell the object what it is supposed to do. Thus it is ensured that knowledge about dependency graphs will not spread over the whole system.

4
Large Refactorings

In this chapter, we are going to address refactorings that are not covered in Fowler's work, i.e. those other than basic refactorings. To this end, we will introduce the term *large refactorings* to clearly distinguish them from Fowler's basic refactorings.

Two exemplary collections of samples form the core of this chapter. They reflect our experiences with and best practices for large refactorings. We differentiate between two types of samples: on the one hand, we address organizational problems and solutions as well as those that are part of the development process. This approach is gaining more and more relevance, especially for large refactorings. The solutions we offer can be applied to your own projects and help you find adequate ways of dealing with large refactorings. On the other hand, we analyze recurring fragments that you can use as elements of your own large refactorings.

4.1   Introduction

During our participation in numerous projects we recurrently observed that – besides small refactorings – larger restructurings are required. If, for example, a pivotal inheritance hierarchy in the system must be rearranged, the impact of such a change can significantly affect the system. It might become necessary to adapt considerable portions of the code. We will call such restructurings *large refactorings*.

Large refactorings may be needed for various reasons. These are the most common ones:

Reasons for Large Refactorings

■ Developers put off small refactorings too long. If software design is not continuously improved, small design weaknesses will accumulate, and a more comprehensive rearrangement might eventually be required.

- Architecture smells emerge – unnoticed first – over time. If one tries to cure them, the respective refactoring can very soon expand beyond the scope of a small and basic refactoring.
- New features or altered software requirements can necessitate large refactorings. While some features will either integrate seamlessly into software or after a couple of minor refactorings, others call for a more elaborate restructuring.

Many development projects avoid executing large refactorings while a project is underway. As a result, the outdated structures will often be left in the system, or they will be tackled with a large redesign after release. We pursue the goal of integrating large refactorings into an ordinary, evolutionary development process.

While many developers possess an intuitive understanding of what constitutes a large refactoring, it is difficult to come up with a *precise definition*. Intuitively, the following characteristics are assigned to large refactorings:

1. *Duration*: large refactorings last longer than one day.
2. *Team*: large refactorings affect the entire project team.
3. *Unsafety*: large refactorings cannot be completely replaced by basic (safe) refactorings. Additional (unsafe) modifications are required.

Unfortunately, these characteristics prevent a totally clear distinction between large and basic refactorings. The manual renaming of a central method in a big system will take more than a day and concern the entire team, but it can be fully realized through applying the basic refactoring *Rename Method*. If the development environment supports the renaming of methods, the refactoring will be done in a few minutes, so that at least the first characteristic of large refactorings listed here no longer applies.

In this book, we will content ourselves with this loose definition because we believe it does not impair the comprehensibility and usefulness of this chapter. The intuitive understanding based on the three characteristics mentioned above offers a sufficiently clear framework.

Even while dealing with basic refactorings, we learned that these are no trivial matter. We observed the same for large refactorings. Often coming up with small steps that are self-contained (i.e. compilable and testable) appears to be particularly complicated.

One of the reasons, among others, is that a large refactoring will affect significantly more code in the system than a small one. Not all effects that a refactoring has on the system will immediately be evident.

The previously mentioned change impact analysis might be of some help here. Moreover, the sections on mechanics in Martin Fowler's book will provide valuable advice on how refactorings should be broken down.

4.1.1 Important Terms

A number of terms will repeatedly come up in the following sections. We wish to explain these briefly. First, we differentiate between basic and non-basic refactorings:

- *Basic refactorings* are those refactorings that are described in Fowler (1999) and mostly refer to basic object-oriented constructs.   *Basic Refactorings*
- A *non-basic refactoring* is a refactoring that exceeds the scope of a basic refactoring as addressed by Fowler. This category includes the large refactorings discussed in this chapter as well as those restructurings which Fowler (1999) calls *big refactorings*.   *Non-basic Refactorings*

Besides distinguishing between basic and non-basic refactorings, the safe execution of a refactoring is also very important to us. In this context, 'safe' means that the developers can be certain not to introduce any new errors in the course of their respective refactoring.

- *Safe refactorings* are refactorings that can be executed without risking changes to the system's behavior or creating new errors. If, for example, a tried step-by-step instruction for a refactoring is available (such as the *Mechanics* in Fowler, 1999), the refactoring can be carried out with no risk of creating new errors.   *Safe Refactorings*
- *Unsafe refactorings* are refactorings for which no tried step-by-step instructions are available that would allow their safe, incremental execution. One example of an *unsafe refactoring* is the renaming of a class (for which no safe step-by-step mechanics exist if you haven't automated it with an IDE).   *Unsafe Refactorings*

Modern, integrated development environments allow a completely automated execution of certain refactorings. Such tools can turn unsafe into safe refactorings. This is, for example, the case for renaming a class. Whereas no mechanics exist for this refactoring that would allow a safe manual execution, it can be carried out automatically via an IDE, which guarantees that the system's behavior will remain unchanged. In consequence, in this case the renaming of a class with an IDE belongs to the category of safe refactorings.

A modern IDE's refactoring support has a quite significant impact on many refactoring activities. Not only is it remarkable that unsafe refactorings can quickly be made safe with the help of an IDE. Moreover, some refactorings can be carried out in a short time although they change many lines of code in the system. For instance, if we rename a method, this step can potentially affect many places in the system (e.g. those calling that method). Even though this refactoring is also considered safe if it's done manually, the IDE's refactoring support changes the work with such a refactoring. We thus make a distinction between automated and manual refactorings:

Automated Refactorings

- *Automated refactorings* are refactorings that are supported by an IDE and therefore can be executed automatically. In this process, the IDE ensures that the system's behavior will not be changed. As a rule, automated refactorings are always safe refactorings.[1] In addition, automated refactorings can be carried out – regardless of the system's size – in a very short time.

Manual Refactorings

- *Manual refactorings* are not supported by the IDE and must be conducted manually by the developers.

4.1.2   Beyond Automated Refactorings

Until now, theoretical works dealing with refactoring issues mainly discussed the functional realization of refactorings. They focused on the automation of basic or even quite complex refactorings or provided mechanics for refactorings. In contrast, the development process aspect has rarely received any attention. While it is often stated that refactorings fit in well with agile development processes, the effects of refactorings on the development process are hardly ever considered. This may not be necessary for many basic refactorings, because they can easily be supervised and handled by a single developer. Here, neither a specific development process is required, nor must particular organizational conditions be provided.

Large Refactorings Behave Differently

Large refactorings behave differently. As Fowler and Beck in Fowler (1999) already remarked for big refactorings, large refactorings can affect the whole team and create certain requirements that must be met by a suitable development process, that is, for large refactorings we must explicitly address problems of how to plan, communicate and execute large refactorings in a team.

4.1.3   Can Large Refactorings Be Avoided?

Large refactorings bring additional development challenges and thus require additional efforts. Here, we notice that the added problems

---

[1]   We regard automated refactorings where the IDE does not gurantee not to change the behaviour as manual refactorings with some IDE support.

can be solved, but they do create an extra demand for planning, communication and discussion, which leads us to the legitimate question of whether there is a way to avoid large refactorings altogether.

First, one could state that continuous refactoring during development renders large refactorings obsolete. This is the basic idea behind refactoring technology as it is applied, for example, in Extreme Programming. Occasionally larger refactorings are needed in XP projects too though.

This is due to the underlying assumption that software development is a learning process. It also means that developers must revise design choices that were made earlier on if new software requirements demand a new software-ergonomic design. Depending on how well the new requirements fit the software's existing structure, these refactoring measures will be smaller or bigger.

For instance, in one project it took us quite a while to find out that *Project Example* we had, until then, misunderstood a part of the field of application. Since our wrong model of that field of application naturally had become a part of the software, the software design needed to be adapted to suit our improved understanding of this field of application.

Surely such effects can be attenuated through the implementation *Spike Solutions* of either spike solutions or prototypes for the basic system's architecture at the beginning of a project. However, of course there is no guarantee that the assumptions leading to the implementation of the new design, made at the beginning of the project, will prove to be right.

Thus we arrived at the conclusion that large refactorings cannot always be avoided. Regular refactoring during ongoing development helps to keep the design flexible and up-to-date. Design problems will be noticed early on and therefore can be solved quickly. This protects developers from postponing refactorings and thus letting the design degenerate (which, in consequence, would require large refactorings). Yet misunderstandings regarding the field of application cannot be avoided entirely.

Furthermore, in connection with our use of the Sotograph, we *Violations of* observed that violations of architecture can easily happen because *Architecture* developers cannot always recognize them right away. If, for example, developers integrate cycles on the subsystem level, there will be no indication that something is wrong. The cycle remains unnoticed in the system. Only a systematic analysis will reveal the potential problem. But even with the aid of the Sotograph, architecture smells cannot be prevented. The Sotograph will help us realize the actual problem only after we have already detected the smell. Nevertheless, a large refactoring will often be required to eliminate it.

Excursion: Refactoring – Not as Hard as Expected

A contribution by Berrin Ileri (berrin.ileri@it-fws.com, it-FWS GmbH)
and Henning Wolf (henning.wolf@it-wps.de, it-WPS GmbH)

Motivation and Background

Together with ten colleagues we are involved in a project for a major
municipal utility. It is our task to develop an individual solution in
Java that mainly serves to support prearrangements for work processes. Since altogether four different organizational units (OU) of
our employer are involved in this project, parts of our solution turn
out to be specific to certain fields of application, in addition to those
parts that serve all units.

Our development background is heavily influenced by the German
metaphors 'Werkzeug' (tools), 'Automat' (automaton), services and
'Material' (materials) that constitute the *WAM* concept. Of course, we
also apply the JWAM framework (http://www.jwam.de), which
already offers a series of abstractions for these design metaphors.

The parts of the system we developed until today comprise
almost 550,000 lines of code with about 3500 classes (of which 1000
classes are anonymous inner classes). Nearly 1000 man-days were
needed to reach the current state. The scale of the scheduled system
upgrading is assessed to require another 3000 man-days.

Our First Target Architecture

In our project work, we adhere to a layered architecture (see figure
below) that was familiar to most developers from other projects.
Each class of a layer is allowed to access any other class of that layer
as well as all classes of the layers beneath, i.e. the layering is not
strict. The corresponding package structure looks as follows (in this
and in the following examples we always show two organizational
units; the other two behave accordingly):

- de.customer.project
    - tools
        - ou1
        - ou2
        - general
    - services
    - materials
    - values
    - util

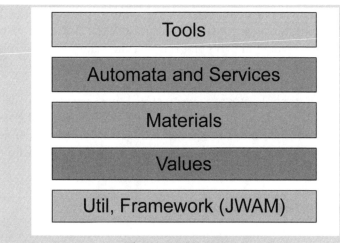

The Original Layering

The First Disillusionment

A short while ago we had our first opportunity to have our software architecture tested with Sotograph. Of course we had hoped that the result would confirm our skills as software engineers. You may take a look at the general survey graph below. The lines represent all kinds of relations (inheritance, usage) between architectural units. The line width as well as the width of the arrows convey the relative number of relations.

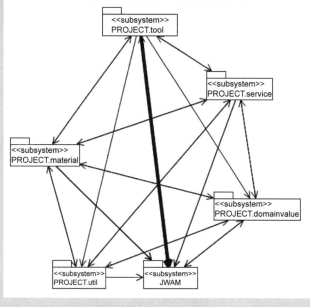

The First Survey Graph

The high number of double arrows (regrettably) shows that the targeted architecture was violated in many places. In defense of our approach we would like to point out that the majority of violations were caused by (JUnit) test classes that we always put in the package next to the class to be tested.

With the aid of Sotograph we analyzed those violations in detail and generated a to-do list containing a significant number of classes to be moved to another package and a large refactoring for our central tool. This tool had until then been insufficiently accessible to the organizational units, forcing them to take turns in using it.

Our Second Target Architecture

Since the project shall become much more comprehensive in the future, we at this point decided to alter organizational units to obtain a clear-cut structure. The package structure now looks as follows :

de.customer.project

- ou1
  - tools
  - services
  - materials
  - values
- ou2
  - tools
  - services
  - materials
  - values
- general
  - tools
  - services
  - materials
  - values
- util

The logical structure is shown in the following diagram:

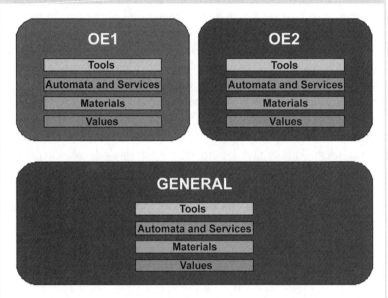

The Targeted Logical Structure

The First Large Refactoring

The already-mentioned to-do list formed the basis of our large refactoring. It mainly consisted of simple relocations of classes into other packages. The big challenge here was the modification of a rather complex tool that needed to be broken down into one general part and specific parts for both organizational units to be supported. Contrary to our misgivings, this restructuring work was dealt with rather smoothly, requiring little more than 100 hours (of which 90 were dedicated to the tool's modification). However, we were aware that this would not solve all our problems, although it erased a remarkable amount of 'white noise' during architecture analyses.

The result of our refactoring can be seen in the following figure if you take a look at the top level. The organizational units are independent of each other, but there are still two double arrows left, which means two subsystems still depend on each other. To put this result into perspective, it should not go unmentioned that only a single reference exists between the subsystems *GENERAL* and *OU2*, whereas subsystem *JWAM* displays six references to subsystem *GENERAL*. Especially the latter references may be confusing, since there can hardly be any calls from general framework classes that address specific project code. The reason is that certain framework classes are overshadowed and project-specific classes are referenced within them. This can easily happen when today's development environments are used, due to the automated generation of import statements. On the other hand, we could break down our project into various source code projects for development purposes to constructively prevent such impermissible calls on the compiler's side.

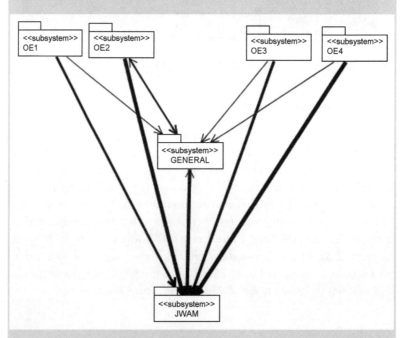

The Refactoring's Result on the Top Level

Beneath the organizational unit level we still have the tool, services and materials levels that we need to consider in context with the subsystem *GENERAL*. When we did this for the organizational unit (OU) 1, the outcome was what you see in the following figure. The architecture we targeted allows the OU tools layer to access all other

OU layers plus all *GENERAL* layers, while the OU services layer should neither access the OU tools layer nor the *GENERAL* tools layer. This rule also applies to the materials and values layers. This aspect was observed, although we were confronted with the following architecture violations:

- 5 references from OU services to OU tools
- 2 references from OU materials to OU services
- 71 references from *GENERAL* services to *GENERAL* tools
- 10 references from *GENERAL* values to *GENERAL* services

In addition, we discovered a reference between *GENERAL* services and *OU materials* that points from *GENERAL* services toward *OU materials*. References in this direction were not planned and thus constitute another violation of architecture.

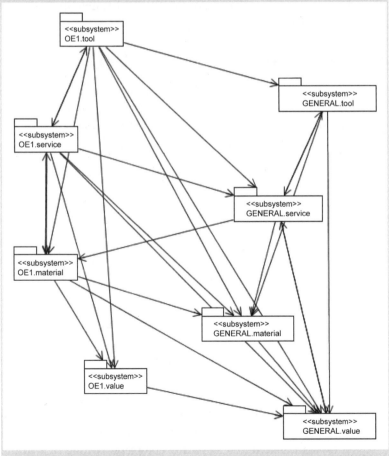

Dependencies on the Next, More Detailed Level

If we add the details of architecture violations we detected when we looked at other organizational units to the ones already discussed here, we get a second to-do list which will become the venturing point of our next refactoring.

Conclusion

Architectures provide an overview of complex software systems. However, architectures are always tailored to meet the status quo. They cannot apprehend changes that occur in the course of a project. Without continuous checks if the targeted architecture's requirements are met, the architecture will merely remain a UML diagram or an outline on paper. It will not noticeably contribute to structuring the source code. Contrary to our negative expectations, most architecture violations could relatively easily be cured with little effort. The less sophisticated refactorings were those most needed though, as they concerned parts of the system that urgently required adaptations of details.

4.2   Best Practices for Large Refactorings

We will dedicate this section to the difficulties that are either of an organizational nature or stem from the development process itself. Such difficulties occur quite often during large refactorings. Typical problems of large refactorings are:

1. *The effects of large refactorings*: a large refactoring can affect big parts of a system.
2. *Breaking down large refactorings*: large refactorings must be broken down into smaller increments.
3. *The use of basic refactorings*: large refactorings can only partly be constructed from basic refactorings. They are more than just a series of basic refactorings.
4. *The process of breaking them down*: the breaking down of large refactorings into single steps is a quite demanding task.
5. *Detours in the code*: the introduction of temporary detours in the code is often necessary. The system structure must deteriorate first before it can be improved.
6. *Assessment of consequences*: it is difficult to predetermine the consequences of single steps in large refactorings.
7. *Unfavorable or wrong refactoring routes*: it will frequently happen during a large refactoring that developers realize they have chosen an unfavorable or even a completely wrong refactoring route.

8. *Interruptions*: large refactorings must repeatedly be interrupted to meet new software requirements.
9. *Loss of orientation*: it is difficult to stay-up-to date as far as the actual state and the goal of the large refactoring are concerned.
10. *Large refactorings are teamwork*: they should not be carried out by single developers without continuously consulting the project team.

To deal with these problems, a number of techniques that are widely applicable have been established in the course of various projects. They range from planning and project organization questions to concrete technical implementations. Because of the vast scope of this field, these techniques are not as elaborate as Fowler's basic refactorings. Even when aided by the techniques described here, large refactorings will still require a lot of thinking and creativity.

4.2.1 Practice: Scheduling Large Refactorings

Problem

Large refactorings might be needed in the course of an evolutionary development process, and they can be executed in various ways. Apart from that fact, in our projects it soon became clear that it is easy to lose track of large refactorings, and that they will not be executed completely if at the same time the project happens to be subject to further development. One of the reasons thereof is probably that new features appear to be more important than a refactoring. Time pressure can contribute to further delay when certain functions need to be urgently realized for a specific iteration.

However, it cannot be our goal to put off large refactorings indefinitely. After all, we already learned that refactorings will become the more difficult to execute the longer they are postponed. This is why we have to make sure that even large refactorings will not perish in everyday development work.

Solution

The ideal way of dealing with large refactorings would be to solve them step by step during daily development while working on new features or parts of the system that should participate in the large refactoring. However, we seldom observe that large refactorings are really handled in this way. Often this leads to unfinished refactorings, or they are never started. Whereas the aforementioned approach might work better in small teams than in larger ones, we tried to find additional ways of making sure that those refactorings are implemented.

This problem can be solved by implicitly integrating refactoring work in the planning process. This means that we will include large refactorings in the iteration and release schedules.

In practice, we observed three different options:

Refactoring Budget per Iteration

▥ *Option 1.* For each iteration, we schedule roughly the same amount of time for refactoring, thus allowing enough time for the team to carry out refactoring work and to advance large refactorings. We are quasi concealing refactorings behind technical requirements.

- *The advantages*: from the customer's point of view, the project progresses continuously. The customer will not get the impression that the developers interrupt the project in order to 'clean up' and to eliminate earlier mistakes.
- *The disadvantages*: refactorings are sacrificed due to technical requirements. For this variety it is very likely that large refactorings will either be forgotten or not even begun.

Refactoring Iterations on Demand

▥ *Option 2.* Specific refactoring iterations are introduced on demand. These iterations only serve the execution of refactorings. In the meantime, system development is on hold.

- *The advantages*: this option constitutes a quite simple approach, since the focus is exclusively on the required refactoring work. Thus interferences between work on large refactorings and the realization of functionalities are ruled out.
- *The disadvantages*: the customer will not be able to observe any technical progress. From the customer's point of view, it looks like the project is dormant while he/she is paying. In consequence, it is possible that refactoring iterations cannot be planned due to time pressure.

Regular Refactoring Iterations

▥ *Option 3.* Frequent refactoring iterations. In one project, for example, we conducted three technical iterations and one refactoring iteration of a week each and created a release from them.

- *The advantages*: this procedure is simple and allows the team to focus solely on refactoring work for a defined period. One achieves an alternation between tense periods (technical iterations) and relaxed periods (refactoring iteration).
- *The disadvantages*: clearly defined refactoring iterations might turn out to be too formal and too strict for the team. If, e.g., the code is very clean and no large refactorings seem necessary, a rigidly scheduled refactoring iteration does not make sense.

In addition, this sort of planning invites the neglect of small refactorings during routine development work. The developers are possibly tempted to put off refactorings.

One cannot generally say that one of these options is better than another. In practice, the decision of which one to choose must be made based on the respective project situation.

4.2.2   Practice: Refactoring Planning Session

Problem

Large refactorings can be noticeably more difficult and complicated than their smaller relatives. They clearly require more time and seriously influence a team's work. Therefore, large refactorings gain more and more importance in the development process. It is no longer safe to assume that they – like small refactorings – can be easily dealt with as part of a developer's everyday routine.

To be able to efficiently integrate large refactorings in an agile development process, we have to bear in mind the larger picture and think beyond the refactoring itself. After all, a large refactoring can affect the work of an entire development team.

The execution of single, partial steps of a large refactoring which are integrated in the common code repository of the development team, creates uncertainties for developers who are not immediately participating in the refactoring work. Once the team has carried out one half of the refactoring, the code contains portions of the new as well as of the old structure. In addition, detours are integrated in the code to allow for these intermediate steps. For the developers it becomes increasingly difficult to keep track of the entire refactoring. The question, asked by developers, why a specific method is suddenly *deprecated* is convincing evidence.

Solution

A simple and at the same time basic means is to discuss and plan large refactorings with the entire team. Similar to a *quick design session* in Extreme Programming, all developers shall participate in a brief refactoring session, during which the design problem and the objective of the refactoring can be discussed and a possible refactoring route outlined. In addition, the developers can discuss a rough time schedule for a large refactoring to permit a rather uncomplicated proceeding.

The refactoring session also fosters direct communication in the team. After such a refactoring session, the design problem has been made known to all team members, and they have all been informed that the respective part of the system will undergo change. Also, all team members are familiar with the goal of the large refactoring and thus able to integrate it in their daily work. Last but not least, this communicates how the system evolves.

For us it has become a significant part of the development process to discuss major design modifications with the team and schedule them as part of the process.

4.2.3   Practice: Refactoring Plan

Problem

Typically, a large refactoring will take place over a longer period. In the course of their development work, the developers will frequently interrupt the refactoring to further develop other parts of the system or generally add new features.

Once the important core of a large refactoring has been implemented, in some cases the refactoring is not completed, i.e. there is no such thing as a 'clean finish.' For large refactorings this means that, for instance, implemented detours will remain in the code, or only parts of the system will be adapted to the new structure. The large refactoring is left incomplete, with the consequence that the system structure is suspended in an intermediate state. This preliminary structure contains parts of the new design as well as parts of the old one, including detours. It becomes much more difficult to understand and change the system.

If the developers totally forget about the refactoring and do not finish it, the system will still be runnable, but it will possess a structure that is inferior to its structure before the refactoring.

Solution

Besides conducting a common refactoring session, it has proven useful for us to write down an outline of the previously discussed refactoring route and put it up somewhere where everyone can read it. For our work, such a refactoring plan typically contains the single steps of the large refactoring. Developers shall place such a schedule in a prominent location. Thus it will be visible and present for all developers.

The refactoring plan initially discussed in the team is by no means written in stone for the whole refactoring period. First and foremost it serves as a representation of the large refactoring, that is, to bring the large refactoring to the developers' attention. It can also serve as a guideline for working on the large refactoring. As a consequence, the single steps of such a refactoring schedule can be altered, or their order can be rearranged. A refactoring plan is no work regulation, but an aid for keeping track of the refactoring process.

It is important to point out that the single steps of a refactoring plan do not exclusively depict modifications of a system (for example changing class names), but also clarify the intention of that particular step (class A inherits from class B). A mere listing of modifications makes a refactoring schedule vulnerable for modifications of the system that take place simultaneously.

It has proven especially helpful to check off which steps were already successfully executed on the refactoring plan. In this way, all developers of the team can see how far the refactoring has progressed, and what steps will probably be tackled next.

However, a refactoring schedule does not substitute direct communication between the developers of a team. Instead it promotes awareness of a large refactoring and its discussion. It helps to keep it in mind and realize its progress.

Excursion: Electronic Refactoring Schedules

Martin Lippert's Vision

The manual schedules we introduced in the previous section already provide some support to the developers of a team for the execution of a large refactoring. Realizing the effect of a refactoring on the system's concrete source code, however, remains difficult for developers. They can see that a large refactoring is being carried out that is not yet finished, and they can recognize what intermediate state it is in. It remains difficult though to reference, for instance, completed steps of a refactoring plan to changes in the source code. The question why a certain method is currently *deprecated* is not answered in this context.

To offer the developers even more comprehensive support, we wish to create a connection between the refactoring schedule and the system's source code. To this end, it evidently makes sense to convert the refactoring schedule into a digital version and make it an integral part of the project's source code.

First of all this means that the refactoring plan must be digitalized and integrated in the shared code repository. Then it can be directly accessed by each developer from his or her workplace.[a] A simple text document would serve the purpose. A comparable result could be achieved if the developers decide to manage their refactoring plans in a project Wiki web.[b]

A much better accessibility can be achieved when the digital refactoring schedule is directly integrated and made visible in the used IDE. In the Eclipse IDE, this could be realized via a special view.

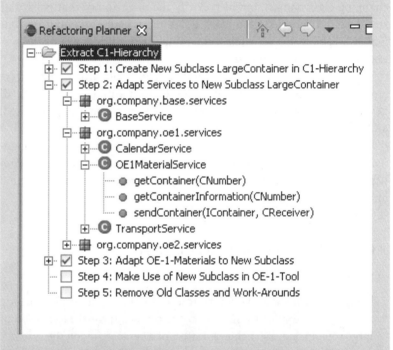

Refactoring Planner View in Eclipse (Mock-up)

The refactoring planner view in the figure above shows the five steps of the 'Extract C1-Hierarchy' refactoring. The single steps are each placed next to a check box which announces whether the respective refactoring step has yet been executed or not. Below each refactoring step the changes brought about by the refactoring are displayed (grouped by packages). The changes are made visible down to the level of single methods.

Optional navigation is possible from classes or methods to either the corresponding editor or to a diff-viewer showing detailed changes for each single refactoring step.

IDE integration enables easy changes of the refactoring plan and committing it back to the common repository. Additionally, IDE integration should allow checking off single steps in the refactoring plan.

With a digitalized refactoring schedule as opposed to a handwritten plan on the development lab's wall, not much has been won yet. Of course it is easier for developers to modify a digital schedule, but this plan does not possess the same charm as a handwritten plan on the wall.

A nice advantage will be won by the adoption of a digital refactoring plan if it is linked to the system's source code. In this case, the developers can detect correlations between single steps of the refactoring schedule and modifications of the source codes. Consequently, a step in a refactoring plan could be assigned certain code-modifications. A refactoring step would then hold the information as to which places in the code were altered.

Once that information is available, a two-way navigation could be realized. On the one hand, developers would get an overview of the altered code sections based on the plan. On the other hand, they could also navigate from the code to the refactoring plan if the former was modified in the course of a large refactoring. If, for example a method has been marked *deprecated*, the developer can find out to which refactoring step this change can be attributed.[c]

Refactoring Maps

Electronic refactoring plans possess a number of advantages (see previous sections). While the refactoring plan serves to visualize the execution of a large refactoring and makes the single refactoring steps transparent for each team member, it does not necessarily help the developers in the team to assess the refactoring's impact on their daily work outside the refactoring context. Often I wish to know how a refactoring will affect my daily routine. Do I have to look at the refactoring plan at all or can I do my job without keeping the refactoring in mind?[d]

I want to be able to see at a glance if the refactoring concerns me, if the part of the system on which I plan to work is already being refactored, or if that part of the system is approaching refactoring. If the latter is the case, the refactoring plan will help me get an idea of the refactoring itself and let me recognize what I have to observe in my work. Should the refactoring take place far away from my own 'construction site,' I can probably ignore the refactoring plan.

But how can I see at once whether the refactoring is 'closing in' or already affecting the part of the system I am working on?

Our idea is to use a so-called *refactoring map* to present the required information in a concise format. A refactoring map represents the system in two dimensions. On this level, the different parts of the system are arranged based on a particular pattern. For very small systems a class diagram will suffice; more comprehensive systems require a package or subsystem diagram.[e] The developer must be able to identify his or her own 'construction site' right away on this map. This can be achieved, for example, if the developer is able to isolate the source code on the refactoring map.

Moreover, a refactoring in progress is visualized on the map through the use of colors. The affected parts of the systems are tinted the color assigned to the refactoring. Thus, each developer can easily see what parts of the systems have already been altered.

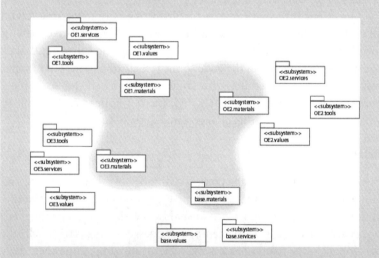

View of a Possible Refactoring Map

This figure shows a first version of a possible refactoring map. It represents the system on the subsystem level. The underlaid area of the map indicates those parts of the system that have already been changed by the refactoring. In our example, until now the refactoring seems to have primarily affected *materials* systems. A single *tools* subsystem has also been included.

a.   In this manner, team members working in different locations can benefit from a refactoring schedule.

b.   We used the Wiki web option in one of our projects and learned that the Wiki web is easy to handle but does not offer the same immediate visibility as a poster on a wall or the source code in the IDE though.

c. The technical realization could be accomplished with meta tags or annotations in the source code. The refactoring annotations could either automatically be submitted to the central repository at check-in, or manually inserted in the code. As of yet, no implementation of this mechanism does exist.

d. This should not replace direct and personal communication among the team members. In fact most of the information should also be disseminated directly in the team, although it would be nice to have a single place to look for backup.

e. The various display formats introduced here are only the first proposals. Other formats are also conceivable.

4.2.4   Practice: Refactoring Detail Plan

Problem

A publicly posted refactoring plan that has been discussed by the team is an important instrument for the coordination of work on a large refactoring. However, since it is kept somewhat vague on purpose, it is hard to determine which risks are involved and how demanding the refactoring will actually turn out to be.

During our project work, we were in for a few nasty surprises: our refactorings proved to be very complex although they had looked rather harmless in their flip chart versions.

Solution

The refactoring plan is supplemented by a chart of refactoring details. This chart should be created by a single developer or a pair of developers (in keeping with the Extreme Programming approach of utilizing pairs of programmers) rather than the entire team. The refactoring plan must be written down, breaking down single steps into basic refactorings as far as possible.

Nevertheless, this does not mean that a large refactoring merely consists of a series of basic refactorings. Additional modifications are required, for example, if one wishes to exchange the superclass of a class.[2] Modifications for which no safe refactorings are available pose the main risk for a large refactoring. Often it is not clear how such a step shall be executed and what consequences would follow in its wake, i.e. during and after refactoring. In the chart of refactoring

High-Risk and Low-Risk Steps of a Large Refactoring

---

[2] Tests can help to make the replacement of a superclass as safe as possible. But there are no mechanics that allows us to safely replace a superclass following the predefined steps easily. The exchange of a superclass will be discussed in more detail later.

details, the distinguishing criterion is whether the single steps qualify as (low-risk) basic refactorings or as (high-risk) other modifications.

Especially high-risk modifications must be analyzed thoroughly. Often it makes sense to begin by simply taking one single step or another. In many cases, the source of the problem will become obvious in a matter of minutes. Once this observation has been made, the respective changes can be discarded.

Visualizing Intermediate Results

It helps to create a graphic representation of the targeted intermediate results as part of the chart of refactoring details (typically using class diagrams). This will help to visualize the larger picture and to stay on top of the overall large refactoring process.

Often large refactorings reach stages where the system structure has already significantly improved. If a large refactoring has reached such a point but is then interrupted, the system structure will nonetheless be better. If a refactoring is stopped prior to reaching a point of improvement, the system will often still contain detours, and the system structure will have deteriorated compared to the original version. In that case, it is advisable to either undo the refactoring completely or at least revert it to its last stage.

The stages that mark improvements of the system structure are called *save points*. They should be highlighted in the refactoring plan as well as in the chart of refactoring details. If you work with branches, make sure to integrate the branches into the main trunk as soon as you reach a save point.

Automating Large Refactorings

When a large refactoring is carried out, the developers will use a number of basic refactorings as a rule, although a large refactoring does not exclusively consist of a series of basic refactorings. It also requires additional development work.

This observation lets us arrive at the conclusion that large refactorings can only be insufficiently automated. It is not enough to plan a large refactoring beforehand, then break it down into small refactorings that can be automated and proceed to apply the sequence of the basic refactorings to the code with the aid of a specialized tool. The developers can execute some steps of a large refactoring aided by refactoring tools, but other steps need to be executed manually. Nevertheless the goal must be to execute as many steps as possible using automated refactorings. The detailed plan can help us find the way through the refactoring that is as close to small automated refactorings as possible.

Excursion: Refactoring Thumbnails

A contribution by Sven Gorts (Sven.Gorts@refactoring.be)

Though modern tool support has made refactoring a lot easier, what remains difficult is expressing one's refactoring ideas to other team members. Especially within the context of a large refactoring, effective communication of the strategic decisions and underlying principles is crucial to a successful completion.

Drawing informal design sketches often helps to visualize refactoring ideas. When developers talk a refactoring through, they sketch small class diagrams, each representing a different stage within the ongoing refactoring. Because these sketches tend to be relatively small, they are called refactoring thumbnails.

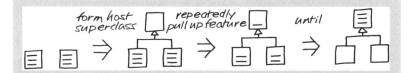

Thumbnail Sequence: Eliminating Duplication by Inheritance

Whether drawn on a whiteboard or a sheet of paper, refactoring thumbnails are drawn as visual additions, not as a replacement for the story being told. In order to enhance communication, thumbnail diagrams are intentionally kept small and concise. This both keeps the noise low and ensures the drawings remain fast and easy to sketch.

Using the thumbnail notation encourages developers to think about a refactoring problem in a more abstract way. At the same time, keeping the diagrams limited to the bare essentials of the refactoring helps to keep the discussion focused.

During the ongoing discussion of a refactoring problem, the informal notation ensures that the sketches retain a tentative flavor. Because of this, developers are less inhibited to grab the sheet of paper and contribute their own thumbnail sketches. The tentative look also causes developers to become less attached to their drawings. If an idea doesn't turn out as expected, only a piece of scribbling paper is thrown away.

Thumbnail sketches are usually short-lived. Indeed, although refactoring thumbnails are being used intensely, adapted and refined for a large refactoring in progress, outdated drawings typically end up in the waste basket once a design smell is factored out.

When a similar situation occurs, the sketches are drawn all over again, which is good. Refactoring thumbnails are about communication. With each sketch we tell a little story about the design. We communicate, discuss and improve.

A Refactoring Conversation

The controlled data flow project (CDF) is an ambitious project that aims to integrate FancyBizz's different data processing systems. Our developers Phil and Steve have been involved with this project for a couple of months. In the upcoming iteration, they need to integrate their software with the automated report generation system (ARG). The ARG code base, known for its legacy, suffers from many problems. During a brief design session, Phil and Steve talk through some of the issues.

Steve: Phil, can we talk? I have some design issues we need to sort out.

Phil: Sure (smiles). It's about the integration with ARG, isn't it?

Steve: How did you guess? (grabs a sheet of paper) What bothers me is this:

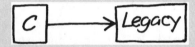

We definitely need the ARG functionality for report generation. If, however, we call ARG directly from our CDF model, large parts of it will inevitably become dependent upon ARG's implementation.

Phil: Yeah, I know. I used to work on the ARG code base during the early days of FancyBizz. Even though the code is rather messy, it has proven stable.

Anyway, we need to prevent dependencies to the ARG abstractions spreading over our domain model. How about encapsulating the ARG functionality with some wrapper classes? Something like this:

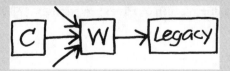

Steve: I see, introducing an indirection level will allow us to deal with those legacy abstractions locally. That's good. I'm more concerned about the runtime dependencies though. The ARG functionality won't run unless it is properly configured and we need to provide its configuration file at startup.

Phil: Indeed, reading the configuration file is part of the initialization sequence. It sets up a connection to the database, initializes the singletons and starts the threads.

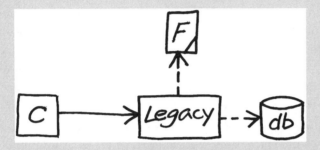

For our CDF unit tests, these dependencies are problematic. Now what do you have in mind? Something with an interface, right?

Steve: Exactly, by using the dependency inversion principle we can break the dependency. At least that would allow us to keep our CDF tests running without carrying the burden of the ARG code. Basically it comes down to this:

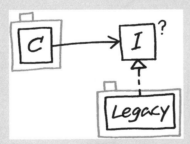

Phil: And we use the interface to write stubs to run our tests against. Seems alright to me.

Steve: Well, maybe not. Let me clarify. (sketches packages)

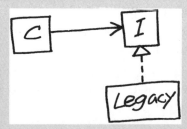

Something's not quite right here. I mean, where does the interface live? According to the interface segregation principle, it should go with the client.

Phil: And then the ARG code would become dependent on us. Na, that's no good. We can't afford the ARG code to become dependent on project-specific code.

Steve: The alternative – keeping the interface with the ARG code base – is not much better. Well, at least it gives us a substitution point for stubbing.

Phil: Wait a minute. The ARG class doesn't have to implement the interface directly. Using a wrapper, there was no need to do so. (grabs his first sketch)

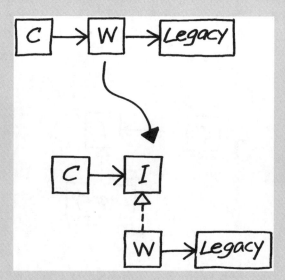

Here. If we extract an interface out of the wrapper solution, we can break the dependency on the ARG module.

Steve: (adds packages) And keep the interface with the client. Brilliant.

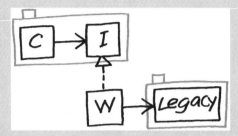

How about the wrapper class?

Phil: We can't move it to either of the packages without reintroducing our dependency problem. So, it needs to live in a separate package, I guess. Which leaves us with the question how to get the wrapper in place.

Steve: That's simple. We pass it as a constructor argument during the creation of the client class.

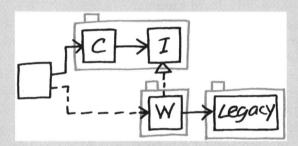

Doing so, the only code dependent on the wrapper, and thus the ARG code, will be the initialization code.

Phil: Hmm, neat. Seems like we're out of dependencies.

Steve: (looks at the entire drawing)

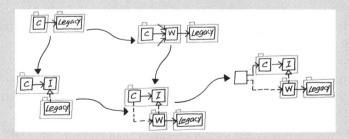

Yeah, guess we're done too. Thanks for helping me sort this out.

Phil: Any time, Steve.

Conclusion

Refactoring thumbnails are a simple means to visualize and discuss software evolution. Using a terse, yet informal notation enables developers to express a refactoring more abstractly while leaving enough room for further clarification and interaction. Such refactoring thumbnails are an effective, lightweight tool which allows the explanation of a refactoring idea in a matter of minutes.

4.2.5   Practice: Assessing Consequences

Problem

In many cases, a refactoring consists of two parts: on the one hand, we alter the structure of the code. On the other hand, we also adapt parts of the system to that altered structure.

Both parts of a refactoring may concern varying amounts of code. Either the changed or to be changed structure itself contains a large amount of code, so that the refactoring will become complicated and comprehensive, or those parts changed via refactoring are used by many other portions of the code. If we modify an interface or a type dependency in the course of a refactoring, the clients of the involved class need to be adapted as well. This may turn out to be a task of considerable scope if many clients exist in the system (see also Section 4.2.8).

The consequences of single refactoring steps are partially hard to assess. Quite often during a large refactoring one will notice that the scheduled single steps cannot be carried out in the originally planned way.

While a refactoring route may be fundamentally wrong, it can also (and quite often) happen during large refactorings that only certain steps turn out to be faulty, or that other necessary steps have been overlooked in the first considerations regarding the refactoring. Those particular refactoring steps must be reorganized and/or supplemented. In a worst-case scenario, the developer team is unable to plan each single step of a refactoring ahead. Whereas the status quo of the system and the goal of the change are clearly defined, the approach to getting there will be established in the process.

In our development processes, we always assume that software development is a learning process. However, this is not only the case for the implementation of new features. Large refactorings are more time-intensive and will restructure complex and/or central parts of the system. Thus it doesn't come as a surprise that large refactorings are subject to a learning process, which is not always completely plannable. What we are learning on our way influences the choices for our further proceedings.

Solution

One source of the problem is that we cannot foresee all consequences of a refactoring beforehand. The larger the system, the more complicated it will be to apprehend even a few refactoring steps.

Modern IDEs allow us to display a system's call graph. This feature enables developers to determine from which other methods in the system a particular method is called.

This function can be used to get a first impression of the possible complexity of changes to a method. Through the call graph's visualization, developers can learn with little effort how many places in the system access the scrutinized method, and how this method is typically used.

Of course this function is only useful when the effect of changes to a single method shall be analyzed. Changes to a class hierarchy cannot be analyzed with this function.

Many IDEs offer functions for displaying the inheritance hierarchies of a class, but the majority of these tools are not able to analyze the effect of changes to such a hierarchy. Often developers are left with the sole option of prototyping single refactoring steps in a branch. The resulting refactoring prototypes will be able to analyze the impact of changes. Such refactoring prototyping can become quite time-consuming. In order to be able to anticipate future steps, the first ones must have been executed almost completely.

Refactoring Prototyping

A similar problem exists in the software maintenance debate. Here, the approach towards mastering the situation is the use of sophisticated *impact analysis* algorithms. Impact analysis aims at enabling an analysis of the effects that modifications of a software system create. Not only are changes to an already modified system analyzed (*comparative impact analysis*), but also the possible impact of future modifications (*predictive impact analysis*).

Predictive Impact Analysis

The equivalents of these tools can be utilized for more comprehensive refactoring work. They let developers analyze how single refactoring steps will affect a system. This can be useful for recognizing complicated refactoring routes as early as possible. Further information can be found, for example, in Hoffman (2003).

Recognizing a Bad Strategy Early On

4.2.6   Practice: Branches

Problem

In fact small steps should support us in breaking down a large refactoring. This procedure also aims at reducing the required merge work, because the small increments can continually be integrated in the shared code repository.

However, some refactoring steps can be executed in a couple of seconds with the aid of modern IDEs. In those cases, taking small steps will not be necessary. If a central method or class is changed though, this will potentially lead to many automated modifications to the rest of the system. If the developers commit these changes back to the shared code repository, comprehensive merge work will very likely be the result.

Today, automated refactorings can be found as part of each professional IDE. They permit modifications of many source code texts at once (for example, if we wish to rename a central class). As simple and comfortable as this functionality appears to be – in some scenarios it can turn out to be quite tricky. If, after such a refactoring, we find out that we took the wrong step, we have to undo that refactoring. Should the IDE neither support such an undo-functionality, nor the complementary refactoring exist in an automated version, the developers will face a lot of work to undo the refactoring.

If developers have proceeded with implementation of application requirements, the new classes may interfere with the refactoring steps. That makes is very hard to undo the refactoring just by going back in the version control system – the application requirements would be undone too.

Solution

If a certain point a branch is separated from the team's current development work, then the team's developers proceed to carry out the refactoring in that branch, while the whole system is further developed in the repository's HEAD. As soon as the refactoring in the separate branch is completed, it is committed back to the up-to-date version of the system.

Advantages of Branches   This option of conducting large refactorings has a number of advantages:

- The large refactoring can be carried out step by step, and developers can continue to work on a system that runs without interruptions.

- The current working version of the system does not contain any detours, which would otherwise be required because of the refactoring.
- A refactoring can simply be 'rolled back' when the developers discover they've decided on a totally wrong refactoring route.

While this option initially sounds quite attractive, it also harbors a couple of disadvantages:

Disadvantages of Branches

- Developers involved in the refactoring are forced to switch between two different versions of the system if they continue to work on it after the implementation of a refactoring increment, or after integration of a new feature to further the refactoring. This switching between contexts is difficult and can delay a large refactoring.
- If the large refactoring is integrated in the current system, a substantial demand for merges is created, because the system development has advanced. Depending on how strong the refactoring's impact on the system is, the merge demands can be rather high. The further the refactoring progresses, the higher these merge demands will become. One of the major risks of such a proceeding is that a refactoring that has been in progress for a long time will no longer be integrated due to the high merge demand, and thus will eventually be discarded.
- As the case may be, a merging of the current system version and the large refactoring can take a relatively long time. During that time, the whole system is no longer runnable. The more time developers need for the merging, the higher is the risk for the entire team of creating a not fully runnable system.
- Once the refactoring has been fully integrated in the system, the developers who are not directly involved in the refactoring work have to familiarize themselves with the new system, because a lot of code may have changed literally from one day to another.

Our experiences made us realize that separate branches are better suited for larger refactoring projects when the changes brought about by that refactoring can be restricted to a part of the system. This is the case, for instance, if a large refactoring only affects the implementation of a fraction of the system. This situation can be evoked by preparing refactorings first (see Section 4.2.8).

Here, it is important to observe that the interface to other parts of the system remains unchanged. In the ideal case the respective part of the system can be replaced with the modified version – as long as its functionality has not been altered during refactoring. If this part has been changed, these changes must be integrated in the refactored version, but the merge demand will be limited.

Eclipse Runtime: An Example

In the course of the Eclipse project, an alternative runtime has been developed as part of the work on the software's version 3.0. The new runtime was developed parallel to the scheduled development of Eclipse version 3.0. Halfway between Milestone M5 and M6, the old Eclipse runtime was replaced with the new Equinox runtime. This was accomplished with minimal effort, because the runtime is accessed by other parts of the system via a fixed interface. In order to ensure an even smoother transition, the developers of the Equinox runtime attached great importance to making sure that compatibility with the old interface was guaranteed (Figure 4-1).

Fig. 4-1
Exchanging Eclipse
Runtime

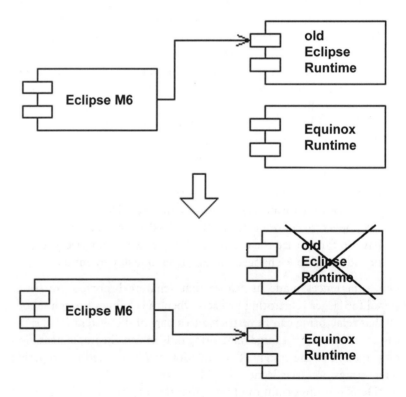

Even though the new Eclipse runtime is a new feature rather than a refactoring of the old runtime, this example demonstrates that the part of the system that shall be modified can be particularly well developed in a separate branch and merged later on, when only implementations are modified.

Unfortunately, large refactorings are not limited exclusively to implementations of system fractions. This seems logical if the refactoring shall improve the system's structure in a significant part of the system. For such modifications, the disadvantages of the branching approach clearly outweigh the advantages. Under these circumstances, we therefore prefer the integration of large refactorings in the main development branch.

4.2.7   Practice: Acceptance Tests

Problem

In our introduction to the refactoring topic we learned that tests and refactorings are inseparable. Refactorings can only be carried out securely when a good test coverage is guaranteed. Of course, a good test coverage is also one of the prerequisites for the success of large refactorings.

Nevertheless, large refactorings do not only require various modifications of the program code, but also modifications of the test code. The effort for the large refactoring will diminish if one occasionally throws away the odd test and executes a new implementation after refactoring.

A similar approach seems to have been chosen by the developers of the C3 project. On the Wiki web, Chet Hendrickson writes:

Experiences from the C3 Project

About every 3 or 4 iterations we do a refactoring that causes us to toss or otherwise radically modify a group of classes. The tests will either go away or be changed to reflect the classes' new behavior. We are constantly splitting classes up and moving behavior around. This may or may not affect the UnitTests.

This is why the traditional unit tests no longer offer a stable framework for large refactorings. In each individual case the developers must decide what a unit test failure during a large refactoring means. Was the last refactoring step faulty, or does the test have to be adapted or deleted?

Solution

Automated acceptance tests (as well as function tests) will prove useful here. They will check the system's behavior from the users' point of view, whereas unit tests check the functionality of single classes from the developers' point of view. Thus modifications of unit tests are often needed during refactorings. Changes to acceptance tests are only permissible to a very limited extent though, because otherwise the refactoring would alter the observable system behavior, not just the

Automated Acceptance Tests

internal program structure. Let us resume: in the course of large refactorings, modifications of unit tests are allowed, but modifications of acceptance tests are not.

For automated acceptance tests, FIT or Fitnesse can be used quite elegantly (see References). Both tools read tests from HTML tables, conduct tests on the application level and document the results in HTML. At the same time, the test results are connected with the application via *fixtures*. The fixtures receive their input values from the HTML tables. With these values, they then call system functions and return their function results. *TestRunner* compares the return values to the expected values based on the test specifications, and again the result is documented. This process is visualized in Figure 4-2.

Fig. 4-2
Acceptance Tests with
FIT / Fitnesse

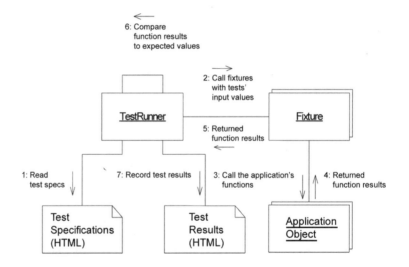

4.2.8   Practice: Refactoring-Enabling Refactorings[3]

Problem

We already discussed that some large refactorings might affect many parts of the system. This makes it a lot more difficult to implement those refactorings because developers have to adapt too many pieces of code. The system shows some kind of resistance against the refactoring.

---

[3]   Thanks to Sven Gorts who came up with this concept of refactoring-enabling refactorings.

Solution

It would be nice if we could lower this resistance against the refactoring. This means, for example, to reduce the scope of the refactoring, the affected parts of the system, to a minimal set.

To realize this, we begin a large refactoring by implementing some smaller refactorings with the goal to reduce the set of affected pieces of code. Therefore the first steps are not aimed directly at reaching the desired design. We first try to refactor the system into a state that makes it easier for us to refactor it.

If the system, for example, makes heavy use of global variables, this could make larger refactorings a lot more difficult than absolutely necessary. In such situations, we first encapsulate those global variables via singletons. This makes it easier for us to start a larger refactoring because access to the previously global variable is now localized in the singleton.

4.2.9   Practice: Detours

Problem

If changes to vital parts of the system are required (e.g. renaming of a vital method), many dependent parts of the system must be adapted as well. During this transition period, the system will neither be compilable nor runnable. Since it is desirable to have a runnable version of the system in the central source code repository, changes can only be integrated when they are complete and the system is runnable again.

Because these changes are rather time-consuming, considerable merge requirements may follow in their wake. Moreover, only after the refactoring is complete, tests can be run to determine if the refactoring process was executed correctly and the system is indeed operational. If the system does not run correctly, it will be very difficult to identify the one error or the errors. In principle, any class that has been changed in the course of the refactoring could be responsible for its misbehavior.

Solution

In order to break down a large refactoring in small increments, detours are built into the code (analogue to the detours for basic refactorings if they are executed stepwise). At the end of a refactoring, these detours must be removed from the code. If the developers additionally integrate single steps of their large refactoring into the shared code repository, the detours that have been introduced into the code will also become visible for other developers.

This leads to a situation that at first sight seems paradox: the detours will first impair the system structure with the goal of eventually improving it. In many cases, the course of a more comprehensive refactoring will look somewhat like Figure 4-3.

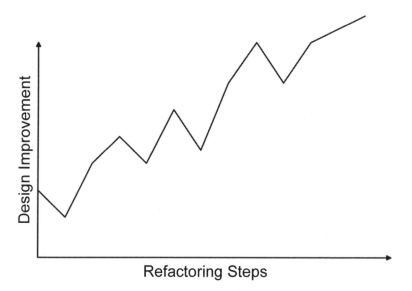

Fig. 4-3
One Step Back,
Two Forward

The graphic illustrates that most steps of a large refactoring will improve the software's design and bring the developers closer to the design they are targeting with their refactoring. However, developers will always have to deal with small steps actually leading in the opposite direction. Usually these steps are identified as being wrong at some point and corrected. However, it is important to recapitulate that a large refactoring can, as a rule, not be planned 100%, from start to end.

Based on the aforementioned observation, we pointed out that single steps of a refactoring might turn out to be wrong. Moreover, in the course of a large refactoring, developers may find that an entirely different refactoring route would have been preferable.

Example: Detours in the Code

The simple refactoring for renaming a method is – unless this is done automatically by an IDE – a good example of such a detour. Let us assume that the following method `print` shall be renamed `print-Document`:

```
public void print (Document obj) {

   ... implementation of print ...

}
```

In a first step we create a new method with the desired name and move the implementation of `print`. We will get:

```
public void print (Document obj) {

   this.printDocument(obj);

}

public void printDocument (Document obj) {

   ... implementation of print ...

}
```

In our next step, we mark `print` as *deprecated*:

```
/**
 * @deprecated use printDocument instead
 */
public void print (Document obj) {
   this.printDocument(obj);
}

public void printDocument (Document obj) {
   ... implementation of print ...
}
```

In the next step, we can adjust all places in the code that until now used `print`. In these places we are simply going to exchange the call `print` with the call `printDocument`.

Once all calls have been replaced, the old method can be deleted. It served as a detour for as long as we were not able to use the new method consistently. During this transitional phase, two versions of the `print` method existed simultaneously. The system's structure was worse than before in this period. Only after the refactoring was complete, was the old method deleted and a better system structure emerged.

4.2.10   Practice: Errors and Warnings as To-do Lists

Problem

Large refactorings harbor the danger of getting lost in minute details. With each step, the number of compile errors grows, and it becomes more and more difficult to integrate a completely functional version of the system into the shared repository. If you are finding yourself in such a situation, you are definitely in trouble rather than accomplishing a refactoring. This is a clear indicator that we are taking too big steps.

In contrast, we want to be able to break down even extremely large refactorings in such small increments that a functional system is guaranteed after each implementation step. We will adhere to this goal even if a large refactoring is carried out in a branch.

Deprecated warnings are a popular way of implementing stepwise changes. The old method or class is marked *deprecated*, and the compiler highlights all sections of the code which still bear references to the element marked *deprecated*. The purpose of this mechanism is an incremental transition of the marked references from the old structure or method to the new one. It is easily possible though that the sections marked *deprecated* in the source code cannot be arranged in any desired order. If, for example, a class with *Inline Class* is removed, all references to this class must be replaced with references to the new class. Should a method call another method while simultaneously passing an object of the old class, the calling class must be modified first and generate an object of the old class prior to the other method's call. If the method of the called class is changed first, the calling method must be adapted as well, because it will expect a parameter of the new class's type. Regarding the calling method, the question arises from where it should get the new class's object. The calling method can no longer simply generate the object because it may need to contain more information than the fields of the class to be deleted.

Solution

Do large refactorings in such a way that:

A Consistent Number of Compile Errors
    ▪ After each refactoring step, a consistent number of compile errors shall occur. This particularly means that the number of compile errors shall not correlate with the size of the respective system, but exclusively with that of the refactoring step. Thus the single steps of a large refactoring can be carried out in as little time as possible.

We will often work with *deprecated* warnings in order to execute successive refactorings. It must be irrelevant in which order *deprecated* warnings are processed because otherwise it will become very hard to determine their correct sequence in large systems. Some system cycles might even prevent a stepwise processing of the *deprecated* warnings. Moreover, arbitrary removal of *deprecated* warnings significantly simplifies planning and – last, but not least – allows the team parallel removal of *deprecated* warnings. You should be aware of the fact that marking something as deprecated is just a step towards the solution – not the solution itself. The refactoring is not finished until after the deprecations are removed, which is the responsibility of each team member. Be aware of using deprecation to put off the 'boring' refactoring work.
No Specific Order for Deprecated Warnings

The single refactoring steps shall leave the system runnable, so that integration is possible on a daily basis.
Continuous Integration

Behavior Conflicts

If we change the type structure of a class hierarchy or single classes of the system, different kinds of conflicts can arise. On the one hand, structure or type conflicts, which are noticed by the compiler, can occur. An example hereof are polymorphic assignments. On the other hand, behavior conflicts that will not be found by the compiler can emerge. For instance, this is the case when methods inside the inheritance hierarchy get overloaded, or when the type is checked via `instanceof`, and, as the case may be, a downcast takes place.
Structure and Behavior Conflicts

Modifications of the type hierarchy are extremely problematic. They must be thoroughly analyzed and planned. Choosing the right refactoring route is of utmost importance.
Modifications of the Type Hierarchy

The overloading of methods in an inheritance hierarchy can lead to unsolicited behavioral changes during large refactorings. For instance, if we change a method's signature, a number of problems will follow in the wake of this change: if the original method overrode a method from the superclass, this must not necessarily be the case with the changed method. The opposite can also occur: a changed method in its new version unintentionally overwrites a method from one of the superclasses. Fortunately, modern tools warn the developer if used for such a signature change.
Additional Problems through Overloading

The relocation of a method to a superclass can cause difficulties when the same method already exists in the superclass, but with a different kind of implementation. This raises the question if the implementation can also be adopted in the superclass. If not, the method cannot simply be moved to the superclass.
Relocating Methods

4.2.11 Practice: Inline Method

Problem

During stepwise refactorings, in most cases old and new structures will exist side by side for a limited time. The old structures are marked with the *deprecated* tag. This procedure primarily serves to track references to the old structure and incrementally remove it. In a Java environment this is particularly easy to do, because the compiler lists references to *deprecated* classes and methods with corresponding warnings.

Developers will often proceed to search all references for the deprecated class or method and adjust the according code to the new method or class. For a very comprehensive system this can cause a lot of work.

Solution

In an article for the XP-2003 conference, Tammo Freese suggests using the *inline method refactoring* in such a refactoring process. The basic idea is an implementation of the method marked *deprecated* based on the new method. The next step is to disperse the deprecated method via the inline method.

Example   Let us look at a brief example: we wish to replace the method `print` with `printDocument`. For this purpose, we already marked the old method `print` as `deprecated` and moved its implementation into the new method `printDocument`.

```
/**
 * @deprecated use printDocument instead
 */
public void print (String doc) {
  printDocument(new Document(doc));
}

public void printDocument (Document obj) {
  ... implementation ...
}
```

Now, we will find several calls of the old method `print` in our system's source code, for example:

```
...
String myDocument = ...;
...
```

```
myPrinter.print(myDocument);
...
```

If we proceed to conduct an inline method refactoring of the method `print` with the aid of the correlating IDE, all calls of the old method will be replaced by its implementation. Cleverly, we implemented the old method in such a way that it simply calls the new method (while converting parameters or return types, if these have changed, where applicable). Thus, after inline method refactoring, the reference to the old method will be directly replaced by a call of the new method:

```
...
String myDocument = ...;
...
myPrinter.printDocument(
            new Document(myDocument));
...
```

In his article, Freese takes this approach even further and shows how refactorings can also be used for APIs. For the large refactorings we are surveying in this chapter, the simple handling of the case described here will be sufficient in most situations. The inline method refactoring lets us elegantly alter those incidents in the code that call *deprecated* methods. Since for an inline method refactoring it doesn't matter how many occurrences in the code must be modified, this refactoring is very helpful in the restructuring of big systems.

Using Inline Method for Large Refactorings

Of course the inline method refactoring will work only if the old method, marked *deprecated*, can be implemented based on the new method. Should it not be feasible to move the implementation into the new method because both implementations are needed, an inline method refactoring does not make sense.

Limitations

The example we just gave also shows that the inline method refactoring can in some cases introduce exactly the kind of 'pollution' that was supposed to be eradicated by the new method (here the use of the string instead of the class `Document`) to the calls.

4.3   Fragments of Large Refactorings

After we have discussed organizational and development process-relevant aspects of large refactorings, we will now deal with functional patterns that can help us with our large refactoring work. However, we must admit that the field of large refactorings is as yet very young. Therefore, we are unable to provide a catalogue similar to Fowler's refactoring catalogue (Fowler, 1999). It may well be possible that there are too many variations of large refactorings to allow the creation of a refactoring catalogue.

Nevertheless, we would like to take a first step towards creating a refactoring catalogue and present fragments of large refactorings. In the last chapter, we saw that architecture smells accumulate in relationships *between* classes, packages, subsystems and layers: often lumps must be disentangled.

A project-specific analysis of what refactoring route makes sense to remove an existing architecture smell is required. In these refactoring routes, certain fragments will recur.

4.3.1 Moving Classes

It is amazing how many architecture smells can be eliminated by simply moving classes. Often cycles between packages, subsystems and layers do not imply the existence of cycles between classes (Figure 4-4).

Fig. 4-4
Moving Classes

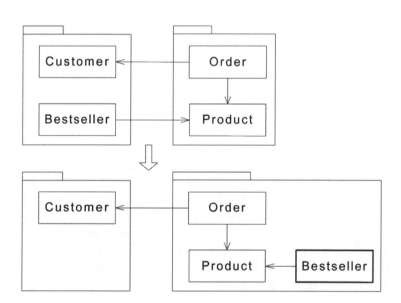

One should be careful though not to make the mistake of moving classes around without heeding their meaning, before all cycles have been eradicated. If single packages, subsystems or layers lose their internal coherence, the damage will be greater than the benefit.

In Java, the moving of a class usually means that the class is put into a new package. Since the package name is part of the fully qualified name of the class, moving means first merely changing the name of the class. In the case of Java, it should be taken into account that package-wide visibility is given (*protected* modifier or leaving out package visibility). Thus moving a class into another package could cause visibility problems.

The single steps for moving a class or an interface are:

1. If the class or the interface are merely visible package-wide: set class/interface to *public*.
2. Set all attributes and methods in the class/interface that are visible package-wide to *public*.
3. For all attributes and methods that are *protected*, check if they are used via classes/interfaces of the same package. Also, set attributes and methods to which this applies to *public*, too.
4. Change the package of the class/interface.

If you are dealing with a development environment that offers refactoring support or a refactoring browser, consider yourself lucky. It will allow you to alter the package name automatically.

- Should there be no support available for automatically changing package names, this process will be quite arduous. This is because the package name of a class cannot be changed in small steps; just as this is impossible for renaming a class [the reason why Fowler (1999) does not offer a refactoring labeled *rename class*].
- In this case, you have to swallow the bitter pill: change the package of the class/interface and then – one by one – fix all error messages. You can either do that in a branch, or you commit the class with a new package name. Afterwards all developers have to adapt all references in a single, concerted effort.

The renaming of a class with IDE support can be made easier if you use the following little trick: Instead of renaming the class directly, introduce a new class with the respective name. The old class's method declarations are copied into the new class and a delegation will be implemented. To this end, an object of the new class must be referenced to an object of the old class, and a temporary cyclic uses relation between the old and the new class be introduced. This uses relation enables skipping between types within the system. It is indispensable to generate a new type for each object of an old type (and vice versa). Thus, all references to the old class can be adapted to the new class step by step.

This approach will be problematic though if the class to be renamed possesses subclasses, because subclasses can either only inherit from the old class or from the new class.

4.3.2   Introducing a Dependency Graph Facade

In order to structure dependencies between packages, subsystems and layers it can be useful to hide a number of classes behind a facade. Whereas in Gamma *et al.* (1994) facades are employed to simplify the handling of multiple classes, we can also use a facade to hide a subsystem's dependency graphs from the client of that subsystem. This allows easier modifications of relations between single classes within that subsystem without having these modifications affect the subsystem's clients.

In the context of the refactoring described here, we assume that the client only depends on the class graph via uses, but not via inheritance. If inheritance relations exist, these must first be removed, for example by replacing them with uses relations (Figure 4-5).

Fig. 4-5
Introducing a Facade

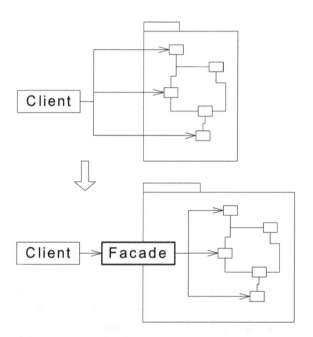

We proceed on the assumption that the client requests all objects to be encapsulated directly or indirectly from a root object. This means that the client uses the class of the root object as well as those classes used by the root object via `get` methods. This situation can easily emerge if the 'Tell don't ask' principle has been violated.

The facade can be introduced in the following steps. The first three steps introduce a level of indirection. The remaining steps ensure that the new level of indirection is used by the rest of the code:

1. Create the facade class, which will generate a root class object in the constructor. The facade class contains the same

constructors as the root class. Add a method to the facade class that can request the encapsulated object.[4]

2. For each method that is called by the client on the root class, create an identical method in the facade class. The methods in the facade class call the respective methods in the root class.

3. Step by step, change all instantiations of the root class to the facade class. Then directly invoke the encapsulated root object on the facade object and proceed to work with the latter.

4. Delay the calling of the root object incrementally and change the method calls from the root object to the facade object. Proceed stepwise. Depending on the circumstances, it might be possible to ease the search for method calls that must be altered by temporarily setting the root class methods to *deprecated*. Add a comment to the source code stating that the *deprecated* tags are only transitional. Otherwise, some over-eager colleagues of yours might accidentally delete them.

5. Proceed similarly to step 4 with all objects that are directly or indirectly referenced to the root class.

6. Remove the temporary *deprecated* tags.

7. Reduce the visibility of the root class to the package, so that the class can only be accessed indirectly via the facade.

The introduction of a facade resembles the 'Hide Delegate' refactoring described in Fowler (1999, p. 157).

4.3.3   Moving a Class within the Inheritance Hierarchy

Errors in inheritance hierarchies can have quite unpleasant consequences. While the hierarchy might be okay for a while, changes to the superclass, particularly semantic shifts, often cause subclasses to be no longer good citizens of the hierarchy. As a result, the system often gets flooded with `instanceof` type checks to adapt the semantic differences on the client side. The inheritance hierarchy will become difficult to understand and to extend. The desired flexibility through polymorphy becomes a source of errors.

Therefore, classes must sometimes be moved within the inheritance hierarchy (see Figure 4-6).

---

[4]   We assume that the root class itself is not going to be used as a facade here to affect its interface as little as possible.

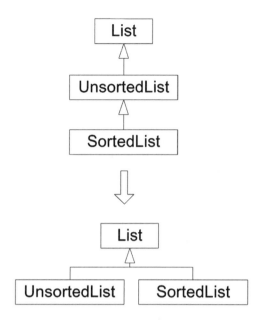

Fig. 4-6
Moving a Class in an
Inheritance Hierarchy

Modifications of the inheritance hierarchy are problematic, particularly the moving of classes within an inheritance hierarchy. The resulting problems and type errors of polymorphic assignments are often not curable in a step-by-step revision. The complete system will only be flawlessly compilable when all type errors have been erased.

This situation can significantly be improved by refactoring clients to use `List` instead of `UnsortedList` or `SortedList`. Unfortunately this is not possible for all cases, for example if clients make use of additional methods that are introduced in one of `List`'s subclasses.

The following single steps can at least contribute to alleviating this problem:

1. To move a class within an inheritance hierarchy, first create a new class in the selected place.
2. Copy the old class's implementation into the new class.
3. Set the old class to *deprecated*.
4. Work off the *deprecated* warnings and step by step adapt all occurrences of the old class in the code.
5. Once the old class is no longer in use, it can be deleted.

Setting Inheritance Relations to deprecated
To support step 4 in a more elegant fashion, we would like to see the compiler alerting us to all polymorphic assignments of the old class as well as their superclasses. Instead of setting the old class to *deprecated*, we would rather mark the inheritance relation between the old class and its superclass as deprecated. The compiler should then issue

warnings to indicate where the obsolete inheritance hierarchy is still in use. This is, for example, the case with polymorphic assignments.

We have implemented an Eclipse plugin as a prototype functionality in the course of the JMigrator project.

In addition, an adapter construct can help to simplify the transition from the old subclass to the new one. The trick is to introduce a temporary uses relation between the old and the new subclass. A method getOld that is also temporary can request an according object of the old subclass from an object of the new one. At runtime, there will always be an object of the new subclass and an object of the old subclass as a pair, and the new subclass delegates its methods to the old subclass (Figure 4-7).

Adapters Ease the Refactoring Process

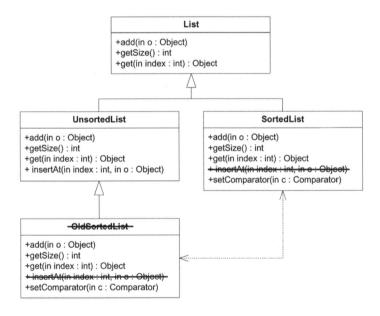

Fig. 4-7
Temporary Uses Relation between SortedList *and* OldSortedList

If a class has until now used the old subclass OldSortedList, the method can be adapted to SortedList in a rather segregated manner. If an invoked method still expects an object from the old subclass, the respective object can be requested from OldSortedList via getOld and passed on to the calling method. The opposite proceeding is also feasible.

Comparisons can be problematic if you use the adapter solution. Naturally, the methods equals and hashCode must be implemented in Java in such a way that the old object and new object are identical. If you check for identity in the system using ==, disparity between the old and the new object will be stated. For each single occurrence, you must decide whether this behavior is desired or not.

Since == does not constitute a method, it is usually not possible in development environments to get a report of all occurrences in the source code where objects of a type are compared via ==.

4.3.4   Changing Class Inheritance to Interface

Inheritance couples classes more strongly than the implementation of interfaces. The reason is that in inheritance relations between classes the subclasses must in principle know the superclass's supervisory control flow. This is not the case for the implementation of interfaces. After all, an interface alone will not implement a supervisory control flow. Of course a class that implements an interface must often know in which context the single interface methods are called by clients. All in all, the dependency is expressed more explicitly though.

Of course inheritance between classes continues to be useful. When dealing with inheritance between classes from different subsystems, you should check if it isn't smarter to have the subsystem define an interface via the superclass (Figure 4-8).

Fig. 4-8
Changing Class
Inheritance to Interface

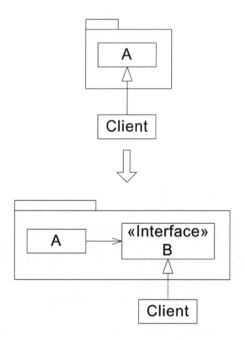

Taking the example from Figure 4-9, we think of class A as a member of a subsystem. The client of the subsystem subclasses A in order to specialize some of the behavior. The functionality of the subclass is used through the superclass A by some other parts of the subsystem in which A is defined. In order to replace the inheritance relationship between A and the subclass, you can utilize the following steps (see also Figure 4-9):

1. Create an interface B with all redefined methods from A.
2. Let all subclasses of A that are located outside this subsystem implement interface B.
3. Step by step, add default implementations from B's methods to each client which has not yet implemented them. The default implementations must display the same behavior as those methods of the same name in A.
4. Adapt A incrementally in such a manner that instead of hook methods, methods from B will be called. This will temporarily create a situation in which A will know the clients via inheritance and use them at runtime (step 3 in Figure 4-9).
5. If A no longer calls any methods on itself which may have redefined clients, delete inheritance relations between the clients and A.
6. In the second step, the new methods of the clients have been implemented in such a way that they adopted the behavior of A's methods of the same name. This may have created redundancies that can be removed by placing the redundant implementations in a help class.

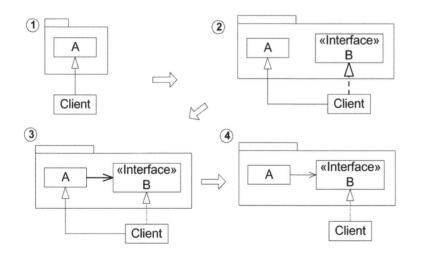

Fig. 4-9
The Single Steps of the Refactoring

The switching from class inheritance to interfaces is a typical step to be executed when a white box framework is further developed into a black box framework (see Foote & Opdyke, 1995).

4.3.5   The Classic Removing of Cycles

Software engineering knows a classic, universal procedure for removing cycles between two artifacts A and B. To this end, B is split into two segments B1 and B2, so that A depends on B1 and B2 depends on A. Depending on the situation, either B1 and B2 are independent from each other, or B2 must depend on B1 (see Figure 4-10, here the variant on the left-hand side). The opposite case – having B1 depending on B2 – would be a mistake in the selection of B1 and B2. Then A would again be part of a cycle (A->B1->B2->A, see Figure 4-10, the variant on the right).

Fig. 4-10
A General Procedure for
Removing Cycles

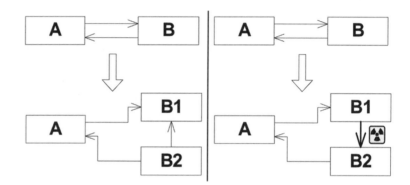

An example for the left variant is the observer pattern (see Gamma *et al.* 1994). There the direct dependency between the subject (A) and the observer (B) is resolved by using an interface Observable (B1).

It is also thinkable that a cyclic dependency exists between B1 and B2. Then the procedure depicted here must also be applied to B1 and B2. In this way, the cycles can iteratively be made smaller and smaller until they eventually disappear altogether (see Figure 4-11).[5]

---

[5]   While this approach removes cycles in dependency relationships, it does not break dependencies. You still need all pieces in order to test one piece, for example.

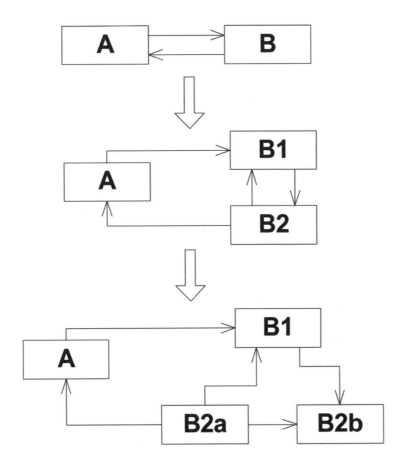

Fig. 4-11
*Iterative Removing of
Cycles*

This method can be used to remove cycles between classes, packages, subsystems or layers.

The previously described moving of classes works like the procedure depicted here, if the moved class is delegated to a new package or subsystem.

The procedure presented here will work universally, but without utilizing the possibilities object-orientation offers: the *removing of cycles with DIP* (see next section) utilizes the inheritance relation for the removal of cycles. This method will often let you remove cycles between classes in a smart fashion.

4.3.6   Removing Class Cycles with DIP

Cycles between two classes A and B can be removed in an elegant manner when DIP (*Dependency Inversion Principle*, see Martin, 1997) is used. For this purpose, we introduce a new interface that contains all methods that A calls on B. A only knows the interface that is implemented by B (see Figure 4-12).

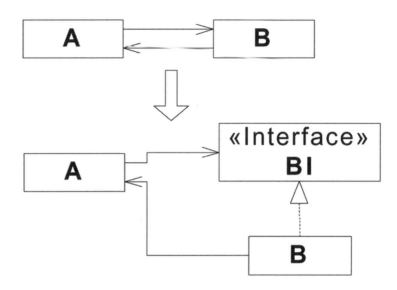

If you compare Figure 4-12 with the structure depicted in Figure 4-10, it becomes obvious that the dependency relations turn out to be identical after restructuring. Only the nature of B2's dependency from B1 will have changed.

This refactoring requires the following proceeding:

1. Extract interface BI from class B. The interface must contain all methods of B that are needed by A. B implements BI.
2. In A, set all references that are not required for object generation from B to BI.
3. If references exist in A for the generation of B, introduce a plugin (see next section).

You will experience the limitations of this refactoring when A does not only use class B, but also generates instances of B. After all, A cannot generate instances of the newly introduced interface BI. Clearly, the generation must be relegated from A. This can happen if, for example, the client of A generates instances of B and passes them on to A. Another approach would be to use a subclass of A to create the appropriate instances or to use factories. Alternatively, you can introduce *plugins* (see next section).

4.3.7   Introducing a Plugin

It is possible to use interfaces to reduce couplings – particularly between subsystems. A client will then no longer directly use a certain class, but only an interface. Thus it is feasible to use any classes at runtime, as long as these classes implement the used interface.

However, this does not answer the question of where the objects implementing the interface come from. If the client itself generates the objects, it must know the concrete classes for their generation (and thereby reintroduce the dependency the interface intended to circumvent). On top of everything, the client must also implement the case statement which serves to determine from which class the object shall be generated.

One solution to this problem can be found in the *Plugin* pattern (see Fowler 2003, p. 499). The interface defines an extension point into which plugins – the classes implementing the interface – can be plugged. To enable the plugin's integration into the system with as little effort as possible, the classes are registered in a `PluginRegistry`. Objects of the plugin classes can be generated using the `PluginRegistry` (see Figure 4-13).

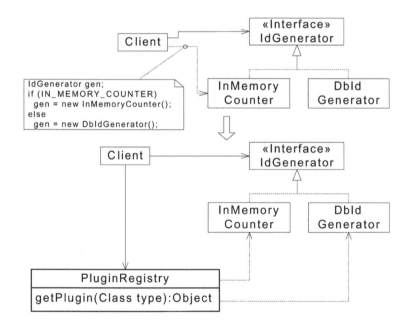

Fig. 4-13
Introducing a Plugin

The following single steps must be taken for this refactoring:

1. Search for all references to those classes that implement the interface. Replace all references that are not used for object generation with the interface. If the interface does not provide a required method, pull it up into the interface. Please note: the method should make sense in the context of the interface.
2. Implement the class `PluginRegistry`. The `PluginRegistry` will be parameterized with information that allows you to find

the suitable class for a requested interface. Alternatively, the `PluginRegistry` itself can get the needed information (for example from a property file). Please make sure not to introduce a mechanism that makes it more complicated to test those classes.

3. Search for all remaining references to the concrete classes that implement the interface. These references can only be object generations, since all other references have been eliminated in the first step. Replace these generations with calls of the `PluginRegistry`'s generation method.

4. To prevent the direct instantiation of subclasses in the future, it is in many cases advisable to set the subclasses or at least their constructors to package-wide visibility. It is recommended that you place the interface, the `PluginRegistry` and the classes implementing the interface in the same package.

The development of plugins is a logical consequence of DIP. They also facilitate the reduction of dependencies during object generation (see also Fowler, 2004).

Today, the plugin concept is discussed in various literary sources. Besides Fowler, Evans describes a similar design for domain modeling with his *Pluggable Component Framework* (see Evans, 2003, p. 475).

The Eclipse development environment offers a plugin model that enables third-party vendors to expand the development environment by their own plugins (see Bolour, 2003]). The Eclipse development environment itself is based on plugins. Therefore, it is possible to use the Eclipse plugin mechanism without the development environment for application development. The developers of Eclipse used this ability to build the *Eclipse Rich Client Platform* for application development.

Excursion: Refactorings are the Work of Human Beings

A contribution by Dierk König, Canoo Engineering AG
(dierk.koenig@canoo.com)

In dealing with refactorings, organizational and functional aspects must be observed. These can be described by scrutinizing the processes and tools that are involved. This is the objectively comprehensible side of refactoring processes.

Moreover, there is another side that is much more elusive: this is the part concerned with the people involved and their interactions[a]. This is the area that I will try to chart here, and I am going to introduce an explanatory framework which helped me at least to find some direction.

In the year 2003, we conducted a nice project: about 7 developers dealt with web technology and a strong database component for more than 5 months. On the agile practice side, we had soon installed automated testing, continuous integration, short release cycles as well as incremental/iterative development. We could cooperate locally and also were in close proximity to our customer. Pairing took place only in part. And the planning procedure was an entirely different story...

The 'basic' refactorings didn't pose a problem. Thanks to the support of conventional tools, only a few errors occurred. Those were recognized and intercepted by functional tests. Typical error sources were the symbolic references in Struts/JSP.

We even managed to get a grip on the 'common' database refactorings including adjustments to the schemas. Here, the first human aspect came into play: all of us had to simultaneously work on the same database instance, and we constantly stepped on each others' toes. This fact continued to get on our nerves until at last one developer took the initiative and – without it being scheduled – extended the database abstraction layer in such a way that everyone could 'virtually' use their own database instance.[b] Time needed: about half a day.

Now we were able to completely erase our own databases prior to each test run, newly construct the schemas and populate them with data. Afterwards, this part ran smoothly.

In the middle of the third iteration, things started to become critical...

Our database abstraction layer and our entire shared work on the code base – our architecture, if you will – became increasingly unclear. Our developer with the strongest knack for architecture took on the task of changing that, saying he wished "to clean up here."

This task had a clear-cut, functional aspect, the usefulness of which was unquestioned. But our developer decided to tackle another aspect that was more about how 'one' can solve such a problem 'correctly' and 'elegantly.'

Our efforts to solve the problem dragged along. For many days no commit would be entered into the repository. A week passed. A second week went by. The developer didn't explicitly refuse pairing offers, but he clearly preferred to work alone. He was also against committing intermediary increments that weren't 'perfect' yet. Team members piped up: "What is he actually doing there?", "Do we really need this?" and so on.

He repeatedly had to interrupt his work to provide support in his field of specialization. This led to further delays.

To keep up with team's progress, he had to increase his synchronization efforts.[c]

In the end, the required integration demand was extremely high by our standards.

We all acknowledged that the new solution actually was an improvement. However, we regretted that it had arrived so late it could no longer be fully effective, and that it had cost so much precious project time.

No-one was really happy with that large refactoring. The solution was not 'perfect' yet. The effort that had gone into it wasn't justified by the result. Spirits were low. Should we have opted for another architecture right from the start? Should we have done without the refactoring altogether? Both seemed wrong alternatives to us.

We certainly would have obtained a better result if we had been able to read this book before taking on that project. Then we would have had:

- the whole team plan the large refactoring; and
- conducted it in pairs; and
- realized it in small increments.

However, the question of how we could have dealt with different tendencies in the team remains: is efficiency more important ('good enough' and quickly developed), or perfection (the only way to do it 'right'). What is valid? What is better?

I am not able to take sides with one party. Both are right. In my view, a fifty–fifty compromise is not an adequate solution here. Instead, I tried to look at the positions from a systemic standpoint.

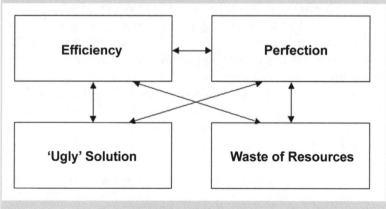

Development and Value Diagram

This is a development and value diagram according to Schulz von Thun (1989).

- Efficiency is a value, and it is good to achieve it. Let's say: E represents this value.
- Perfection is also a value, and it is good to achieve this value too. Let's say: P represents this value.
- If you overdo your striving for efficiency, you will obtain a solution that is 'ugly.'
- If you overdo your striving for perfection, you will waste resources.

The arrows in this diagram are pivotal. The diagonal arrows represent fears and (possibly unspoken) accusations:

- P accuses E of building 'unclean solutions,' having no sense of quality, etc. At the same time, P is afraid of being reproached for the same things.
- Vice versa, E accuses P of wasting resources. On the other hand, E fears that he could face the same accusations.

One should keep in mind that "fear and aspiration are siamese twins" (Schulz von Thun, 1989).

- P would like to be as efficient as E, if he could only maintain his quality level at the same time.
- E would like to be as perfect as P, if this were possible without losing time.

This recognition forms the basis for a development approach that unites the striving for perfection with the striving for efficiency.

This approach does not imply that you do less of what you think is important. It is about uniting one's own position with the other's point of view, so that you – speaking in terms of our diagram – 'develop upwards.'

How can this be accomplished?

Sometimes it is enough to let all team members participate in the creation of the development and value diagram, to let them find their own solution. If no solution is found, here are a few suggestions:

- The advice to take small steps is backed up by another argument: small steps lead to an added value within a short time, and this will appease E. Smaller tasks can be handled more easily in sufficient quality. This will alleviate P's fears.

- The team's 'Go!' in favor of a refactoring usually diminishes the risk of accusations.
- E and P team up in a pair for the refactoring to keep each other in line. This is not possible if both – which is often the case – have problems on the relationship level. Such problems must be settled first. "[The] technology [group] (detached, controlling, bent on proving themselves and aggressive-debasing) [has] to learn most in this scenario: Used to operating argumentatively and solution-oriented on the content level, they will often oscillate between exaggerated distancing themselves from others, dogmatism, help-lessness and aggression on the relationship level" (Schulz von Thun, 1989, p. 248).
- A coach can help to hear voices coming from the lower corners of the diagram, to put them into perspective and offer possible sup-plementing values. Typical phrases are: "let's finish it quickly before...," "only this one here" and on the other end "one," "cor-rectly," "elegant," "architecture," etc.

As our project's coach, I wasn't as successful with this approach as I would have liked to be. As far as I can judge, I could contribute to fostering the mutual understanding and appreciation between those involved, but their actual behavior did not change visibly for the short term.

Mutual respect is the basis for each progress in a dialogue. Once Kent Beck and I had a long e-mail discussion with differing opinions. He finally replied: "Progress comes from the disagreement of friends." There is a whole world of meaning summed up in this one sentence.

What is valid for a team can also be valid for a single person. Friedemann Schulz von Thun explains in his book the analogy between a team that consists of various persons and the various 'voices' that are united inside a single person (see Schulz von Thun, 1998). He calls this phenomenon 'the inner team.'

Whenever I am facing a refactoring, I can feel the dispute between E and P in myself. At best, a programming partner will be at my side, with whom I can discuss openly to resolve stalemate situa-tions. At worst, I will reproach myself until I have a bad conscience or until I suppress any thought of either E or P.

If the previously described model finds your favor, you can find an even wider field for its application, for example:

- To counteract the fear of an unnoticed introduction of mistakes through refactorings and of 'encrusted' code.

- To counteract project-bureaucracy (fear of loss of control) and hacking (fear of loss of freedom).
- To obtain a concrete, detailed view of the code, e.g. through unit tests that deliver fast feedback and an abstract, architectural view – for example with the aid of Sotograph.[d]
- Etc.

Where do I stand in this system if I either adamantly refuse to apply Big Design Upfront, the Life Cycle model, or MS project charts, or if I think that they are indispensable?

- [a.] The Agile Manifesto: "...people and interactions over processes and tools...."
- [b.] Realized with conventions for the table names.
- [c.] Merging of the HEAD with its branch.
- [d.] I call it 'programming distance.'

Excursion: Sustainable Architecture

A contribution by Klaus Marquardt, marquardt@acm.org

Redesign

You may be familiar with the following situation because of your own, painful experiences: a project has been finished, but with a lot of stress for all involved. Many goals have been reached, but the more experienced developers are left with a very bad feeling: they know that the code basis will continue to exist, but on the way to the last milestone, too much of the originally wanted structure has been changed and undermined by faulty, half-hearted solutions. They'll walk up to their boss or customer and ask for two team months to carry out a 'redesign,' i.e. to 'clean up' – and they won't get permission to do so.

When I assume the customer's position, I can perfectly understand this decision. The project came dangerously close to failing, now it's time for it to make money. If I were in the customer's position, I wouldn't allow any further budgeting without seeing clear cut advantages for my business either. What value can an investor possibly gain from a struggling team that even admits to working sloppily, if not even new functions are being added?

Dependency Management

There are projects where the software's internal structure directly serves to achieve business success. I will use the project Olymp[a] as an example here: Olymp is a plugin architecture[b] for the software of a family of medical devices. The basis of all these devices forms a framework for shared functions and abstractions. Via this framework, specific domain components (applications) are implemented as plugins. Products are created by 'plugging together' various applications with as little integration effort as possible. The software required for integration is also realized as a plugin.

This architecture suits the underlying organizational structure very well. Each department can manifest its specialized knowledge in an application software. Each single department is responsible for its software. Each product has a definite source, which is also responsible for production, marketing and customer relations. However, all applications profit from the extension of the framework, and all products will potentially profit from powerful applications. The architecture enables parallel development as well as congruency of tasks and competencies; the placing of functions rather 'low' in this building set system increases their reusability and also fosters a uniform exposure of the products to and behavior in the market.

On this level, the architecture of Olymp consists almost entirely of the definition of responsibilities, dependencies and their management. All further technology and complexity are secondary to these aspects. This level directly supports the organization and its internal business model. Thus the existence and maintenance of the architecture makes sense. Refactorings that serve to maintain the structure or increase its reuse will be actively supported by the investor.

Recognition

Each of these different plugins contributes to a series of layers, among others, data, rules, algorithms, displays and operating elements. This view builds orthogonally on the separation of single plugins. In its entirety, the structure of the whole software is almost ideal for a static analysis. As a matter of fact, I built a kind of software tomograph for my own purposes and used it to analyze the system in rather long intervals. Due to the system's clear organizational structure, I was very rarely surprised.

If I feel that dependency structures are important, these violations will document a communication problem. Violations that are discovered in the course of formal checks are always found too late, and pointing them out will only be partially convincing. This is why I always perceived the use of these tools as a last resort which would offer me an apparently objective justification for my goals.

It is much more difficult to assess if a class or a package have been assigned to the correct unit regarding its task. I have not yet come up with an idea for an automated test for this purpose. Instead,

I made the question of what would be the right location into a standard issue in design reviews. For each possible placement, I worked out criteria and defined a specific order, stating which unit should preferably contain classes.

Relocation within the logical structure frequently occurred in the course of the project. It was suitably infamous, and eventually it was dubbed 'Cat-Ball.'[c] Relocation wishes stated in the design reviews were not always popular, but for the sake of the greater good they were accepted and the refactorings executed.

No Change Without Suffering

Actually, several projects are part of the Olymp architecture: one for each plugin. The plugins in turn contain subprojects, because these usually comprise code for various processors and embedded systems. In such a complex system, it is hard to make progress, especially during the early learning phases, because each change caused by a refactoring has political consequences. To reach easier controllability and escalation paths, the first of these projects were united under a common management. For some projects, this would happen by and by.

Nevertheless, fundamental changes concern many places in the code of various subprojects. In most cases, the developers that are involved perceive refactorings as disturbances of their routine – after all, their own code works well, and they will not experience any improvements that concern them. This perception goes as far as having an imaginary barbed wire fence run around one's 'own' field of work; a fence that has even been established by the immediate project manager. Our motto for compromises made under a common project management was: *Those who want to bring about change must suffer.* The person who carries out a refactoring is also responsible for modifying the entire code of all affected plugins right away and for getting the refactoring to run properly.

In spite of this at first glance frightening prospect, this proceeding has proven to work well in the Olymp project. It reduced the developers' fear of interferences, because no-one could be accused of having introduced thoughtless and arbitrary changes. At the same time, the path was cleared for really important changes. We decided we would (and wanted to) do without aids such as *deprecated* tags. Last but not least, *deprecated* means that we are dealing with a 'slow' refactoring – one that has been partly put off to maintain compatibility. Such a careful approach was not necessary for a clear-cut, comprehensive project under common management. The prerequisites for our approach were a certain amount of shared code ownership, continuous integration, automated build & test, active support by the version control system, as well as a team with a common goal.

Inside the Booth

Developments and modifications that cannot be completed in the course of a few days or that require the combination of various expert competencies are separated from the normal development process and relegated to a booth. A booth is a separate branch of the version control system that is being run parallel to the main development process. As a rule, each developer (or pair of developers) will have their own branch and deliver their results into the integration stream. Here, a baseline will be drawn every couple of hours or days. Prior to delivery, each developer must synchronize with the latest baseline and carry out the required merges.[d] This leads to pressure in exactly the right place: synchronization with colleagues can be timed individually, but those who neglect synchronization for a longer period will eventually have a lot to catch up with. However, it is important that the decision when to synchronize can be made individually and is thus able to suit each project situation as well as each work style.

Bigger refactorings, like those that concern an API and several components, can even take a couple of weeks. Afterwards, the colleagues in the booth must merge a lot – unless they had the foresight to regularly synchronize with the current stage of integration during this period. This synchronization cannot only affect the main branch, but also occur inside the booth.

The booth creates a setting which makes sure that customers who use a component or interface will not notice the modifications that are going on, nor are they forced to make the necessary adjustments themselves. Instead, they can go through with their original plan. As long as all projects and partial projects can be handled as a unit, no compatible interface must be serviced.

Active, But Patient Waiting

Once the software architect working with such a system has completed the preparatory work of creating a fitting structure and mutual understanding and has established an adequate work process, he can lean back and relax a bit. Further interventions are not productive as long as the developers are coping well – on the contrary, it is more likely that they would evoke defensive reactions from the developers.

Nevertheless, the architect must be alert at all times and respond at once when problems or irregularities emerge.

This status quo reminds us of the work technique that is occasionally dubbed 'active, but patient waiting' in the medical profession.[e] It is a matter of one's personal experience to keep the balance between waiting and intervening and to recognize when threshold values have been reached.

Many aspects that an architect must consider in the course of the project can wait until the right moment for dealing with them has arrived. I like to document the points of recognition when these moments have arrived in the form of diagnoses and the according remedies as therapies. The advantage of this description method is that very different solution strategies from different points of view that are all valuable on their level of application (technological, process-oriented and that of human interaction) are all summarized in one place. Similar to a doctor of human medicine, a software architect can treat problems solely based on their symptoms or try to find the cause of these symptoms. He or she can work in an exclusively technical way or choose a holistic approach. Some of the smells in this book are also depicted as diagnoses.[f]

Sustainable Architecture

The blend of a decent technical solution, two-way adaptations of both architecture and organizational structure, compliance of technology and a process that heeds the developers' pace, the architect's attitude, as well as far-sighted concepts for handling the software's entire lifecycle – all these aspects account for a sustainable architecture in my opinion. Such an architecture meets today's needs without existing at the expense of future releases or the developers.

[a.] Depicted in Marquardt & Völter (2003).
[b.] See Marquardt (1999).
[c.] Derived from the tossing of a category.
[d.] This is the typical mode of work under ClearCase UCM.
[e.] Thanks to Dr. Kerstin Marquardt for this verbalization.
[f.] See Marquardt (2001).

4.4   Example: Lists

Let us take a look at an example to illustrate the discussions in this chapter. This example is similar to a real-life large refactoring in one of our projects.

4.4.1   The Starting Point

Initially, a system contains a class List[6] to allow the saving of objects in lists. During development, it turns out that a sorted list is also required. Its behavior is very similar to that of the already existent class List. Consequently, we will derive SortedList from List (see Figure 4-14).

Fig. 4-14
List *and*
SortedList

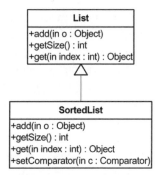

The problems we depicted in the List class example also recur in domain-specific classes. We, too, had trouble cracking these nuts. We had the following experience.

System development proceeds and the method insertAt is introduced to the class List (see Figure 4-15).

Fig. 4-15
insertAt *in* List

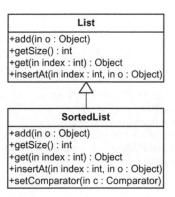

---

[6]   Naturally, one will very rarely implement one's own list classes. There is no need to, because the required container classes are provided by standard libraries for all popular programming languages. List classes are well suited for our example though, because they are easy to understand.

In practice, it can take a lot of time until somebody realizes that the design is somewhat crooked: insertAt is meaningless in SortedList, since the sort sequence specifies its position. Imagine you are inserting an object into a list in a specific position and afterwards ask for the object in that position. You would assume to get exactly the same object you put into the list (as this is the contract with the interface). In case you have created a SortedList, this contract would be violated. As there is no reasonable way of not inheriting methods from superclasses, something must be wrong with the inheritance hierarchy.

The inheritance hierarchy though can effortlessly be corrected by introducing another class labeled UnsortedList, which contains the method insertAt (see Figure 4-16).

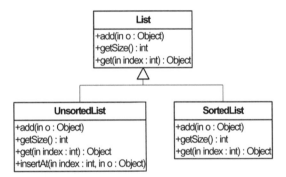

Fig. 4-16
Target Design:
insertAt *in*
UnsortedList

Getting there is not quite that simple, because the classes List and SortedList are already being used all over the system and other design smells (like the use of instanceof) impair a straightforward refactoring. A quick sanity check to verify the impact of a refactoring is to put the insertAt method in comments and then compile. The compile errors give an indication of the size of a refactoring and hint at places where you may want to clean up first.

In one project, we were facing a related problem and chose the following (dangerous) approach.

4.4.2 The First Approach

The class List is renamed UnsortedList to emphasize the problem in the inheritance hierarchy (see Figure 4-17). It is worth integrating this change to avoid merge conflicts because of double meanings of UnsortedList before and after refactoring.

Fig. 4-17
Renaming List *in*
UnsortedList

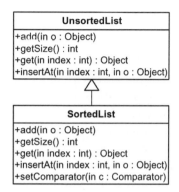

Now the new class List is introduced as the superclass of Unsort-edList. List receives the common methods add, getSize and get (see Figure 4-18). In most cases the new class List should be declared abstract to indicate that implementation subclasses are expected.

Fig. 4-18
New Superclass List

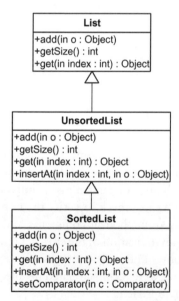

Positive is the fact that until now the changes of the inheritance hierarchy took place mainly locally. Only the renaming affected other parts of the system. Since most development environments carry out renamings automatically and adjust all references, no significant effort on our side was required.

The next step will be to move the class UnsortedList within the inheritance hierarchy (see Figure 4-19).

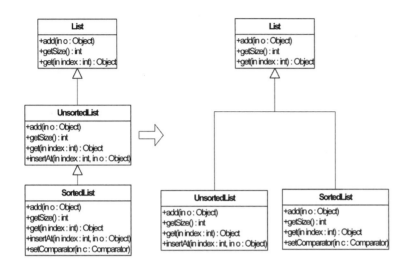

Fig. 4-19
Correct Insertion of
UnsortedList

The class `UnsortedList` is moved in a split second. And now the *The Drama Unfolds* drama unfolds: we get pelted with hundreds of error messages. Soon enough, the reason becomes clear: some hundred or thousand times we find method declarations of the following sort:

```
public void doSomething (UnsortedList list)
```

Originally, the parameter type `List` was in this place, but now it's been changed to `UnsortedList` in the course of renaming the classes. Not only unsorted, but also sorted lists were generated in the system. The latter create type problems:

```
SortedList list = new SortedList();
...
doSomething(list); // here the typo occurs
```

So, what can be done now? The initial impulse might be to swallow this bitter pill and eradicate the type errors one after another. Unfortunately this means that no compilable system state will be available for quite some time. Depending on the number of occurrences that need to be corrected, it might take unacceptably long for all errors to be eliminated.[7]

---

7   Of course a better way would be to switch back right away and think of a better way to perform the change. This is definitely what we would suggest. Nevertheless, sometimes you get caught in the trap. This is what we wanted to demonstrate here.

Actually, things can get even worse, because faulty inheritance hierarchies are often accompanied by very unpleasant long-term consequences. The inheritance hierarchy will be straightened out in the client code; usually with direct type queries (instanceof) and downcasts.

Most likely, our project example will present us with code of the following kind:

```
public void doSomething (UnsortedList list) {
  if (list instanceof SortedList) {
    SortedList sl = (SortedList) list;
    sl.setComparator(comp);
  }
  doSomethingElse(list);
}
```

However, we do remember that the parameter type was originally called List, and the method implementation did not always look so devastated.

Of course, another type error arises here. The compiler knows that UnsortedList cannot be casted after SortedList. After all, UnsortedList is no longer a superclass of SortedList.

It is obvious how the method is supposed to look like instead. Fortunately, we did correct the parameter of doSomethingElse beforehand.

```
public void doSomething (SortedList sl) {
  sl.setComparator(comp);
  doSomethingElse(sl);
}
```

Now, the whole matter is getting weird: two type errors have disappeared because the initially protested call and the invalid cast were corrected. Instead, ten brand-new type errors have popped up. All of a sudden, new portions of the code show type errors. A closer look reveals code like this one:

```
UnsortedList list = new UnsortedList();
doSomething(list);
```

Wait a second – what is going on here? doSomething always used to work with sorted lists, although this could not be deduced from the method declaration. Now, this must be some glitch: due to the if-construct in the original method implementation of doSomething, the method call was without effect. Accordingly, it seems safe to delete the doSomething call in this instance. If we weren't so busy eliminating all those type errors, we could run our tests now. And they would clearly prove that our assumption of a useless method call is wrong. There was a trick hidden in the original implementation of doSomething: the method basically executed doSomethingElse – for the sorted as well as for the unsorted lists. Only if a method with a sorted list was called as a parameter, would the comparator produce a certain sort sequence.

Thus we find ourselves in major chaos with our refactoring. The only means of escape from this scenario seems to be this one: we'll throw away our entire refactoring work, retrieve the latest working version from the version control system and start over with a different strategy. Admittedly, this is a worse idea than it appears to be at first sight, because we have not only carried out the refactoring in a single branch of the system, but also integrated at least its first steps into the shared repository. This means that all developers have to return to the last status quo prior to refactoring. Thus a couple of man weeks or even months can easily be completely lost. Alternatively, one can try to reverse the commenced refactoring step by step or execute it in a branch, but the latter procedure is not without its drawbacks either. We will come back to the discussion of branches later on.

Starting All Over

Perhaps you will first deem the representation of this refactoring somewhat hypothetical. Who would assemble such a messed-up system without noticing it? We have actually repeatedly seen such systems (and worse). Especially during long-term projects, unspeakable accumulations of oddities appear to be the rule rather than the exception.

Interruptions of Large Refactorings

We already talked about how large refactorings can be broken down in small increments. Furthermore, large refactorings often cannot be completed within a short time frame. A development team will need several days or even weeks until the whole large refactoring is finished.

In many projects, the developers do not have the option of dedicating several days or even weeks exclusively to one large refactoring. At the same time, the software system's development is supposed to progress as well. To enable this, developers will put down the large refactoring after a few steps have been carried out and continue with another task (e.g. work on a new feature). Normally, they will resume the refactoring at a later date.

4.4.3   The Second Approach

Let's have another look at our list example. How should we have executed it otherwise to successfully circumvent the cited pitfalls? Look at Figure 4-20.

Fig. 4-20
Start and Goal of the
Refactoring

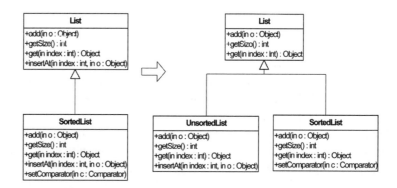

In our first attempt, we argued that List actually is an unsorted list and renamed the class. Then we extracted a new superclass List.

Step 1

Now we'll assume a slightly different perspective and argue that there is nothing wrong with the class List. Only the method inser-tAt has no business in this particular class. We set the method to *deprecated*. In our next step, we generate a new subclass of List that we label UnsortedList. The implementation of the insertAt method is copied to UnsortedList. See Figure 4-21.

Fig. 4-21
Step 1: New Subclass
UnsortedList

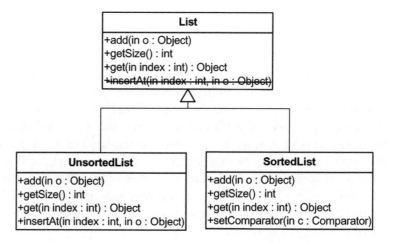

In our first step, we followed the advice not to move classes inside inheritance hierarchies, but to expand the hierarchy instead by creating new classes. Immediately, we can see one positive effect of our action: we didn't get any compile errors. In their place we merely received a number of *deprecated* warnings. They point to uses of the method insertAt under the type List in our system.[8]

Step by step, we can now analyze the calls of List.insertAt and adapt them to UnsortedList.insertAt. This process can be quite time-consuming, if the method insertAt is called on the type List. However, it doesn't matter in which order the *deprecated* warnings are processed.

Let us take a closer look at various code sections in the system that use insertAt. These sections reveal to us how these sections of the code can be rearranged.

Step 2

Replacing insertAt with add

The simplest option is to substitute the insertAt call with the call add. This is only feasible though if it doesn't matter in which position the new object is inserted.

```
public void whatever (List list) {
  ...
  list.insertAt(0, myobject);
}
```

... becomes ...

```
public void whatever (List list) {
  ...
  list.add(myobject);
}
```

Adapting Parameter Types

Naturally, we cannot replace all calls of insertAt with add calls. If we did this, we could delete the method insertAt altogether from List. Therefore, we will again use a method that calls insertAt and gets an object of the type List as parameter:

```
public void something (List list) {
  ...
  list.insertAt(i, myobject);
}
```

---

[8] As nice as the use of deprecated warnings is, these warnings always harbor the risk of never getting tackled. Therefore the use of the deprecation feature requires some discipline to make sure the refactoring is not finished until all deprecations are resolved.

For this method, the method `insertAt` is called on purpose to allow insertion of the object `myObject` in a certain position in the list. This means that in future the method will no longer get an object of the *List* type, but one of the type `UnsortedList` instead. We want the method `something` to look like this:

```
public void something (UnsortedList list) {
   ...
   list.insertAt(i, myobject);
}
```

If we change the parameter type of this method in a single step to `UnsortedList` though, it is very likely that we will be confronted with a multitude of compile errors, because the method is still used in its old version in some places in the system. For instance:

```
public void useList () {
   List list = new List();
   ...
   something(list);
}
```

Or:

```
public void useList (List list) {
   ...
   something(list);
}
```

Now, we actually need to adapt all these references to our recently altered method `something` to make the system compilable again. However, such a proceeding is against both the principle of taking many small steps rather than a single big one and the principle of adhering to a consistent number of compile errors. So what can we do instead?

Let us recall what our method looks like:

```
public void something (List list) {
   ...
   list.insertAt(i, myobject);
}
```

As an alternative to simply changing the parameter type to `UnsortedList`, we will create a new method with the parameter `UnsortedList` and proceed to copy the old implementation.

```
public void something (List list) {
  ...
  list.insertAt(i, myobject);
}

public void something (UnsortedList list) {
  ...
  list.insertAt(i, myobject);
}
```

Initially, the new method is not going to change the system's behavior, because the methods are bound to the parameters via static types. It is only applied where the new type UnsortedList is also already being used, which suits us just fine here.

Now we only have to set the old something method to *deprecated* and incrementally adapt its references to the new method.

```
/**
 * @deprecated
 */
public void something (List list) {
  ...
  list.insertAt(i, myobject);
}

public void something (UnsortedList list) {
  ...
  list.insertAt(i, myobject);
}
```

instanceof

In the section about the first refactoring route the following piece of code gave us quite a headache:

```
public void doSomething (List list) {
  if (list instanceof SortedList) {
    SortedList sl = (SortedList) list;
    sl.setComparator(comp);
  }
  doSomethingElse(list);
}
```

The new refactoring route has rendered the same code less critical. As long as the method doSomethingElse continues to expect an object of the type List as parameter, the method can remain as it is. If doSome-thingElse is adapted to require a parameter of the type Unsort-edList, the method doSomething must be duplicated as well.

Step 3   Once we have removed all calls of deprecated methods, we can finish the refactoring in a third step. To this end, we must merely remove those methods that are obsolete and marked *deprecated*.

References and Further Reading

Bolour, A. 2003. *Notes on the Eclipse Plugin Architecture.* http://www.eclipse.org/articles/Article-Plugin-architecture/plugin_architecture.html. Article about the Eclipse plugin model.

Coplien, J.O. & Schmidt, D.C. 1995. *Pattern Languages of Program Design.* Addison-Wesley. Contains many important articles about software architectures and patterns.

Eclipse. http://www.eclipse.org. Website focusing on the open source development environment Eclipse. Here you can download Eclipse itself. You will also find documentations about various aspects of Eclipse.

Evans, E. 2003. *Domain Driven Design.* Addison-Wesley. This excellent book discusses domain driven design. For the context of this chapter, the Pluggable Component Framework is relevant. (see p. 475).

FIT. http://fit.c2.com. FIT is a tool for conducting automated acceptance tests (including function tests). The tests are specified via HTML tables (e.g. for tables containing input values and expected output values for specific system functions), which are executed by a test runner. Using fixtures, the test runner binds the application to be tested to the tables containing the tests. In turn, the test results are documented in HTML pages.

Fitnesse. http://www.fitnesse.org. Fitnesse is based on FIT. In addition to FIT, it also offers a Wiki web which allows easier specification and organization of tests.

Foote, B. & Opdyke, W.F. 1995. *Lifecycle and refactoring patterns that support evolution and reuse.* In Coplien, J.O. & Schmidt, D.C. (eds); *Pattern Languages of Program Design.* Addison-Wesley, pp. 239–257. Groundwork article about frameworks.

Fowler, M. 1999. *Refactoring–Improving the Design of Existing Code.* Addison-Wesley. This standard work on refactorings contains a chapter about big refactorings that belong in the category of the large refactorings addressed in this chapter of our book. Fowler describes big refactorings as significant and recurring refactorings.

Moreover, four typical larger refactorings are explained, but there is no information whatsoever available on how large refactorings should be treated in general.

Fowler, M. 2003. *Patterns of Enterprise Application Architecture.* Addison-Wesley. Contains many important design patterns for the programming of comprehensive business applications, also the plugin pattern (among others).

Fowler, M. 2004. *Inversion of Control Containers and the Dependency Injection Pattern.* http://martinfowler.com/articles/injection.html. Here, Fowler focuses on the inversion of control containers and discusses several approaches to the generation of plugins.

Freese, T. 2003. *Inline method considered helpful: an approach to interface evolution.* In Marchesi, M. & Succi, G. (eds), *Proceedings of the 4th International Conference on Extreme Programming and Agile Processes in Software Engineering, XP 2004,* Genova, Italy. Springer, LNCS 2675. In this article, Freese depicts how the Inline Method Refactoring can be used to enable a stepwise evolution of interfaces. In our book, we are using a simplified variety of that technique to resolve deprecated methods.

Gamma, E., Helm, R., Johnson, R. & Vlissides, J. 1994. *Design Patterns. Elements of Reusable Object-Oriented Software.* Addison-Wesley. The design pattern bible. Also contains the facade pattern.

Hoffman, M.A 2003. *Automated impact analysis of object-oriented software systems.* In *OOPSLA 2003 Companion.* ACM Press. In this extension of his abstract, Hoffman writes about a tool that allows the conduction of several types of impact analyses. Particularly interesting is the predictive impact analysis option to anticipate the impact of changes.

JMigrator. *http://sourceforge.net/projects/jmigrator.* JMigrator is an open source project that provides support for modifications to subsystem APIs. Parts of its functionality can be utilized for large refactorings, e.g. for the detection of polymorphic assignments. JMigrator is realized as an Eclipse plugin. At press time of this book, JMigrator is still in an early stage of development.

Lippert, M. 2004. *Towards a proper integration of large refactorings in agile software development. In Proceedings of XP 2004 International Conference on Extreme Programming and Agile Processes in Software Engineering.* Springer, LNCS. This XP-2004 conference contribution elaborates on the problems of large refactorings in an agile development process. It focuses on the organizational aspects and obstacles and suggests the use of refactoring plans.

Marquardt, K. 2001. *Patterns for plug-ins.* In Dyson, P. & Devos, M. (eds), *Proceedings of the Fourth European Conference on Pattern Languages of Programming and Computing* (EuroPLoP 1999). Universitäts-Verlag Konstanz. This article describes typical patterns of a plugin architecture and offers a number of patterns. In addition to patterns on the architectural level, it contains patterns for organizational and process-related issues and scrutinizes some design decisions.

Marquardt, K. 2002. *Dependency structures. Architectural diagnoses and therapies.* In Ruping, A., Eckstein, J. & Christa, S. (eds). *Proceedings of the Sixth European Conference on Pattern Languages of Programming and Computing* (EuroPLoP 2001). Universitäts-Verlag Konstanz. In this article, a series of bad smells is portrayed in the shape of diagnoses and therapies. The collection of diagnoses primarily refers to architectural aspects and offers a series of possible therapies for each smell that will help to cure it.

Marquardt, K. & Völter, M. 2003. *Plug-ins–Applikationsspezifische Erweiterungen.* In *JavaSpektrum 2/2003.* Available online at: http://www.sigs-datacom.de/sd/publications/pub_article_show.htm?&AID=1117&TABLE=sd_article. The functional concepts of plugin architectures are introduced in this source and compared to those of other component architectures. The main topic is the impact of a plugin architecture and related contract issues as well as a decision guidance, if this architecture type is useful for a specific project or not.

Martin, R.C. 1997. *Stability.* C++ Report. Even though this contribution is several years old, its content has neither collected dust, nor is it C++-specific. In this article, DIP (Dependency Inversion Principle) is also described.

Schulz von Thun, F. 1998. *Miteinander reden,* Vol. 2. Rowohlt Taschenbuch. Volume Two of this bestselling series. How to develop a systemic view of mutual restraints and vicious circles in communication. Development and Value Diagram, personal ways of communication, approaches to communication improvement.

Schulz von Thun, F. 1998. *Miteinander reden,* Vol. 3. Rowohlt Taschenbuch. Volume Three of this bestselling series. Analogies between teams consisting of several persons and the inner team, the various voices within one person. Work methods of these teams: side by side (without contact), disordered (without structure), against each other (restraining), with one another (fostering). How to remove blockades, integration of all members, team development, coherent presentation of the (inner) team to the external world.

5
Refactoring of Relational Databases

In application development, mostly relational databases are employed nowadays. Other than object-oriented programming languages, relational databases hardly offer any options for building modules. Therefore, there is no way of locally limiting the effect of changes to a single module.

Changes to relational database schemas (e.g. removal of a foreign key from a table) will often affect expansive areas of the schemas and thus create a need for comprehensive adaptations of the program.

This chapter addresses what modifications of relational database schemas occur, and how these can effectively be embedded in large refactorings.

Modifications of relational database schemas and the required work in their wake (program adaptations, data migration, etc.) were much discussed in the context of agile methods. This chapter will survey several of the discussion results, which means that the authors of the concepts quoted here should be honored rather than us. We merely assembled the information.

5.1   Differences between Databases and OO Programming Languages

Before we get started, it is helpful to take a closer look at the differences between relational databases and object-oriented programming languages:

■ The focus of relational databases is on the definition of data structures. Encapsulation through methods or the like is not possible. In consequence, data access cannot be sensibly restricted.

■ Tables are connected via foreign key relations. These links too cannot be encapsulated.

▓ Data in databases is persistent and outlasts a program run. If the database schema is altered, the data must migrate.

▓ If more than one installation of the system exists (e.g. at different customers), there will also be different databases. Should the database schema be changed, the respective change must be made for each installation and the data of each schema must migrate.

▓ Different users can access data simultaneously, while conceptually each single user has his or her own copy of the program.

▓ Classes can inherit from each other; tables and data can't.

▓ Source code can be changed locally from the developers' terminals and tested prior to reintegration in the shared code repository. Conflicts can be recognized and eradicated with the aid of powerful tools. In most projects, the database is run centrally for all developers.

▓ Source code can be managed with the support of version control systems and administrated in variants. Database structures and data can only be versioned with significantly greater effort.

▓ Accessing data in the database takes a multiple of the time required for accessing objects in the RAM.

▓ The data structures in relational databases are shallow, whereas they are deep and interlaced in OO systems.

5.2   Problems in the Interaction of Programs and Database

The interaction of programs and database creates additional problems:

▓ Program and database are often not coupled typesafe (as happens to be the case with JDBC, for example). The compiler has no means of assessing if program and database are structurally compatible. Suitable mapper classes or persistence layers will take the problem elsewhere without solving it. Typesafety will be lost inside the mapper classes or the persistency layer, not already outside.

▓ Databases will 'hide' objects when in one place of the program objects are written to the database and then read out somewhere else. Thus objects can be exchanged between parts of the program without this process becoming visible at the program's interfaces.

▓ Frequently, a 1:1 relation between classes and tables is assumed, which is often not correct for data-intensive applications. Specifically for reading in objects from the database, several tables must be joined, or certain views must be applied for performance reasons. As a result, there is no simple way of determining which classes must be adapted in the course of database modifications.

Conversely, it is not always clear how changes of class will affect queries and views.

■ There is the odd case where a mapping between types in the database and the primitive data types of the programming language used will cause difficulties. For instance, the granularity of time stamps (TIMESTAMP), floating point numbers of varying precision or strings of various character sets can deviate (milliseconds versus nanoseconds).

■ In object-oriented systems, containment relations are modeled based on the container (i.e. an account will know its balance). In relational databases, 1:N relations are modeled precisely and vice versa (due to foreign key relations balances knowing to which account they belong). This means that there is no predefined course of action for a refactoring.

Thus we have to consider three major areas for refactoring:

1. Refactoring of the database schema/the data model.
2. Migration of data between different versions of the database schema.
3. Refactoring of the database access code.

5.3   Refactoring of Relational Database Schemas

In practice, a number of database schemas will exist in parallel. There are at least *two* variations: one for the developers (the *development database*) and one for the users (the *production database*).

Development and Production Database

Thus developers can try out modifications of a database without affecting the system's users. Only when the changes to the database have been thoroughly tested and adapted to the system on which the database is built, will the program and the new database schema be made available to users with the next release.

Moreover, each developer should have his or her own database instance to be able to test changes to the database in isolation from the rest of the team. The existence of several database instances makes the migration of data between various types of database schemas a pivotal topic. We are going to discuss this topic in the following section.

One Database for Each Developer

In many refactorings a central principle of a stepwise evolution of programs as well as of data structures is recurring: old structures are not immediately replaced with new ones. Instead, old and new structures will exist side by side for some time. The old structure will be marked *deprecated* to keep new parts of the program from accessing it. Then the existing programs are modified; step by step they will be adapted from the old structure to the new one. Once this has been

Refactoring a Database Schema

accomplished, the old data structure will finally be deleted. Figure 5-1 shows the evolution of the table *Customer*. Initially, first and last name were stored together in one field labeled *Name*. The two pieces of information shall now be submitted to the fields *First Name* and *Last Name*. To this end, both fields are added to the *Name* field and the latter marked. After all programs have been adapted to use *First Name* and *Last Name*, the *Name* field is deleted.

In its intermediate state, the table *Customer* contains redundant information (*Name*). Either the application can ensure that the data will be consistent, or the problem is solved with the support of suitable triggers.

Customer	Customer	Customer
Number	Number	Number
Name	*Name*	
	Last Name	Last Name
	First Name	First Name
Street	Street	Street
Zip Code	Zip Code	Zip Code
Town	Town	Town

In Java, program elements can be marked obsolete with the *deprecated* tag. In other programming languages as well as in the database field, the search for an equivalent of this tag will be fruitless in most cases.

In the relational database field, columns, tables, views or even entire schemas will be marked *deprecated*, depending on the refactoring that is applied. How these elements are marked as being obsolete is primarily determined by how the database is accessed. If, for example, an OR mapping tool that generates Java access classes is used (such as Apache's *Torque*), the generated classes or single methods can simply be marked *deprecated* – on the one condition that no other system directly accesses the database. Figure 5-2 shows this proceeding. The application only accesses the database via mapper classes. Therefore, it suffices to mark the access methods for the field *Name* as *deprecated* in the second version (crossed-out methods).

If access does not take place strictly channeled via specific access classes, one usually will have to make do with conventions. One can either maintain a list of all obsolete elements or add comments to the elements that state that those elements are deprecated. Of course it is important that all developers know the convention agreed upon and observe it.

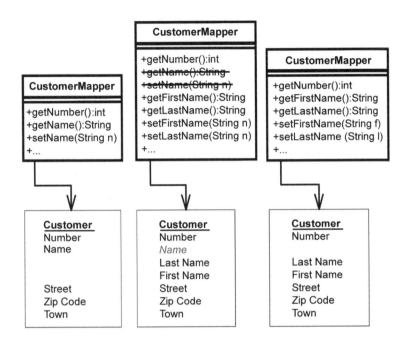

Fig. 5-2
A Database Access Layer Makes the Marking of Deprecated Elements in Data Structures Easier

5.3.1   Database Refactorings

On his website, Ambler (2003b) has collected frequently required refactorings for relational database schemas. The refactorings depicted there are a useful reference source.

Ambler's refactorings aim at improvements of database schemas. Therefore, the addition of a column alone does not constitute a refactoring. The added column by itself will not improve the database schema.

Database refactorings fall into various categories: refactorings that will either improve the data quality, structure, performance, referential data integrity, or the database architecture.

The descriptions of refactorings refer to the database structure. The adaptation of programs or the migration of existing data is only mentioned as a side note.

The *deprecated* concept is also applied to database refactorings. Since tables and columns cannot be marked as being deprecated in relational databases, another way for communicating what is deprecated must be found (see previous page).

5.4   Migration of Data between Different Versions of a Database Schema

As soon as the system has been released for users, a refactoring of only the development database schema will no longer be sufficient. For instance, if a column is moved from one table into another, this will be realized with SQL. The column is deleted in the source table and newly generated in the target table. As soon as the restructured system is released, we must face the problem of migrating the data from the old to the new version of the database schema. We will also have to observe how the selected migration strategy impacts the database refactoring.

5.4.1   Versioning Database Schemas

Therefore, we need to migrate the existing data to the new schema after the database schema has been changed. Of course the old and the new schema need to exist side by side during migration. Only after data migration has been completed, can the old database schema be deleted.

The coexistence of two schema versions can be realized in different ways. One option is to define a schema exclusively for the respective version. The version number is then incorporated into the schema's name, i.e. schema *V1*, schema *V2*, etc.

Alternatively, the version number can also be incorporated into the table name, e.g. *Customer V1, Product V2*, but this will also have consequences for the refactoring of the database schema. After all, foreign key relations, constraints and triggers all contain references to the tables' names. Once a new version of a schema has been created, all these references must be adjusted.

For this purpose, we assume that for each schema version a corresponding database schema is created.

The schema name enables the application to identify in which version the schema exists. This is an important prerequisite for the data migration of software products that are used by numerous customers. In such a scenario, one cannot take for granted that each customer uses the most recent version of the system. Thus it should be possible to migrate data from any older version to the newest one. To achieve this, one has to discern in which schema version the data originally exists.

5.4.2   Connecting Migration Steps

As mentioned before, when developing software products for a greater number of customers, it is not safe to expect that each customer uses the most recent version of a system software. Customers are likely to skip one or another version of the system.

Each migration transfers a database schema's data into the new version of that schema. This new version will be the starting point of the next migration.

Consequently, the newly installed system version must determine in which schema version the data is available and then proceed to carry out all required migrations until the process is complete for the youngest version. This presupposes that each installation must contain all migration programs that were ever created. For very expansive systems which have been in use for a long time, this can pose a problem, because very old migration programs might not work, for example, with the current version of the operating system. In such cases, the system must be broken down into generations and only deliver those migration programs as part of the installation which belong to the youngest generation.

The customer cannot expect that a migration from an older generation to the most recent one can be executed in a single step. If necessary, several migration steps must be carried out.

Figure 5-3 illustrates the principle of connected migration. If migration takes place from one version to the next, only one of the migration programs *MigA*, *MigB* or *MigC* will be carried out. Should migration happen from *V2* to *V4*, the application system will first execute the migration program *MigB* and then *MigC*.

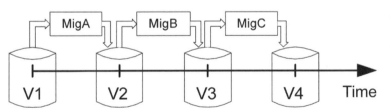

Fig. 5-3
Connecting Migration Steps

5.4.3   Migration of Very Large Data Amounts

When dealing with very large amounts of data, a single migration program can cause time problems: the migration of one billion data sets is hardly a feat that will be casually accomplished. Shutting down, for example, the main system of a bank house or an insurance company for 24 hours in the middle of the week to migrate their data is out of the question.

Problem: Very Large Amounts of Data

However, this problem can be approached either from an organizational or a technical perspective. For the organizational solution, one

Organizational Incorporation

has to precisely schedule modifications of the database system and conduct the migration when there is enough time. The Christmas and Easter holidays are ideal for this purpose.

Incremental Migration   If the overall technical conditions allow such a proceeding, the migration can be executed incrementally. The data will be migrated only when the system needs it. The migration period is thus prolonged, but the system's operation will not be interrupted. In a scenario with strict 7×24 runtime requirements, an incremental migration is often the only feasible solution.

Parallel Versions of Database Schemas   One prerequisite for incremental migration is that the application system is able to handle various versions of the database schema simultaneously. When accessing the database, the system must know in which schema to find the required data. Altered data will always be committed back to the new database schema though, and then deleted from the old one. Once the old schema no longer contains any data, it can be deleted.

Many Parallel Versions of Database Schemas   If the incremental migration takes longer than one release cycle, more than two variations of the database schema will exist at the same time.

An elegant way of keeping data simultaneously in different database schemas is to save the objects in BLOBs as well as fieldwise saving (see Section 5.9).

5.4.4   Data Migration Techniques

ETL tools can greatly simplify data migration. ETL stands for *Extract, Transform, Load*. ETL tools support the extraction of data from a data source, transformation of that data, plus loading it to another data storage. ETL tools are generally used to exchange data between applications which are not integrated. This makes them important tools in the EAI (*Enterprise Application Integration*) field.

Using ETL tools for data migration between different versions of database schemas was originally only a by-product – as a matter of fact, ETL tools have capabilities that go far beyond such application. Unfortunately, herein also lies the main disadvantage in utilizing them for data migration: they are very expensive. Buying them solely to deal with typical migration tasks is often not worth the money.

Fortunately, a less costly ETL tool is available for each relational database: SQL. With the help of SQL, data can easily be extracted (SELECT) and reloaded into the database (INSERT, UPDATE). However, SQL does not offer any direct support for transformation tasks, but often recoding tables or stored procedures will come in handy here. In such recoding tables, source and target values are specified for single fields. A problem-free migration of field contents is enabled by the *Insert-Select* command. This course of action is recommended if one decides to change the display of enumeration types. If a field was, for instance, coded with the character M for 'male' and 'F' for 'female' and is now supposed to be displayed with the digits 0 for 'male' and 1 for 'female', we have an ideal area of application for a recoding table.

If more complicated data migrations are necessary, programs that will carry out the data transfer must be written. Today, many databases allow the running of Java programs directly in the database. This can be beneficial for data migration, because the data no longer needs to be transferred from the database server to the machine handling the migration over the network. Thus migration can be speeded up noticeably.

5.5 Refactoring Database Access Codes

One of the oldest demands in software development is the call for encapsulating database access in a database access layer. A database access layer provides the option of exchanging the persistence medium. The developers only have to adapt the database access layer instead of rewriting the whole application system.

With agile methods and large refactorings, the demand for a database access layer is supported by another argument: the effects of changes to the database schema will be limited to the database access layer. This is the only means of keeping the subsequently needed efforts sufficiently small. Figure 5-4 shows the schematic architecture of an application with a database access layer.

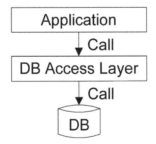

Fig. 5-4
Database Access Layer

5.5.1 Synchronized Changing of the Database Schema and Database Access Code

Generally speaking, application systems store data in databases to read them out later on (see Figure 5-5).

Fig. 5-5
Dataflow of the
Database Connection

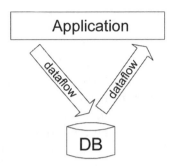

Redundant Structures of
Business Objects

At least when integrating relational databases, structures that are in part redundant will be created: the structures of business objects in the application as well as in the database bear a strong resemblance to each other. This is why usually both application *and* database must be adapted in the course of refactorings of such business object structures.

This means there are four potential places that must be modified during refactoring:

1. The portions of the database schema that are relevant for the altered business object structure.
2. The classes that define the modified business object structure in the application.
3. The database read-in operation for the business object.
4. The database write operation for the business object.

In principle, the read and write operations addressing the business objects can be arbitrarily distributed over the whole system. A well-designed system will at least ensure that there is only one place in the system where a business object is stored in the database. During read-in from the database this is unfortunately not always possible, because for performance reasons entire business object graphs are at once loaded in the *select* instructions via joins.

The most common case for refactorings of business object structures is execution of the following procedure:

1. Changing the table in the database exclusively in increments.

   ▣ New fields are added.
   ▣ Fields to be deleted remain in the code and are marked *deprecated*.
   ▣ Modified fields are duplicated; the old fields are marked *deprecated*.

2. New fields in the database are assigned appropriate default values.

3. Business object classes are changed in such a manner that the new data fields from the table can be stored in the business object and values for the *deprecated* fields can still be delivered; if necessary, the fields of the business object class must be set to *deprecated*.
4. All database write operations must be extended by the option to fill new fields.
5. All database read operations must be adapted to allow the read-in of these new fields; all read access to *deprecated* fields in the table must be eliminated.
6. All write access must be removed from *deprecated* fields.
7. *Deprecated* fields must be deleted from the table.
8. *Deprecated* fields must be deleted from the business object class.

This procedure does not constitute a generic, universal solution. It should specifically be amended for the respective refactoring.

Let us now assume that we wish to add a new field for country *A Simple Example* codes to the class *Customer* (so far, we only had German customers; now we will deal with customers from all over the world). To this end, we will first introduce the new field into the class *Customer*. Here it is assigned the default value 'G' for Germany. As of yet, the field will not be saved and loaded.

In the next step, the new field is added to the database schema, and all existing data sets are assigned the default value 'G' for the new field. Now the loading of customers will be adapted, followed by saving. Finally the new field is made visible in the GUI.

Here is a short version of each single step:

1. Add a new field to the class and assign the default value.
2. Introduce a new field to the database schema and assign the default value.
3. Enable loading of the new field.
4. Enable saving of the new field.
5. Make the new field visible in the GUI.

After each single step, the system is in a consistent state.[1] The desired effect will be achieved with the last step. Until this step has been taken, the system can only handle customers from Germany.

Things are not always so simple: let us assume that we wish to *A More Complex* store the country code no longer as a character code, but as a number *Example* instead. To realize this, the country code field must be changed from

---

[1]   Steps 1 and 2 as well as 3 and 4 can also be executed in reverse order.

the type *String* to *Integer* in the database as well as in the program code. At the same time, the persistent data must be recoded.

The following refactoring steps will render the desired result:

1. Add a new field to the class and assign the default value.
2. Introduce a new field to the database schema and assign the default value. Add the new field to saving.
3. Add the new field to loading.
4. Switch the GUI and all other access to the old field to the new field.
5. Remove the old field from loading.
6. Remove the old field from saving.
7. Delete the old field from the class.
8. Delete the old field from the database schema.

Concerning points 1 and 2: here a static default value cannot be employed because the default value depends on the existing country code. A recoding algorithm is required to calculate the numeric country codes for the existing *string* country codes. For this purpose, the recoding algorithm will probably have to access a recoding table in the database.

A closer look at the single steps makes it clear that the modifications for loading and saving cannot be finalized in one step. As a matter of fact, both parts of the system must be adapted several times.

Of course making the final adaptation in one step is extremely seductive. If loading of the field in step 3 is removed at once, the system initially appears to be in a consistent state (no compile errors will be reported, and tests working with the new field will also run error-free). Admittedly, after loading, the field in the objects would show a default value that does not match the field's new value. This constellation can create all kinds of problems in the rest of the program code.

5.6   Roles in a Project

In projects that use agile methods, the previously described database refactorings and the procedures following in their wake (data migration) are the rule, not the exception. The whole procedure must be organized without impairing its progress.

Foremost this means that the understanding of the DBA's (database administrator's) role undergoes change. He or she will not personally make every single change to the database. This would encumber the developers' work and overburden them with the sheer number of modification requests.

Instead, the DBA has to accept the role of the person who supports the developers with changes to the databases. After all, he or she usually has a more detailed knowledge. As a side-effect, the DBA can also keep track of which modifications to the database are made and can intervene, if – in his or her opinion – development takes a wrong turn.

This changed understanding of the DBA's responsibilities will last but not least be reflected in the allocation of rights. Developers in agile projects need more database rights. At least for their local database and the shared development database they must have the right to make changes to the database schema. Modifications of other schemas can, as before, be executed by the DBA, who will also function as a quality-ensuring checkpoint.

5.7 Tools

Graphical administration tools are available for most database types. Normally, they also allow changes of database structures. However, these tools cannot be considered refactoring tools for databases. On the one hand, the effects of modifications are simply ignored, on the other hand they don't offer any mechanisms to take back changes or to version them, etc.

However, the majority of projects that apply refactorings will not execute changes of the database schema with the aid of such tools. Should no other tools be at the developers' disposal, SQL scripts will serve instead to realize modifications of the database schema. The scripts are versioned in the version control system. The gradual execution of these scripts enables migration of a database schema existing in any version to any successive version. Thus, writing additional migration programs for the migration of production databases will often be unnecessary.

5.7.1 OR Mapping

The mapping of objects to relational databases is supported by a variety of commercial and open source tools. For Java, often *Torque*, *Castor* or *Hibernate* from the open source field as well as the commercially available *TopLink* are used. With the introduction of *JDO* (Java Data Objects), a standardized programming interface for such an OR mapper in a Java environment has now also been defined. For the future it is expected that the existing OR mappers will be able to support JDO.

Most OR mappers generate SQL scripts and source code for database access from a description of persistent data structures. Rarely will the application developer have to deal with SQL directly.

The source code generated in such a way constitutes a good basis for the database access layer and significantly improves typesafety of the database access. Access is not always 100% typesafe, because direct changes of the generated classes or the database schema will again result in a loss of typesafety. In addition, the formulation of queries can lead to type errors.

Overall, the generated source code brings about a clear enhancement of the situation compared to direct database access. In this way, code-generating OR mappers support large refactorings in a minimalist way: the effects of changes to persistent data structures will become visible as soon as the OR mapping source code is newly generated. The affected parts of the application will now display compile errors. We are yet far away from having achieved a refactoring in small steps, let alone an automation. The application developer must still ponder which refactoring steps he or she wishes to take.

Equally, OR mappers are of little help for the migration of existing data. Here again, the application developers must decide what is to be done.

5.7.2 ETL Tools

ETL tools (see also Section 5.4.4) read out data from a data source, transform this data and load the results into another data source. ETL tools are, for example, used in the EAI field (*Enterprise Application Integration*) to synchronize the data of different applications.

A welcome side-effect is the usefulness of ETL tools for data migration between different versions of a database schema. In comparison with the writing of individual migration programs, the application of ETL tools saves a lot of work. However, it should not go unmentioned that the licensing costs for commercial ETL tools range in the five-digit dollar zone. Many projects will discard such an investment that will 'merely' speed up development in a fringe area right away.

Should ETL tool licences have been purchased for other reasons though, their application is an extra benefit.

5.7.3 Scripting

If no ETL tool is at the developers' disposal, most of the data migration for refactoring purposes should be done with scripts. After all, the migration programs/scripts will be used only once for data migration and then never again. Thus their maintenance requirements are not as high as those for the actual production system.

5.8 Tips

- Develop a database access layer that hides the database structures completely from the application. As a result, modifications of the database schema will be limited to the database and the database access layer.

- Define all table and column names as constants and use the constants for database access. Typical OR mappers will generate the constants from the description of persistent data structures. If no OR mapper is at your disposal, write your own program to generate the constants from the database.

- Adhere to the naming conventions for primary and foreign keys to enable easier detection of dependencies in the database schema.

- Use different database instances or at least different database schemas for *staging*: Unit test DB per developer, DB for integration testing, DB for acceptance testing, DB for production.

- Do not use the database manufacturer's tool to change the database schema. Write SQL scripts instead for changing the schema. Write the scripts in such a way that existing data can be migrated. Developers can use these scripts to adopt modifications of the local database instance to the development database, but also to migrate the database schema and data from the production database.

- Apply the following strategy in regard to the database: make sure that each database instance contains both an old and a new version of the database schema. It is the only way of migrating the data with minimal effort when switching the schema.

- If you are using OR mappers, version the definition of persistent data structures in the version control system.

- If you are not using OR mappers, version the SQL scripts for creating and changing the database schemas in the version control system. Alternatively, in many cases you can let the database itself generate the description of its structure (SQL Create Statements) and then version it.

- Ensure that your source code stays independent from the concrete data that is stored (i.e. it should not presuppose the existence, for instance, of customer no. 999). Should this not be feasible, proceed to make the dependency explicit, e.g. let the program verify the existence of the required data at program start.

- Unit tests should see to the existence of the required data themselves. They should either generate the data directly from the program code or load it to the database, using a script. Then the script must be versioned together with the source code.

■ More complex data models do not always permit that tests generate their own required data. Thus the tests will depend on data in the database. In such cases, make sure that the tests will exclusively depend on the data in the unit test database instance.

■ When the system expands, the performance of database-dependent unit tests can become problematic. In these cases, design patterns such as *ObjectMother* or *MockTypes* are useful. Where appropriate, an in-memory database can be utilized for testing.

5.9 Typical Data Models

If an application system requires extremely flexible data structures (for example, because the users need to be able to change the data structures themselves), developers will often work with data modeling on a meta level. They will create a data model that allows saving any type of data structure. In principle, this can be realized in two ways: *saving of BLOBs* and *fieldwise saving*.

Such data models enable a flexible handling of constantly changing data structures and simplify the refactoring process.

5.9.1 Saving of BLOBs

When saving BLOBs (*Binary Large Objects*), information about the actual data structures is only present in the application system. Only the application knows how these BLOBs are structured internally. Often such systems work with two tables: a data table and a search table. The data table possesses only two columns: ID and object. In the ID column the unique ID of the saved object can be found, whereas the object can be found in the object column as a BLOB. The ID column is the primary key.

Searching for BLOBs in the Database

All criteria which are potentially searched for are listed in the search table. The search table has two columns too: the ID as well as the search criterion. The ID column is a foreign key to the data table ID. For each search criterion which can be looked for with an object, a data set is stored in the search table. The primary key consists of ID and search criterion. Figure 5-6 gives an overview of the two tables.

Fig. 5-6
Saving Objects as BLOBs

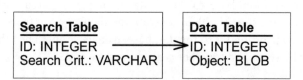

When saving in BLOBs is desired, developers must decide how uses relations between objects can be circumvented. Here, a distinction is made between *containment relations* and *references*. Objects that are contained in other objects will be saved and also read as a whole in a BLOB with the parent object.

References between BLOBs

References in class definitions are specially marked (e.g. through saving only the referenced object's ID in the field instead of applying a uses relation). In this way, at first only the original object will be loaded. The referenced objects will either be loaded directly afterwards or when they are actually required.

The advantages of this type of modeling are:

- Changes of the data structure require only modifications of classes in the application system, not of the database schema itself. Therefore, no simultaneously active database schema variations are needed.
- A refactoring of data structures is limited to changes of the program code and the migration of existing data.
- Data can be migrated stepwise from an old to a new data structure during loading. The old and new *BLOB-Mapper*[2] versions are required for migration, but only *one* database schema.
- OR mapping is simplified altogether.
- Objects with a complex structure can be read and written easily.
- It is easy to realize flexible data structures that allow adjustments by the user.

The disadvantages are:

- The stored data cannot be used without the application system.
- As a rule, the stored data cannot be used by other systems, i.e. such that were written in other programming languages. The database cannot be utilized as an integration medium for different systems.
- Report and list generators based on the database cannot be applied.
- Data can only be analyzed as far as this function has been programmed into the application.
- Inconsistent data cannot be repaired manually via the provided database mechanisms.
- The saved objects constitute the smallest locking level.
- Where high transaction rates are present, search and data tables can turn into a bottleneck for locking.

---

[2] If, for instance, Java serialization is used directly, the classes must be able to load objects of earlier class versions.

▨ The number of data sets, especially in the search table, can be very trying regarding the database's performance capacity when a large amount of data is involved.

5.9.2   Fieldwise Saving

For fieldwise saving, like for saving with BLOBs, basically two tables exist: the search table and the data table. However, the data table contains no BLOBS, but a data set for each stored field instead, so that for each field of each saved object a data set is created. The number of data sets in this table is easy to calculate: number of objects * average number of fields for each object. To make sure that objects can be reconstructed from the data table, at least columns for the object ID and the field name are needed besides the ID and field value columns.

Figure 5-7 shows both tables. The ID in the data table constitutes the unique primary key. This key is not imperative though. It is also possible to define the primary key as a composite of object ID and field name.

Fig. 5-7
Fieldwise Saving

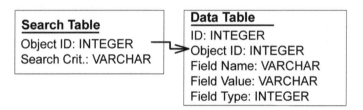

The advantages of this type of modeling are:

▨ Changes of the data structure require only modifications of classes in the application system, not of the database schema itself. Therefore, no simultaneously active variations of the database schema are needed.

▨ A refactoring of data structures is limited to changes of the program code and the migration of existing data.

▨ Data can be migrated stepwise from an old to a new data structure during loading.

▨ OR mapping is simplified altogether.

▨ It is easy to realize flexible data structures that allow adjustments by the user.

▨ Advantages as compared to saving in BLOBs:

   – The data can be used by other systems and tools.
   – Inconsistent data can be manually repaired.
   – Ad hoc analyses can be carried out directly with SQL.

In contrast, these are the disadvantages:

- Where high transaction rates are present, search and data tables can turn into a bottleneck for locking.
- The number of data sets, especially in the search table, can be very trying regarding the database's performance capacity when a large amount of data is involved.
- Access to the database is slowed down, because now not only one data set per object, but many data sets must be processed.
- In comparison, the ratio between the share of user data and the overhead is relatively bad. For many values less bytes would suffice for storage (e.g. for integer fields), but storage capacity is always reserved for string saving. Moreover, for each persistent field its own key information is stored. Sometimes this key information requires more storage than the actual, saved data.[3]

5.10   An Example

This section will use a more comprehensive example to further elaborate on the previously introduced principles for refactoring with databases. We will use a time recording system for IT consultants, which lets all consultants access a web interface to enter their actual work hours. This input serves as the basis for calculating the consultants' salaries as well as for billing their customers.[4]

5.10.1   Our Starting Point

The subsystems are depicted in Figure 5-8. The consultants access the systems via the subsystem *Web*. The accounting department uses the subsystem *Report* to generate the necessary print lists and analyses.

Subsystems in a Time Recording Example

The subsystem *Web* works with the subsystem *Business Objects*, which provides concepts such as *Employees* and *Time Entries*. These business objects are saved in the database and reconstructed from the database with the subsystem *Administration*. To this end, a purchased subsystem *DB* (the driver for accessing the concrete database; for Java this will usually be JDBC) is utilized.

Subsystem Web

The subsystem *Report* employs the subsystem *Analysis* in order to carry out all necessary analyses for the print lists (e.g. all hours for

Subsystem Report

---

[3]   This problem can be solved by placing field name and field type in a table of their own (normalized variation).

[4]   This example is also used in Chapter 6. We decided to reprint it here in its entirety, so that both chapters can be read independently of each other.

each employee for one project). Of course, the subsystem *Analysis* uses the subsystems *Business Objects* and *Administration* to access the persistent business objects. The print lists are created with the aid of a commercially available report tool (subsystem *Report Tool*).

Fig. 5-8
Subsystems of the
Time Recording
Example

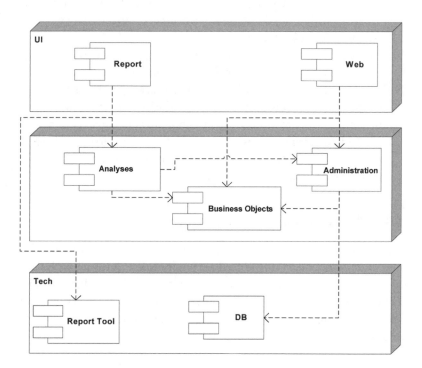

The subsystems are arranged in three non-strict layers: user interface (UI), domain model and technology.

Essentially, the time recording system is based on the business objects from Figure 5-9. *Time Entries* has a vital position here: besides date, start and end time, *Time Entries* also displays references to *Project*, *Activity* of the project, as well as to *Employees*.

Figure 5-10 shows a simple data model for storing business objects.

5.10.2   Motives for a Refactoring

The modeling of the subsystem *Business Objects* strongly influences the API of the subsystem *Administration* and thus also the interaction between *Analysis* and *Administration*.

Basically we have to implement the respective low-level functions for most analyses in *Administration*. The business objects are too 'stupid' to allow the subsystem *Analysis* to execute complex functions on them. Theoretically, it is also possible for the subsystem *Analysis* to directly access the database. However, this would also mean that the subsystem *Administration* no longer encapsulates the database, thus making modifications of the database schema more difficult.

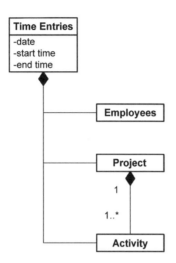

Fig. 5-9
Business Objects

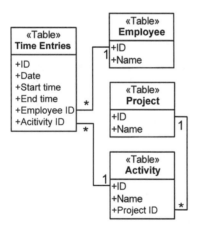

Fig. 5-10
Data Model for
Business Objects

Therefore, the subsystem *Business Objects* should be restructured in such a way that it becomes 'smarter' and the API of the subsystem *Administration* does not inflate so strongly.

5.10.3 Goal of the Refactoring

This object model of the subsystem *Business Objects* shall now be modified in such a manner that the model of the core business objects will look as follows: each one of the *Employees* has got a *Month Folder* for

The New Object Model
for Business Objects

each month with a *Calendar Sheet* for every work day. On the *Calendar Sheet* all *Time Entries* are recorded, including start and end time, *Project* and *Activity* in the project (see Figure 5-11).

Fig. 5-11
Business Objects After Restructuring

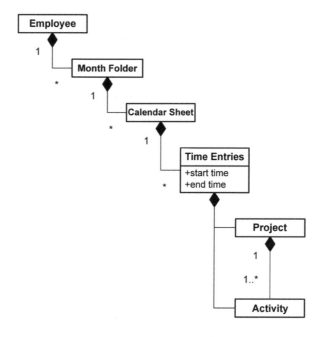

Figure 5-12 shows the corresponding data model.

With this restructuring of the subsystem *Business Objects* we venture deeply into the system's vocabulary. We can expect a demand for comprehensive restructuring measures of the entire system. Here, we are going to focus on the refactoring's impact on database access, that is, on the data model and the *Administration* subsystem.

5.10.4   Refactoring Proceeding

The Refactoring Challenge

The difficulty this refactoring poses lies in the coordination of changes to the classes and those to tables. Both have to match for each separate step.

Unfortunately it is impossible to first view the class structure or the data model isolated from the rest and then deduce the respective other model from it. The main obstacle is that the uses relations in 1:*N* relations of the class model constitute a reversal of the data model. The *Calendar Sheet* does have a number of *Time Entries*, whereas in the data model *Time Entries* knows to which *Calendar Sheet* it belongs. If you transfer this example to the whole model, you will get a smell because cyclical relations are present.

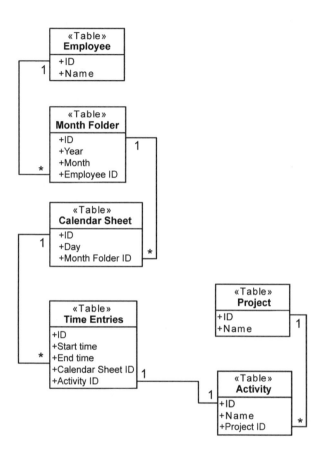

Fig. 5-12
Data Model After
Restructuring

Therefore, we will proceed step by step, as we are used to. First, we are going to reverse the relations between *Time Entries* and *Employees* in the class model: now *Time Entries* will no longer know the *Employees*, but *Employees* is assigned a certain amount of *Time Entries*. Figure 5-13 illustrates this refactoring step.

The First Step

The class structure we just created must correspond with the data model, of course. Interestingly, no modification of the data model is required to achieve this. The data model shown in Figure 5-10 can also display the new class model.

We will now extract the date information from *Time Entries* and put it in the class *Calendar Sheet*. For now, we will work without the *Month Folder* and store the complete date in *Calendar Sheet*. Figure 5-14 visualizes this refactoring step on the class model.

The Second Step

Fig. 5-13
Reversing the Relation
between Employee
and Time Entries

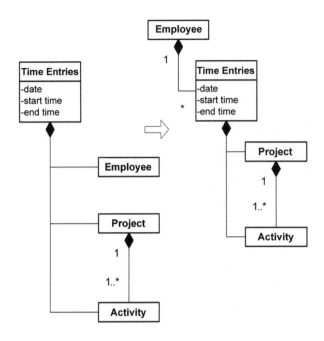

Fig. 5-13
Reversing the Relation between Employee *and* Time Entries

Fig. 5-14
Calendar Sheet
Contains Date
Information

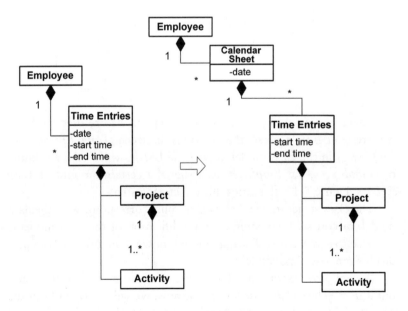

Figure 5-15 describes the matching data model. If the data model's tables have been used exclusively to load and save the business objects, the restructuring explained in Figure 5-15 can be executed as described, together with the class model's restructuring:

1. Add the new table *Calendar Sheet* to the data model.
2. When existing data shall be adopted: copy data per SQL script from the existing tables into the new table.
3. Delete the fields *Date* and *Employee ID* from the *Time Entries* table.
4. Rearrange the business objects' class structure.
5. Adapt the mapping functionality in the subsystem *Administration*.

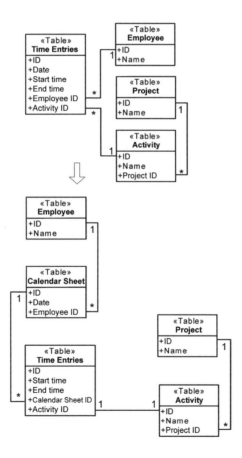

Fig. 5-15
Calendar Sheet
Contains Date Information

Should, however, several parts of the system access the tables, one cannot simply remove fields from the tables (*Date* and *Employee ID* from the *Time Entries* table). In this case, the fields must be set to *deprecated*, resulting in the data model shown in Figure 5-16.

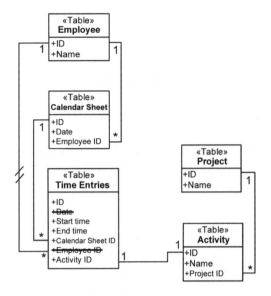

Fig. 5-16
Calendar Sheet
Contains Data
Information:
Deprecated *Fields*

The following steps are executed during this refactoring:

1. Add the new table *Calendar Sheet* to the data model.
2. Set the *Date* and *Employee ID* fields in the *Time Entries* table to *deprecated* (e.g. through an entry in the file *deprecated_db.txt*).
3. Rearrange the business objects' class structure.
4. Adapt the mapping functionality in the subsystem *Administration* so that it will also write the new table and its fields; if necessary using INSERT, should the respective set of data not yet exist in the *Calendar Sheet* table.
5. Step by step adjust all other write access instances in the system in such a way that old and new fields are written parallel.
6. When existing data shall be adopted: copy data per SQL script from the existing tables into the new table.
7. Adapt the mapping functionality in the subsystem *Administration* so that none of the *deprecated* fields will be read any more.
8. Step by step delete all other read access to the *deprecated* fields.
9. Step by step delete all other write access to the *deprecated* fields – thus enabling reading from the new fields.
10. Delete *deprecated* fields.

Here it becomes clear that modifications of database structures can become quite tedious if access is not unambiguously channeled by few classes: in the beginning, *all* write access instances must be modified in such a way that they will write to old *and* new fields. Only then the read access instances can be adapted stepwise.

It is crucial not to deliver any releases to customers between single refactoring steps. Otherwise, there is a high risk that the fields won't be completely written to. Inconsistent data would be the consequence.

The third big step is extraction of the *Month* information from the *Calendar Sheet*. This step follows the same pattern as the second one and therefore isn't described here.

The Third Step

References and Further Reading

Agile Databases, mailing list:
> http://groups.yahoo.com/group/agileDatabases.
> This mailing list discusses database-related topics with a focus on agile methods.

Ambler, S.W. 2003a. The process of database refactoring.
> http://www.agiledata.org/essays/databaseRefactoring.html.
> An article that gives an overview of database refactorings, including descriptions of the development processes.

Ambler, S.W. 2003b. Catalog of database refactorings.
> http://www.agiledata.org/essays/databaseRefactoringCatalog.html.
> A catalogue of frequently used refactorings of database schemas.

Celko, J. 1999. *SQL for Smarties – Advanced SQL Programming*, 2nd ed. Harlekijn. This book provides an introduction to advanced SQL concepts and presents suggestions for solutions for recurring modeling problems, such as the mapping of tree structures to relational databases.

Fowler, M. & Sadalage, P. 2003. Evolutionary database design.
> http://www.martinfowler.com/articles/evodb.html.
> This article explains the basic concepts of evolutionary database design. Refactorings of database schemas, the migration of data as well as refactorings of database access codes are examined.

Sadalage, P. & Schuh, P. 2002. The agile database: tutorial notes. Presented at XP/Agile Universe 2002, www.xpuniverse.com. Here, among other issues, the deprecated marker of database elements is discussed.

6
API Refactorings

In this chapter, we are going to examine the effects of refactorings on application programming interfaces (APIs) and the clients based on them. We will primarily focus on Java in this context. With justifiable effort, the results should be transferable to other object-oriented programming languages.

6.1   Subsystems

In each non-trivial software system, partitions can be found that are used by other partitions of the same system. Often this kind of structuring is specified: we talk about subsystems, class libraries, frameworks or components. To simplify matters, we will from now on summarize all these different partition types under the label *subsystems*. They all have in common that they are clearly distinguished from other subsystems. A class always belongs to precisely one subsystem and is used by the rest of the system via an interface (API, i.e. application programming interface). See Figure 6-1.

Subsystems

The division into subsystems as well as the API's definition can either be implicit or explicit. For implicit subsystems, there is no specification of which subsystems exist, what these subsystems are called, which classes belong to them, or which classes and methods constitute their API. The system's structure becomes much clearer when all these things are explicitly defined. For the explicit definition of subsystems, so-called component models are used, such as the Eclipse plugin model, CORBA, COM, or a business/project-specific component model.

Besides ensuring a clean structuring of the system, subsystems support reuse. First of all, they can be reused in a company's different projects. If a subsystem is rather common, it can either be commercially marketed or distributed as an open source component.

Subsystems for Reuse

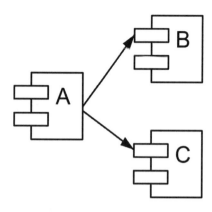

6.2   Problems of API Refactorings

Unfortunately, modifications of subsystems cannot always be limited to internal implementations. Occasionally, an API must be adapted as well in the course of a refactoring.

At first this sounds paradoxical, since refactoring means changing the design without changing the observable behavior. Now if you regard the API of a subsystem as a part of its observable behavior, a change to the API would mean that you change the behavior and therefore do something different than refactoring. But what happens if you recognize that the name of an API's method is misleading? Naturally you would refactor it to a better name and therefore do a refactoring. The difficulty arises because you cannot adapt all clients of the API right away.

Anonymous Subsystem Users

If a subsystem is not only used for one project (internal reuse), but for various projects instead, maybe even in different companies (external reuse), the refactoring of APIs will become more difficult because the concrete code, which is based on the API, is unknown. This is the reason why code based on that subsystem cannot be changed instantaneously in the course of an API refactoring. If the API is broken, the dependent code has to migrate. A subsystem A depends on a subsystem B when interfaces or classes of subsystem B are used in subsystem A's source code. See Figure 6-2.

For the purpose of API modifications, often a distinction between source code and binary compatibility is made. A modification is source code-compatible if the system can be compiled and its runtime behavior will still be the same after it has been modified. A modification is binary-compatible if the system will be operable without prior new compilation. Interestingly, neither does source code compatibility imply binary compatibility or vice versa. However, we are concerned with source code compatibility, not binary compatibility in this chapter (the latter is discussed in Rivières, 2001).

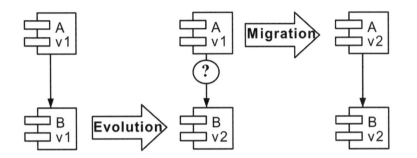

Fig. 6-2
Evolution and
Migration

Sometimes, demands are made not to change a subsystem's API any further after its publication. In practice, it soon becomes clear that meeting this demand would be purpose-defeating: on the one hand, the API will not be altered any more; on the other hand, increased usage of the subsystem results in new requirements that can only be met through changing the API. Hence, we will try to build as stable APIs as possible, although we know that we'll have to modify them sooner or later.

Stability of APIs

6.3 Compatibility Classes

Not every change of a subsystem's API will generate a demand for migration. At worst, compatible changes to the API will require a new compilation of the dependent code.[1] Regrettably, many more changes are incompatible than one would expect at first sight. Therefore, adding methods appears not to be a critical step. If an abstract method is added to an API class though, subclasses can be rendered invalid: they lack the implementation for the new, abstract method. The following tables convey an impression of compatibility classes[2] (we assume that non-constant fields are private and can thus be disregarded in this context). Non-private attributes can, if applicable, be adapted using the *Encapsulate-Field* refactoring.

Compatible and Incompatible Changes

---

[1]   In Java, usually not even a new compilation is necessary. There are a couple of interesting exceptions though, e.g. the changing of constant values, which is generated by the compiler in the client classes.

[2]   The comments on each compatibility class can be found in the descriptions of the different changes (see Section 6.5).

Changes to Interfaces

No.	Change	Compatibility
1	Adding an interface	Incompatible
2	Removing an interface	Incompatible
3	Renaming an interface (also: moving an interface into another package or renaming a package)	Incompatible
4	Adding a superinterface	Incompatible, because dependent classes can become abstract
5	Removing a superinterface	Incompatible

Changes to Classes

No.	Change	Compatibility
1	Adding a class	Incompatible
2	Removing a class	Incompatible
3	Renaming a class (also: moving a class into another package or renaming a package)	Incompatible
4	Changing a superclass	Incompatible
5	Adding an interface	Incompatible
6	Removing an interface	Incompatible
7	Expanding visibility	Compatible
8	Restricting visibility	Incompatible
9	Setting a class from final to non-final	Compatible
10	Setting a class from non-final to final	Incompatible
11	Setting a class to abstract	Incompatible
12	Setting a class from abstract to non-abstract	Compatible

Changes to Constants in Classes and Interfaces

No.	Change	Compatibility
1	Adding a constant	Compatible
2	Removing a constant	Incompatible
3	Changing a constant type	Incompatible
4	Changing a constant value	Compatible

Changes to Methods in Interfaces

No.	Change	Compatibility
1	Adding a method	Incompatible
2	Removing a method	Incompatible
3	Renaming a method	Incompatible
4	Changing a method's parameter list	Incompatible
5	Changing a method's return type	Incompatible
6	Adding an exception to a method in the interface	Incompatible
7	Removing an exception from a method in the interface	Incompatible

Changes to Constructors in Classes

No.	Change	Compatibility
1	Adding a constructor	Incompatible, if the classes until now did not have an explicit constructor
2	Removing a constructor	Incompatible
3	Changing a constructor's parameter list	Incompatible
6	Expanding a constructor's visibility	Compatible
7	Restricting a constructor's visibility	Incompatible
12	Weakening a constructor's precondition	Compatible
13	Strengthening a constructor's precondition	Incompatible
18	Adding an exception to the constructor	Incompatible
19	Removing an exception from the constructor	Incompatible

Changes to Methods in Classes

No.	Change	Compatibility
1	Adding a method	Incompatible, if the method is abstract; also incompatible, if the new method is final and 'accidental' redefinitions take place in subclasses
2	Removing a method	Incompatible
3	Renaming a method	Incompatible
4	Changing a method's parameter list	Incompatible
5	Changing a method's return type	Incompatible
6	Expanding a method's visibility	Incompatible, if the method is redefined in subclasses
7	Restricting a method's visibility	Incompatible
8	Setting a method from final to non-final	Compatible
9	Setting a method from non-final to final	Incompatible, if the method is redefined in subclasses
10	Setting a method from static to non-static	Incompatible
11	Setting a method from non-static to static	Incompatible, if the method is redefined in subclasses
12	Setting a method to abstract	Incompatible
13	Setting a method from abstract to non-abstract	Compatible
14	Weakening a method's precondition	Incompatible, if the method is redefined
15	Strengthening a method's precondition	Incompatible, if the method is called
16	Weakening a method's postcondition	Incompatible, if the method is called
17	Strengthening a method's postcondition	Incompatible, if the method is redefined

No.	Change	Compatibility
18	Setting method to synchronized	Incompatible, if the method is used in a multi-threaded context
19	Setting method from synchronized to non-synchronized	Incompatible, if the method is used in a multi-threaded context
20	Adding an exception to a method in a class	Incompatible
21	Removing an exception from a method in a class	Incompatible

It turns out that most API changes are incompatible. In Java, the *deprecated* tag will provide some first assistance: it allows us to mark interfaces, classes and methods as obsolete. A class that shall be deleted will not be deleted right away but identified as *deprecated*. The class can still be used, although the compiler will generate a warning each time this happens. The dependent code can migrate step by step while staying compilable and executable at all times.

Deprecated *Tag*

The following source code depicts how the *deprecated* tag denotes deletion of the class `MyClass`:

```
/**
 * @deprecated
 */
public class MyClass
{...}
```

Use of the deprecated tag creates a new compatibility class. Such 'denoted' incompatible changes are called *deferred-incompatible*.

Deferred-Incompatible Changes

When we take a closer look at the table above, we will see that, in principle, the renaming of interfaces, classes and methods could be carried out automatically. One would merely need a machine-readable description of the changes to the API plus a program that reads in these descriptions and makes the necessary changes to the client. Especially for renamings, a simple mapping file in which the old as well as the new name is listed would suffice. Such a function for automated migration when package names are altered is already integrated in some development environments.

In this case, we speak of automatable changes and get the following compatibility classes:

No.	Compatibility Class	Migration
1	Compatible	No migration required
2	Automatable	Automatic migration is possible in a single step; rather little effort needed
4	Deferred-incompatible	Stepwise migration is possible. The system stays compilable and executable all the time
5	Incompatible	Migration must be carried out completely. During migration, the system is neither compilable nor executable

6.4   Refactoring Tags

To simplify the migration of dependent subsystems and enable *merciless
refactorings*[3] also for published interfaces, we are going to introduce the
concept of refactorings tags (see Roock, 2004), which serve to improve
the compatibility of changes. Incompatible changes will become either
deferred-compatible or even automatable.

In the following subsections, we will show how the new meta tags
affect the refactoring work on published APIs. Based on possible modifications of APIs, we will also show in detail how these can be executed in such a manner as to ensure compatibility.

6.4.1   The Future Tag

The *Future* tag demonstrates which form an interface, a class or a
method will have in the future. If an API client uses an element with a
Future tag, the developers can verify whether their usage of the element will still be valid in the future.[4]

---

[3] The term *Merciless Refactoring* is derived from agile methods practice and
emphasizes that here refactorings are a central part of everyday development
work.

[4] This requires that the developers adapt those tags if they change their opinion
regarding the modification.

The simplest form of the *Future* tag specifies that the respective element will be deleted in the future. The following source code sample shows how the *Future* tag announces deletion of the class `MyClass`:

```
/**
 * @future #undefined
 */
public class MyClass
{...}
```

With the *deprecated* tag, Java offers a similar mechanism. The *deprecated* tag can be used as an acronym for the *Future* tag displayed above, supplemented with *#undefined*. The *deprecated* tag is interpreted by the Java compiler. Whenever an element marked deprecated is referenced, the compiler will give out a warning. The element will be compiled correctly though, and the system will remain completely operational.

However, no warning will be generated if the obsolete element as well as the referencing element can be found in one and the same class.

For classes, the *Future* tag can also denote changes to the modifier (visibility, *final*), as well as changes to the superclass and to implemented interfaces. For interfaces, this tag can also be used to mark changes to superinterfaces.

The inheritance relation between *Customer* and *Partner* can be marked as obsolete in the *Customer* class's comment. Here, the *Future* tag is used to denote that the inheritance relation will be deleted at some point:

An Example

```
/**
 * @future public class Customer
 */
public class Customer
  extends Partner
  ...
```

Thus, all direct uses of *Customer* and *Partner* stay valid. It is important that the client will no longer be allowed to make use of the inheritance relation between *Customer* and *Partner*, as is the case with polymorphic assignments, for instance.

Even several changes can be described with the *Future* tag. In the following example, in the future the class *Customer* will no longer inherit from *Partner* and also no longer implement the *Serializable* interface. Instead, only the *Comparable* interface will be implemented:

```
/**
 * @future public class Customer implements Comparable
```

```
*/
public class Customer
    extends Partner
    implements Serializable, Comparable
    ...
```

For methods, changes of the modifiers can be described. Especially switches from non-final to *final* as well as changes of visibility can be elegantly expressed with the *Future* tag.

The following example shows how the *Future* tag denotes that the method setName will become *final* in the next version. Until the next subsystem version release, the client developers can eliminate all redefinitions of setName.

```
/**
 * @future public final void setName (String name)
 */
public void setName (String name)
    ...
```

Additionally, the tag can be supplemented with an informal description of what is to be done now that the element can no longer be used in the old way.

6.4.2   The Past Tag

Whereas the *Future* tag shows what an element will look like in the future, the *Past* tag describes what the element looked like in the past. This enables developers to see what the element's name was in the previous version. For classes and interfaces, it also contains information about the packages in which the classes and interfaces were stored before.

The *Past* tag serves to visualize renamings and moves. In principle, the changes thus become automatable. The following example shows the *Past* tag for renaming a method setName to setLastName:

```
/**
 * @past public void setName (String name)
 */
public void setLastName (String name)
    ...
```

Migration can be accomplished in an even smoother manner not simply through renaming the method, but through duplicating it. The new

version will refer to the old one via the *Past* tag, and the old version
will be marked *deprecated*:

```
/**
 * @deprecated
 */
public void setName (String name) {
  setLastName(name);
}

/**
 * @past public void setName (String name)
 */
public void setLastName (String name)
   . . .
```

In JDK, the succession method is often directly and informally appended
to the *deprecated* tag:

```
/**
 * @deprecated Replaced by setLastName(String)
 */
public void setName (String name) {
  setLastName(name);
}

public void setLastName (String name)
   . . .
```

6.4.3 Working with Refactoring Tags

The refactoring tags introduced here can also be applied usefully without the aid of special tools. The search options offered by modern development environments (e.g. Eclipse) are completely sufficient here.

First, the source code of a subsystem can be searched for all *Future*   Future *Tag*
tags. Based on the elements found and supported by the development
environment, one can determine in which places they are used. The
developer must check the elements used and adapt them where necessary.

Similarly, *Past* tags in subsystems can be searched with the source   Past *Tag*
code search function. The results will let developers conclude how
these elements used were labeled before. The uses of the renamed elements can be roughly determined with a source code search, followed
by a check of the detected uses and – if required – changes of their use.

Using the *deprecated* tag is even simpler. The compiler will point at
the places in the client code where deprecated elements are used. These
places must merely be analyzed. The more information that has been

added to the *deprecated* tag (e.g. 'replaced with'), the easier migration will be.

6.4.4   Tools for Migration

Specialized tools facilitate the handling of refactoring tags. Aided by the *Past taglet*, the subsystem developers can analyze the subsystem APIs' *Past* tags. The Past taglet will write the detected renamings to a file. Then this file is – together with the new subsystem version – delivered to the subsystem's clients. Here, the renaming file serves as input for the *Renamer*, which carries out the required renamings in the client code.

A first version of these open-source tools is available for download as an Eclipse plugin at https://sourceforge.net/projects/jmigrator.

In addition, we plan to implement the *Future Warner*: it will check the client code for future invalid use of the API. Whenever such an invalid use is identified, a warning will be issued. Then the client developers could change the client code in such a way that it would function with a future subsystem version.

6.5   API Refactorings in Detail

If a subsystem's API is modified, two kinds of conflicts can emerge: structural conflicts and behavior conflicts. Structural conflicts prevent the system's compilability. In the case of a behavior conflict, the system will still be compilable, although its execution will be faulty. However, a clean test coverage will at least help to identify and systematically eradicate behavior conflicts.

In this section, we are going to explain for each API modification which conflicts it will create and how it can best be carried out compatibly.

The goal of changes to APIs is always to maintain compatibility with existing clients. 100% security can hardly ever be reached. Many of the techniques for API refactorings presented here function based on copying a method and then pasting it with a new name. Admittedly, the generation of a method in turn will be incompatible. In practice though, such change hardly ever leads to problems. Therefore, we accept that there is no such thing as 100% security. We will content ourselves with a high compatibility probability.

Next, we describe typical modifications. We always adhere to the premise that non-constant attributes in classes are private. That is why

we won't consider the possible changes to attributes and their consequences any further.

During the following refactorings, you will frequently encounter
situations in which methods are not simply deleted or modified.
Instead, they are copied and saved with a new name. Only later on
will the old version of the method be deleted. The problem here is to
find good, i.e. meaningful, names for the methods. Let us assume
that the old name was meaningful. Now we have to find an equally
good, i.e. meaningful, name to replace the old one. Alternatively, we
can mark the new name as temporary, adhering to the respective
convention (for example, the old name could be supplemented with
the ending _TEMP) and change it back in the next version of the
subsystem.

*New and Temporary
Method Names*

6.5.1 Changes to Interfaces

Adding an Interface

In most cases, adding an interface is compatible. The change will
become incompatible though if an interface of the same name already
exists in another package. Should the client import both packages with
*, an ambiguity will result, and the client can no longer be compiled.

The change will not even become compatible when a subsystem's
interface names are unambiguous without package names. Last but
not least, an interface with an identical name can also be defined in
another subsystem. Nevertheless, interface names should be unique for
each subsystem. Thus the risk of ambiguities will not be entirely eliminated, but at least reduced.

Removing an Interface

The removal of interfaces is incompatible. If the interface is not immediately removed but set to *deprecated* instead, the change becomes
deferred-incompatible.

Renaming Interfaces

The renaming of an interface is incompatible. One could copy the
interface with the new name and set the old version to *deprecated*.
However, this approach could easily create type problems, even if the
new interface inherits from the old one or vice versa.

If the interface is renamed and the old name annotated with the
Past tag, the change will become automatable.

Here is an example for renaming the *Customer* interface into *Partner*:

```
/**
 * @past public interface Customer
 */
public interface Partner
...
```

It should not go unmentioned that a change carried out with the *Past* tag is not always automatable. If an interface of the new name does already exist in another package, this can lead to an ambiguity (see also 'Adding an Interface').

Adding a Superinterface

When another interface is added to the list of interfaces that inherited, we will receive an incompatible change. Client classes that implement this interface will become abstract because they do not implement the methods of the new superinterface.

If the client class previously owned methods that now 'coincidentally' implement the superinterface's methods, a behavior conflict can emerge.

The change will become deferred-incompatible when the interface is not directly added to the interfaces that inherited and the change is denoted only with the *Future* tag instead. The Future warner can detect those classes that must implement the new interface in the future. In this way, the client developers can adapt their code before the actual change is executed.

Here is an example of how the *Future* tag is used:

```
/**
 * @future public interface Customer
 *              extends Partner
 */
public interface Customer
...
```

Removing a Superinterface

If an interface is removed from the list of those interfaces that inherited, we are faced with an incompatible change. Client classes that use the interface for typing demand more methods than the interface will offer after the change.

This change will become deferred-incompatible if the interface is not directly removed from the list of interfaces that inherited, but the change is merely denoted with the *Future* tag instead. The Future warner can detect those classes that will expect methods which no longer exist in the future. The client developers can adapt their code before the actual change is executed.

An example of the *Future* tag's use:

```
/**
 * @future public interface Customer
 */
public interface Customer extends Partner
 ...
```

6.5.2   Changes to Classes

Adding a Class

Normally the addition of a class is compatible. The change will become incompatible though when a class of the same name already exists in another package. If the client imports both packages with *, an ambiguity will emerge, and the client can no longer be compiled. The only exception to this rule is the occurrence of a client coincidentally compiled with the wrong class. In such a case it is very likely that a behavior conflict will emerge.

The change will not even become compatible if the class names of a subsystem are unique without being assignable to package names. After all, a class of the same name can also be defined in another subsystem. Nevertheless, class names should be unique for each subsystem. The risk of ambiguities will not be eradicated entirely, but at least reduced.

Removing Classes

The removal of classes is incompatible. If the class is not immediately removed but set to *deprecated* instead, the change will become deferred-incompatible.

Renaming Classes

The renaming of a class is incompatible. Theoretically, one could copy the class, assign it the new name and set the old version to *deprecated*. This can easily lead to type problems though, even if the new class inherits from the old one or vice versa.

If the class is renamed and the old name annotated with the *Past* tag, the change will become automatable.

Look at the example for renaming the class *Customer* in *Partner*:

```
/**
 * @past public class Customer
 */
public class Partner
...
```

Unfortunately, changes using the *Past* tag cannot always be automated. If a class with the new name already exists in another package, an ambiguity might be created (see also 'Adding a Class').

Changing a Superclass

Changes of the superclass are incompatible. At first, polymorphic assignments will become invalid. For example: if *Customer* is a subclass of *Partner*, and *Partner* is exchanged as a superclass, all assignments of *Customer* to variables of the *Partner* type will become invalid. Moreover, the subclasses of the modified classes will become abstract if the new superclass defines abstract methods. Should the subclasses 'coincidentally' define the abstract methods, a behavior conflict will be the outcome.

If the *Future* tag is used to denote changes, it will be rendered deferred-incompatible. The Future warner can identify those classes which will either expect methods that no longer exist in the future or no longer implement defined abstract methods. This allows client developers to adapt their code before the actual change is made.

The following is an example of the *Future* tag's use:

```
/**
 * @future public class Customer
 *              extends Person
 */
public class Customer extends Partner
...
```

Adding an Interface

The adding of an interface to the list of interfaces that are implemented by the class is incompatible: existing subclasses will become abstract. If the subclasses 'coincidentally' define the methods, a behavior conflict will emerge.

The change will become deferred-incompatible if the addition of the interface is denoted with the *Future* tag.

For example:

```
/**
 * @future public class Customer
 *            implements Storable
 */
public class Customer
...
```

Removing an Interface

The removal of an interface from the list of interfaces implemented by the class is incompatible: the class's objects are no longer assignable to the remote type.

The change will become deferred-incompatible if the removal of the interface is denoted with the *Future* tag.

For example:

```
/**
 * @future public class Customer
 */
public class Customer implements Storable
...
```

Expanding Class Visibility

The expansion of class visibility is compatible.

Restricting Class Visibility

The restriction of class visibility is incompatible.

The change will become deferred-incompatible if the visibility restriction is denoted with the *Future* tag.

For example:

```
/**
 * @future class Customer
 */
public class Customer
...
```

Setting a Class from *Final* to *Non-final*

If a class that is declared *final* is set to *non-final*, the change is compatible.

Setting a Class from *Non-final* to *Final*

If a class is set from *non-final* to *final*, a structural conflict will be the result: existing subclasses will be rendered invalid.

The change will become deferred-incompatible if it is not executed directly, but denoted with the *Future* tag instead.

Here is an example of the *Future* tag's use:

```
/**
 * @future final public class Customer
 */
public class Customer
 ...
```

Setting a Class to *Abstract*

If a concrete class becomes abstract, we are faced with an incompatible change. When objects of this class are created, those create statements will become invalid.

The change will become deferred-incompatible if it is denoted with the *Future* tag.

For example:

```
/**
 * @future public abstract class Customer
 */
public class Customer
 ...
```

Setting a Class from *Abstract* to *Non-abstract*

If an abstract class becomes concrete, we are faced with a compatible change – at least as long as no new methods that were previously abstract must be added to the class. If that was the case, we could get a behavior conflict.

6.5.3   Changes to Constants in Interfaces/Classes

Adding a Constant

The addition of a constant is compatible.

Removing a Constant

If a constant is removed, a structural conflict will occur.

The change will become deferred-incompatible if the constant is not deleted, but marked as *deprecated* instead.

Changing a Constant Type

The changing of a constant type is incompatible.

The change will become deferred-incompatible if a new constant with the desired type is created while the old constant is set to *deprecated*.

For example:

```
interface Printer {
  /**
   * @deprecated
   */
  public static final int LASERPRINTER=1;
  /**
   * @deprecated
   */
  public static final int INKJETPRINTER=2;

  public static final String
    LASERPRINTER_TYP="laser";
  public static final String
    INKJETPRINTER_TYP="ink";
}
```

Changing a Constant Value

In most cases, the changing of a constant value is compatible. However, if a number of constants constitutes the value range of an enumeration type, the change can create a behavior conflict. This is the case when the client's value range has been expanded by constants of its own and the values used there are in conflict with the new constant value.

6.5.4 Changes to Methods in Interfaces

Adding a Method to an Interface

If a method is added to an interface, a structural conflict will be created. Existing implementations of the interface will become abstract, because they don't possess an implementation of the new method. If, by chance, a suitable method already happens to exist in an implementation, this method will be implemented 'accidentally.' This can lead to a behavior conflict.

The change will become compatible if the interface is not directly implemented in the application, but application classes are derived from default implementations instead. Then the subsystem developers can provide a suitable method implementation in the default implementation.

For example:

```
public interface Window {
  public void setWidth(int w);
  public void setHeight(int h);

  // new method: setSize
  public void setSize(int width, int height);
}

public class DefaultWindow implements Window {
  private int width, height;

  public void setWidth(int w) {
    width = w;
  }

  public void setHeight(int h) {
    height = h;
  }

  // new method: setSize
  public void setSize(int w, int h) {
    setWidth(w);
    setHeight(h);
  }
}
```

Removing a Method from an Interface

The removal of a method from an interface is incompatible. The change will become deferred-incompatible if the method is not directly deleted, but set to *deprecated* instead.

Renaming a Method in an Interface

If a method in an interface is renamed, a structural conflict will be the result. Generally, the change will become automatable if the method's previous name is defined in the *Past* tag.

For example:

```
public interface Customer {
  /**
   * @past void setName(String name)
   */
  public void setLastName(String name);
}
```

Yet it is possible to experience situations where the changes will remain incompatible. This is going to be the case if a method of the same name and parameters but with a different return type already exists in either a subinterface or an implementation of this interface. If a method with the same parameters and a matching return type exists in an implementation, a behavior conflict can occur because the renamed method will be implemented automatically by the method in that implementation. If a default implementation exists for the inter- *Default* face and classes are never directly implemented in that interface, but *Implementations of* succeed the default implementation instead, the change can also be *Interfaces* handled with the *deprecated* tag: in this case, the method must be duplicated in both the interface and the default implementation. Also, the old method must be set to *deprecated*.

Changing the Parameter List of a Method in the Interface

If the parameter list of a method in an interface is changed, a structural conflict will emerge. The change will become deferred-incompatible unless it is executed directly. Instead, the method will be copied and the copy will be changed. The old method must be set to *deprecated*.

For example:

```
public interface Customer {
  /**
   * @deprecated
   */
  public void setName(String name);
  public void setName(String lastname,
                      String firstname);
}
```

Changing the Return Type of a Method in the Interface

If the return type of a method in an interface is changed, the change will be incompatible. Existing implementations of this method in the client will become invalid.

The change will become deferred-incompatible when a new method with a new name and the desired return type is created. The old method will be marked with the *deprecated* tag.

We will have to find a new name for the new method if the programming language (in this case Java) does not allow for defining a number of methods in one class that can only be distinguished by their return type.

For example:

```
public interface Customer {
  /**
   * @deprecated
   */
  public String getName();
  public Name getCustomername();
}
```

Adding an Exception to a Method in the Interface

The addition of an exception to a method is incompatible because the client code will have to catch this exception.

The change will become deferred-incompatible if the method is copied and generated together with the desired exception list under a new name. The old method must be set to *deprecated*.

For example:

```
public interface Printer {
  /**
   * @deprecated
   */
  public void print(Document d);
  public void printDoc(Document d)
    throws PrinterException;
}
```

Removing an Exception from a Method in the Interface

The removal of an exception from a method is incompatible because the client code is not allowed to catch this removed exception. In addition, redefinitions of the method will become invalid because they expand the exception list.

The change will become deferred-incompatible if the method is copied and generated with a new name together with the desired exception list. The old method will be set to *deprecated*.

For example:

```
public interface Printer {
  /**
   * @deprecated
   */
  public void print(Document d)
    throws PrinterException;
  public void printDoc(Document d);
}
```

6.5.5   Changes to Constructors in Classes

Adding a Constructor

When a new constructor is added to a class, incompatibilities will emerge, as long as no explicit constructor exists. In this case, the compiler will no longer generate the default constructor. Clients that until now have been using the default constructor will become invalid.

The change will become compatible if one always creates an explicit default constructor whenever the first constructor is inserted. This problem can be avoided right from the start when always at least one explicit constructor is created.

Removing a Constructor

The removal of a constructor from a class is incompatible. The change will become deferred-incompatible if the constructor is not directly deleted, but set to *deprecated* instead.

Changing a Constructor's Parameter List

If the parameter list of a constructor is changed, a structural conflict will occur. The change will become deferred-incompatible unless the change is made directly. Instead, the constructor will be copied and the copy will be changed. The old constructor will be set to *deprecated* and call the new constructor.

For example:

```
public class Customer {

  /**
   * @deprecated
   */
  public Customer(String name) {
    this(name, „");
  }

  public Customer(String lastname,
                  String firstname)
  {..}
}
```

Expanding Constructor Visibility

If constructor visibility is expanded, the change will be compatible.

Restricting Constructor Visibility

If constructor visibility is restricted (e.g. from *public* to *protected*), an incompatible change will be the result. Clients that use the respective constructor will become invalid because the constructor is no longer visible to them.

The change will become deferred-incompatible if the restriction of the constructor's visibility is denoted with the *Future* tag.

For example:

```
public class Customer {
  /**
   * @future protected Customer(String name)
   */
  public Customer(String name)
  {..}
}
```

Weakening of a Constructor's Precondition[5]

If a constructor's precondition is weakened, a compatible change will be the outcome.

---

[5]   Pre- and postconditions refer to the contract model based on the design-by-contract principle (Meyer, 1992).

Strengthening of a Constructor's Precondition

If a constructor's precondition is strengthened, its uses will become invalid. Thus the change will be incompatible.

Adding an Exception to a Constructor

The addition of an exception to a constructor is incompatible because the client code has to catch this exception.

Removing an Exception from a Constructor

The removal of an exception from a constructor is incompatible because the client code is not allowed to catch this removed exception.

6.5.6   Changes to Methods in Classes

Adding Methods to a Class

If a new, non-private method is added to a class, incompatibilities will arise. If a method of the same name and parameters but with a different return type exists in a subclass, a structural conflict will emerge. Even if the method is defined with identical parameters and an identical return type in the subclass, the structural conflict will be inevitable if the method in this subclass is less visible. Should the method's signature happen to be the same as the signature of the new method, a behavior conflict is likely to result, because the new method will accidentally be overwritten by the subclass.

Removing Methods from Classes

The removal of a method from a class is incompatible. The change will become deferred-incompatible if the method is not directly deleted but set to *deprecated* instead.

Renaming Methods in Classes

If a method in a class is renamed, a structural conflict will be the result. As a rule, the change will become automatable if the method's previous name is defined in the *Past* tag.

For example:

```
public class Customer {
  /**
   * @past void setName(String name)
   */
  public void setLastName(String name);
}
```

Alternatively, the old method can also be copied and saved with the new name. Then the old method must be set to *deprecated*. In this case, the change will not become automatable, but at least it will be deferred-incompatible. Yet it is possible to experience situations where the changes will remain incompatible. This is going to be the case if a method of the same name and parameters but with a different return type already exists. Should a method of the same name, the same parameters plus a matching return type exist in the subclass, a behavior conflict can emerge because the renamed method will be overwritten by the method in the subclass.

Changing Parameter List of a Method in a Class

If the parameter list of a method in a class is changed, a structural conflict will emerge. The change will become deferred-incompatible unless the change is not made directly. Instead, the method will be copied and the copy will be changed. The old method will be set to *deprecated* and call the new method.

For example:

```
public class Customer {

  /**
   * @deprecated
   */
  public void setName(String name) {
    setName(name, „");
  }

  public void setName(String lastname,
                      String firstname)
  {..}
}
```

Changing the Return Type of a Method in a Class

If the return type of a method in a class is changed, the change is incompatible. Existing redefinitions of this method in the client will become invalid. If the new return type is no subtype of the old one, the uses of the respective methods will also be rendered invalid.

The change will become deferred-incompatible if a new method with the new name and the desired return type are created. The old method will be marked *deprecated* and their implementation will refer to the new method.

For example:

```
public class Customer {

  /**
   * @deprecated
   */
  public String getName() {
    return getCustomername().toString();
  }

  public Name getCustomername()
  {..}
}
```

Expanding Method Visibility in a Class

If method visibility in a class is expanded (e.g. from *protected* to *public*), we will get an incompatible change. Existing redefinitions of this method will become invalid because they restrict visibility.

The change will become deferred-incompatible if a copy of the method with the desired visibility is generated and saved with another name. The old method will be set to *deprecated*. The new method will refer to the old method.

For example:

```
public class Customer {

  /**
   * @deprecated
   */
  protected String getName()
  {..}

  public String getCustomername() {
    return getName();
  }
}
```

Restricting Method Visibility in a Class

If method visibility in a class is restricted (e.g. from *public* to *protected*), an incompatible change will result. Clients of this method will become invalid, because the method will no longer be visible to them.

The change will become deferred-incompatible if a copy of the method with the desired visibility is generated and saved with another name. The old method will be set to *deprecated* and refer to the new method.

For example:

```
public class Customer {

  /**
   * @deprecated
   */
  public String getName() {
    return getCustomername();
  }

  protected String getCustomername()
  {..}
}
```

Setting a Method in a Class from *Final* to *Non-final*

If a method declared *final* is set to *non-final*, the change will be compatible.

Setting a Method in a Class from *Non-Final* to *Final*

If a method is set to *final*, the change will be incompatible because existing redefinitions of that method have become invalid.

The change will become deferred-incompatible if the old method is copied and inserted under a new name. The new method will be declared *final* and call the old method.

For example:

```
public class Customer {

  /**
   * @deprecated
   */
  public String getName()
  {..}

  public final String getCustomername() {
    return getName();
  }
}
```

Setting a Method in a Class from *Static* to *Non-static*

If a method is set from *static* to *non-static*, the change will be incompatible. Calls via the class name will be rendered invalid through the change. Now, one instance of the class will always be required.

The change will become deferred-incompatible if a new, non-static method is generated under a new name. At the same time, a static variable that contains a default instance of the respective class will be introduced into the class. The old method will be set to *deprecated* and call the new method on this default instance.

For example:

```
public class Printer {

   private static Printer defaultPrinter =
                                new Printer();

   /**
    * @deprecated
    */
   public static void print(Document d) {
     defaultPrinter.printDoc(d);
   }

   public void printDoc(Document d)
   {..}
}
```

Setting a Method in a Class from *Non-static* to *Static*

If a method is set to *static*, the change is incompatible. Redefinitions of methods in client classes will be rendered invalid through the change.

The change will become deferred-incompatible if a new, static method is generated under a new name. The old method will be set to *deprecated* and call the new method.

For example:

```
public class Printer {

   /**
    * @deprecated
    */
   public void print(Document d) {
```

```
        printDoc(d);
    }

    public static void printDoc(Document d)
    {..}
}
```

Setting a Method to *Abstract*

If a method that was until now concrete is changed into an abstract method, the resulting change will be incompatible: existing subclasses will become abstract.

The change will become deferred-incompatible if the change is denoted with the *Future* tag.

For example:

```
public abstract class Printer {
    /**
     * @future abstract print(Document d)
     */
    public void print(Document d)
    {
        printDoc(d);
    }
}
```

Setting a Method from *Abstract* to *Non-abstract*

If an abstract method becomes non-abstract, we will get a compatible change.

Weakening of a Method's Precondition in a Class

If a method's precondition is weakened, uses of this method will remain valid. However, redefinitions of this method will become invalid, because they expect the old precondition. It is not permissible though to strengthen the precondition in a class. Thus the change is incompatible.

The change will become deferred-incompatible if a new method with the desired precondition is created under a new name.

For example:

```
public class Printer {

  /**
   * @deprecated
   * @require d != zero
   */
  public void print(Document d) {
    printDoc(d);
  }

  /**
   * @require true
   */
  public void printDoc(Document d)
  {..}
}
```

Strengthening of a Method's Precondition in a Class

If a method's precondition is strengthened, redefinitions of this method will remain valid. However, uses of this method will become invalid. Thus the change is incompatible.

The change will become deferred-incompatible if a new method with the desired precondition is created under a new name.

For example:

```
public class Printer {

  /**
   * @deprecated
   * @require true
   */
  public void print(Document d)
  {..}
```

```
    /**
     * @require d != zero
     */
    public void printDoc(Document d) {
      print(d);
    }
}
```

Weakening of a Method's Postcondition in a Class

If a method's postcondition is weakened, redefinitions of this method will remain valid. However, uses of this method will become invalid. Thus the change is incompatible.

The change will become deferred-incompatible if a new method with the desired postcondition is created under a new name.

For example:

```
public class Printer {

    /**
     * @deprecated
     * @ensure d.hasbeenprinted()
     */
    public void print(Document d)
    {..}

    /**
     * @ensure true
     */
    public void printDoc(Document d) {
      print(d);
    }
}
```

Strengthening of a Method's Postcondition in a Class

If a method's postcondition is strengthened, uses of this method will remain valid. However, redefinitions of this method will become invalid. Thus the change is incompatible.

The change will become deferred-incompatible if a new method with the desired postcondition is created under a new name.

For example:

```
public class Printer {

  /**
   * @deprecated
   * @ensure true
   */
  public void print(Document d) {
    printDoc(d);
  }

  /**
   * @ensure d.hasbeenprinted()
   */
  public void printDoc(Document d)
  {..}
}
```

Setting a Method in a Class to *Synchronized*

If a method that is declared *non-synchronized* is set to *synchronized*, there will be the rare case in which this change is incompatible. It can trigger deadlocks, and a behavior conflict will be the consequence.

The change will become deferred-incompatible if the method is copied and inserted as *synchronized* under a new name. The old method will be set to *deprecated*.

For example:

```
public class Printer {

  /**
   * @deprecated
   */
  public void print(Document d)
  {..}
```

```
        public synchronized void printDoc(Document d)
        {..}
}
```

In contrast to the usually applied duplicating of methods, the original method will not be simply delegated to the new method. If this was done, the aforementioned deadlock situation would occur. Instead, the new method can either call the old one or the implementation itself will be copied.

Setting a Method in a Class from *Synchronized* to *Non-synchronized*

If a method that declared *synchronized* is set to *non-synchronized*, the change will be incompatible. Multi-threaded applications can display an aberrant behavior after this change has been made. A behavior conflict will emerge.

The change will become deferred-incompatible if the method is copied and inserted as *non-synchronized* under a new name. The old method will be set to *deprecated*.

For example:

```
public class Printer {

  /**
   * @deprecated
   */
  public synchronized void print(Document d)
  {..}

  public void printDoc(Document d) {
    print(d);
  }
}
```

Adding an Exception to a Method in a Class

The addition of an exception to a method is incompatible because the client code must catch this exception.

The change will become deferred-incompatible if the method is copied and generated under a new name with the desired exception list. The old method will be set to *deprecated*.

For example:

```
public class Printer {

  /**
   * @deprecated
   */
  public void print(Document d)
  {..}

  public void printDoc(Document d)
    throws PrinterException {
    print(d);
  }
}
```

Removing an Exception from a Method in a Class

The removal of an exception from a method is incompatible because the client code is not allowed to catch this removed exception. Moreover, the method's redefinitions will become invalid because they expand the exception list.

The change will become deferred-incompatible if the method is copied and generated under a new name with the desired exception list. The old method will be set to *deprecated*.

For example:

```
public class Printer {

  /**
   * @deprecated
   */
  public void print(Document d)
    throws PrinterException {
    printDoc(d);
  }

  public void printDoc(Document d)
  {..}
}
```

6.6 Converter

The refactoring tags described here clearly aim at keeping the new interface of the modified subsystem temporarily backwards-compatible with the old version. Thus the interface gets 'polluted' with methods that are not needed by the new client in the subsystem.

Converters that convert object structures between different versions are an alternative here. If they are used, the subsystem's API will not be altered. The subsystem is copied instead, so that the old as well as the new version of the subsystem can be used in parallel. Often the new version of the subsystem will receive the suffix '2'.

Since in many cases it is not possible to adapt the entire application at once, some parts of it will continue to work with the subsystem's old version for the time being, while other parts are already using the new subsystem version. If the different parts of the application have to communicate with each other, the object structures of the old and the new subsystem versions must be bidirectionally convertible.

For this purpose, developers of a duplicated subsystem can supply one converter or more. In this way, the system's 'pollution' will be limited, and the convention of adding the suffix '2' will make it sufficiently clear to anyone that the old subsystem version will soon be history. Moreover, all classes of the old subsystem version will be set to *deprecated*, of course.

Converters do display definite limitations though, if classes of the modified subsystem have been inherited by other subsystems. In such a case, it will no longer be feasible to construct a general converter with simple means.

6.7 Application Migration with Incompatible Subsystem Changes

Unless the subsystem developers alleviated their modifications of the subsystem API by using the aforementioned tags, the application developers will be in for an unpleasant surprise: after the subsystem's new version has been installed, the application will no longer be compilable. The compiler will generate countless error messages. Unfortunately, the number of error messages provides little valuable information. Several of them will be sequence errors, so that fewer changes must be made than the mass of messages at first suggests. But single migration steps can in turn produce new sequence errors – for example, because a developer notices that a parameter list of a method in the application must be adapted. All in all, the demand for adaptation can hardly be projected precisely. This creates a lot of insecurity for further project planning. Thus the migration to a new subsystem version becomes a relevant risk.

In addition, the application will remain uncompilable during the entire migration period. This means that neither the application itself nor tests can be executed. Whether all single parts of the application migrated correctly or not will only become clear at the very end of the migration process.

This problem can be countered with a stepwise, new construction of the application. Please proceed as follows:

Migrating an Application Layer by Layer

1. Install the new version of the subsystem.
2. Create a new, empty version of the application project, including references to the new subsystem version.
3. Copy the application's lowest layer into the new project.
4. Make the copied application classes compilable again.
5. Change the copied application classes so that they will pass the tests again. The tests will also let you discover and resolve semantic conflicts (which requires a good test coverage, of course).
6. Copy the next application layer. Proceed with step 4.

Figure 6-3 visualizes this procedure. However, of course the migration effort will not become smaller when these instructions are being followed, but at least the already migrated parts of the application will be compilable and run the according tests. This migration method will significantly reduce the risks involved.

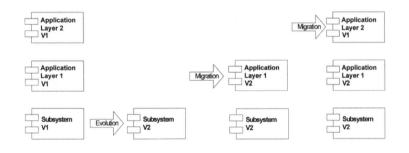

Fig. 6-3
New Construction of the Application for Migration

6.8   Tips for Designing APIs

Only a few, simple tips will help to design APIs in such a manner that they will be stable regarding changes.

Design Tip 1: Planning Inheritance

Inheritance must be planned. If inheriting from an API class hasn't been explicitly planned and scheduled beforehand, the class should be set to *final*. Methods that are not explicitly meant for overwriting should be declared *final* or *private*. Methods that in principle inherit from subclasses but do not belong to the class's normal API, can be labeled *protected*.

The keyword *final* constitutes a very powerful restriction for clients and can thus lead to problems. Especially when writing tests with JUnit, often scenarios will be created where a referenced class must be replaced by a specific version (e.g. Mock or Dummy). If the referenced class has been declared *final*, the testability via Mock or Dummy classes (which, as a rule, inherit from the class) will be impaired. Interfaces come in handy here: the actual implementation class is declared *final*, whereas the interface can be utilized for Mock and Dummy implementations.

Design Tip 2: Avoiding Inheritance

If inheritance between API classes can be avoided, it should be avoided: otherwise API clients can build on these inheritance relations.

Design Tip 3: Abstract Implementations for Interfaces

API clients that implement an API interface will become more stable regarding changes to the interface if they do not directly implement the interface, but inherit from an abstract class. If a new method is added to an interface, a default implementation will be defined in the abstract class, so that API clients must not be adapted.

Here, we are facing an area of potential conflict: in the chapter about architecture smells, we argued that list-like inheritance hierarchies point at speculative generalization. Now, in this chapter, we are suddenly suggesting use of exactly these list-like inheritance hierarchies. The reason for this suggestion is easily explained: in the case depicted here, the list-like inheritance hierarchy has deliberately been applied in order to smooth the way for modifications of subsystem interfaces. This is an ostensive example of the fact that not every smell automatically signals the existence of a problem.

Of course the abstract implementations for interfaces will function only as long as the client classes implement only a single interface (Figure 6-4). If several interfaces are supposed to be implemented, inheritance from several abstract implementations will prove impossible (at least in languages with single inheritance).

A way out of this dilemma is provided by the *Adaptable pattern* used in Eclipse (see Gamma and Beck, 2003).

Design Tip 4: Small APIs

The smaller the API is, the lower the probability that the API must be changed incompatibly. Subsystems should be designed in such a way

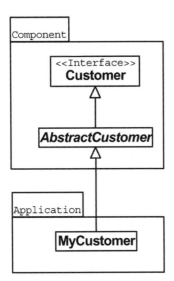

Fig. 6-4
Abstract Implementations for Interfaces

that as many classes as possible are hidden behind an as small as possible API.

All elements should have as little visibility as possible.

Design Tip 5: API in Its Own Packages

If the API as well as the implementation of a subsystem are respectively organized in packages of their own, changes to the implementation can more easily be kept separate from the API (Figure 6-5).

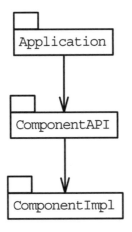

Fig. 6-5
Division between API and Implementation

Design Tip 6: Unambiguous Class Names

Class names in a subsystem API should be unambiguous, even without package names. Otherwise, problems can arise during migration when classes are moved into other packages.

Design Tip 7: Avoid Wildcard Imports

The problem that the previous design tip addresses can be attenuated by avoiding wildcard imports (as from implicit imports). Instead use explicit imports, maybe using an automated import feature of an IDE to remove wildcard imports.

Design Tip 8: Explicit Default Constructor

Each class should have at least one explicit constructor to prevent the compiler from generating the default constructor. Otherwise, the compiler-generated default constructor can be deleted 'accidentally' when a parameterized constructor is added.

6.9   An Example

This section aims at clarifying the previously explained principles of API refactoring, using the framework of a more comprehensive example. To this end, we will choose the example of a time recording system for IT consultants. The consultants can access the system via a web-based interface to feed in their work hours. The values fed into the system form the basis for payroll accounting as well as for generating invoices to customers.[6]

6.9.1   Our Starting Point

Subsystems in the Time Recording

The subsystems are displayed in Figure 6-6. The consultants access the system via the subsystem *Web*. The accounting department uses the subsystem *Report* to produce the required print lists and analyses.

Subsystem Web

The subsystem *Web* works with the subsystem *Business Objects* which provides concepts such as *Employees* and *Time Entries*. These business objects are saved in the database and reconstructed from the database with the subsystem *Administration*. To this end, a purchased subsystem *DB* is utilized.

---

[6]   This example is also used in Chapter 5. It is described here in its entirety so that one can read both chapters independently.

The subsystem *Report* employs the subsystem *Analysis* in order to carry out all necessary analyses for the print lists (e.g. all hours for each employee and for one project respectively). Of course, the subsystem *Analysis* uses the subsystems *Business Objects* and *Administration* to access the persistent business objects. The print lists are created with the aid of a commercially available report tool (subsystem *Report Tool*).

Subsystem Report

Of course, the subsystem *Analysis* uses the subsystems *Business Objects* and *Administration* to access the persistent business objects. The print lists are created with the aid of a commercially available report tool (subsystem *Report Tool*).

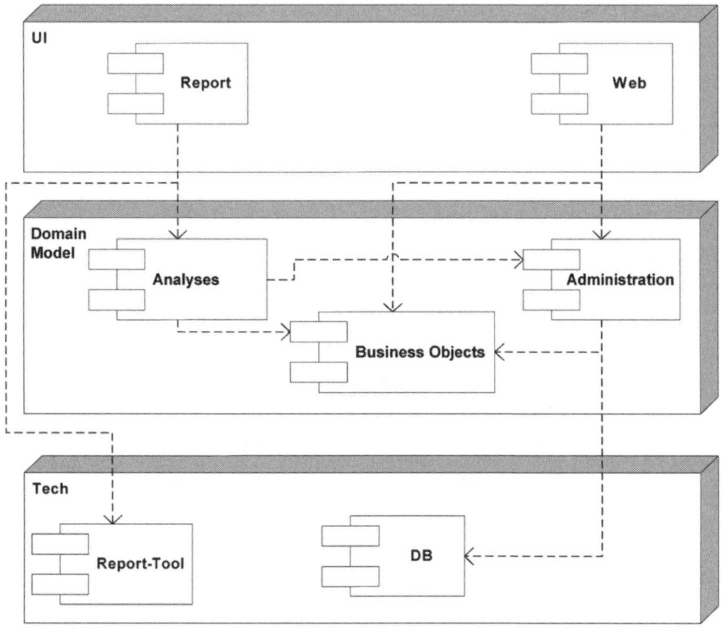

Fig. 6-6
Subsystems of the Time Recording Example

The subsystems are arranged in three non-strict layers: user interface (UI), domain model and technology.

At its core, the time recording system builds on the business objects displayed in Figure 6-7: *Time Entries* holds a central position. Besides date, start and end time, it contains references to the *Project*, the project's *Activity* and the *Employees*.

The Business Objects

The subsystem *Business Objects* has a special role in our example. It is used by many other subsystems, and its API contains many classes of the subsystem. Consequently, we are confronted with the architecture smell 'subsystem API too large' here. In our example, this smell is wanted though. The subsystem *Business Objects* shall provide the vocabulary for the other systems' communication among each other.

Fig. 6-7
Business Objects

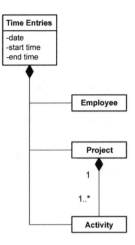

Based on this vocabulary, the API of the subsystem *Administration* looks as follows:

API of the Subsystem Administration

```
public interface Administration {
   public void enter (Time Entries z);
   public void cancel (Time Entries z);
   public Time Entries[] getEntry
      (Project p, int year, int month);
   public Time Entries[] getEntries
      (Employee m, int year, int month);
   public Time Entries[] getEntries
      (Employee m,
       int year, int month, int day);
   ...
}
```

6.9.2   The Reasons for this Refactoring

The modeling of the subsystem *Business Objects* strongly influences the subsystem *Administration*'s API and thus also the interaction of *Analysis* and *Administration*.

Basically, we have to implement the respective low-level functions for most analyses in *Administration*. The business objects are too 'stupid' to allow the subsystem *Analysis* to execute complex functions on them.[7] Theoretically, it is also possible for the subsystem *Analysis* to

---

[7]   This could also be a smell in the design: maybe the business objects are merely data structures.

access the database directly. However, this would also mean that the subsystem *Administration* no longer encapsulates the database, thus making modifications of the database schema more difficult.

Therefore, the subsystem *Business Objects* should be restructured in such a way that it becomes 'smarter' and the API of the subsystem *Administration* does not inflate so strongly.

6.9.3   The Goal of this Refactoring

This object model of the subsystem *Business Objects* shall now be modified in such a manner that the model of the core business objects will look as follows: each one of the *Employees* has got a *Month Folder* for each month with a *Calendar Sheet* for every work day. On the *Calendar Sheet* all *Time Entries* are recorded, including start and end time, *Project* and *Activity* in the project (see Figure 6-8).

The New Object Model of the Business Objects

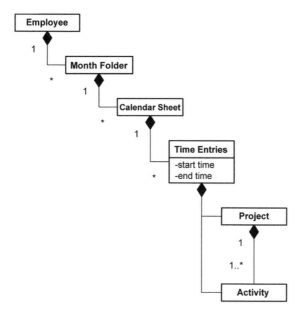

Fig. 6-8
Business Objects after Restructuring

With this restructuring of the subsystem *Business Objects*, we venture deep into the whole system's vocabulary. We should expect a demand for comprehensive restructuring measures of the entire system.

Here, we are going to focus on the refactoring's impact on the API of the *Administration* subsystem. We can imagine the new API as follows:

The New API of the Administration Subsystem

```
public interface Administration {
   public void save (Employee m);
```

```
        public Employee getEmployee
          (String name);
        public Employee[] getProjectEntries
          (Project p);
        ...
      }
```

In principle, it would be possible to leave the old methods in *Administration* and simply set them to *deprecated*:

*Backwards-Compatible
API of the Subsystem
Administration*

```
public interface Administration {
  public void save (Employee m);
  public Employee getEmployee
    (String name);
  public Employee[] getProjectEntries
    (Project p);

  /**
   * @deprecated
   */
  public void enter (Time Entry z);

  /**
   * @deprecated
   */
  public void cancel (Time Entry z);

  /**
   * @deprecated
   */
  public Time Entry[] getEntries
    (Project p, int year, int month);

  /**
   * @deprecated
   */
  public Time Entry[] getEntries
    (Employee m, int year, int month);

  /**
   * @deprecated
   */
  public Time Entry[] getEntries
```

```
   (Employee m,
     int year, int month, int day);
  ...
}
```

Regrettably, this does not solve the problem of how changes of the subsystem *Business Objects'* API should be dealt with. There, not only the interfaces of the classes have changed, but also the relations between the classes themselves were completely rearranged.

6.9.4   Refactoring Procedure: Business Objects Omnipotent

We will proceed based on the assumption that the single subsystems in our example are developed by different teams. In the course of a subsystem's refactoring, it is therefore not feasible to reconstruct all this subsystem's dependent subsystems. We must find a way to execute the refactoring step by step, and in such a manner that the subsequent migration will cause as little effort as possible.

Different Teams for Each Subsystem

The evident refactoring course would be to model the subsystem *Business Objects* in such a fashion that it can be used like the old subsystem. To this end, all classes with their respective methods would be kept and the new methods merely added to them. Naturally, the old methods would be set to *deprecated* to indicate that migration must be directed at the new methods. The outcome would be the class structure that can be seen in Figure 6-9.

Omnipotent Business Objects

This example too proves that a large refactoring will often lead to an initial deterioration of the system's structure. Here, we have provoked two extremely bad smells because we created two cyclical relations. For this reason it is pivotal that we finish our refactoring: in the next version of the subsystem *Business Objects*, the cyclical references will be gone, as will the *deprecated* methods.

Anyhow, the 'deteriorated' version of the subsystem will enable us to adapt the remaining application to the business objects' new structure. Likewise, we will let the API of the subsystem *Administration* 'deteriorate,' so that both the old and the new structure can be processed.

Afterwards, the deprecated methods are removed from the API. We will get the targeted API of the subsystem *Administration*:

```
public interface Administration {
  public void save (Employee m);
  public Employee getEmployee
    (String name);
```

New API of the Subsystem Administration

Fig. 6-9
Backwards-
Compatible Subsystem
Business Objects

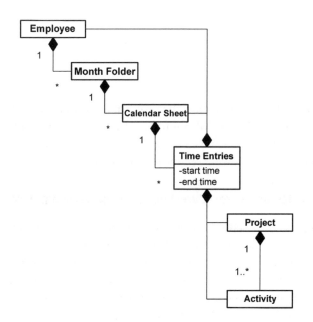

```
public Employee[] getProjectEntries
    (Project p);

    . . .

}
```

6.9.5   Refactoring Procedure: Duplicating Business Objects

Duplication of the Sub-
system Business Objects

Another option for a step-by-step restructuring is duplication of the subsystem *Business Objects*. First, a new subsystem labeled *Business Objects2* is created in the same location as the subsystem *Business Objects*.

In this subsystem *Business Objects*, all classes are then set to *depre-cated*. The new subsystem *Business Objects2* contains – besides the new business object classes – a converter that is capable of transferring object structures of the subsystem *Business Objects* into object structures of the subsystem *Business Objects2* and vice versa. This gives us the opportunity to restructure the remaining parts of the application step by step. Once the application has been completely restructured, both the converter and the subsystem *Business Objects* will be deleted and the subsystem *Business Objects2* renamed into *Business Objects*.

Preconditions for Pro-
gramming a Converter

To enable programming of such a converter for object structures while keeping the effort to this end acceptable, the object graphs must be rendered convertible without information loss. In our example, the conversion of a time entry of the old model into *Employee* with his or her *Time Entries* is only feasible if access to the database is possible. There, all further time entries for *Employee* must be determined. During reverse conversion, the opposite can easily occur: too much information is provided for one class *Time Entries*. In that case, several *Time Entries* for one *Employee*, based on the old model, must be generated.

This problem can be addressed by creating a 'streamlined' model of the new business objects, i.e. one that allows conversion without information loss (see Figure 6-10).

In this 'streamlined' model, one employee is always assigned one calendar sheet, and each calendar sheet only one time entry. In effect, the time entry's date information has been moved to a class of its own: the class *Calendar Sheet*. Additionally, the uses relation between *Time Entries* and *Employee* has been reversed. Now, the business objects' new structure can be changed relatively simply with the help of a converter.

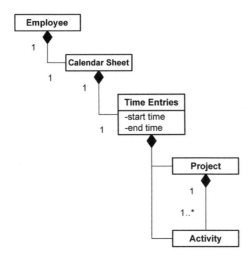

Fig. 6-10
The 'Streamlined' Model of the New Business Objects

As soon as we deployed the new object structure, we can install the new API of the *Administration* system:

```
public interface Administration {
   public void save (Employee m);
   public Employee getEmployee
      (String name);
   public Employee[] getProjectEntries
      (Project p);
   ...
}
```

New API of the Sub-system Administration

In the next step, the refactoring of the business objects will be completed. The new class *Month Sheet* and the transition from 1:1 relations to 1:*N* relations is relatively easily accomplished.

6.9.6   Evaluation of Both Approaches

Option 1   The application of the first refactoring option did not require any particular amount of creativity. It did have the disadvantage of degenerating the system structure though. In a very large system, this can have significant negative consequences. Therefore, this kind of 'pollution' must be eradicated as soon as possible.

Option 2   The second option created far less 'pollution' of the system due to use of the converter. Especially the dependent system's APIs did not inflate. The duplication of the subsystem *Business Objects* definitely constitutes a smell (code duplication), but both units are kept strictly separate. Of course, it is important to finally delete the old version of the subsystem as soon as possible. Since 'as soon as possible' harbors the danger of getting deferred for ever (in favor of more urgent matters), it is often advisable to set an explicit target version where the old version will be removed.

The second option seems to be more appealing for migration, but unfortunately it is not universally valid. If classes from the subsystem *Business Objects* had inherited from other subsystems, writing a universally applicable converter would have become impossible. Converters will work well if it is guaranteed that no subclasses exist. This is the case if at least all dependent subsystems are available for analysis, or if constructive subclasses have been excluded, for example through declaring the classes of one's subsystem *final*.[8]

Excursion: Black Box Refactoring

A contribution by Jens Uwe Pipka
(jens-uwe.pipka@daedalos.com, Daedalos Consulting)
One often-made implicit assumption during a refactoring process is that the entire code basis of a software system is at the programmers' disposal. If this is the case, all relations and uses of a subsystem to be refactored are known. They can be analyzed and adapted accordingly. This procedure constitutes a so-called *White Box Refactoring*, because the changes are made to the whole system. After the whole system has been adapted, the refactoring is complete. No further steps are required. This scenario is shown in the following figure:

---

[8]   See the comments regarding testability in Section 6.8.

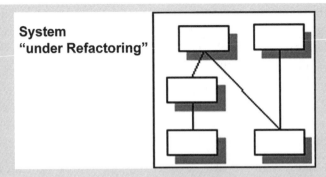

White Box Refactoring

We face a more difficult situation if a refactored system has a number of potential clients that are not familiar, as is e.g. the case when object-oriented libraries or a framework are applied. In such a situation, different systems use the common code basis. Therefore, we speak of a base system. An external subsystem that uses and specifies this base system is called the using system (see next figure).

If a refactoring is carried out in the base system, it is in most cases not feasible to identify all potential effects on the using systems, because multiple couplings between systems are possible. Thus, not all options can be taken into account fully during refactoring processes concerning the base system: a so-called *Black Box Refactoring* takes place, since there is no guarantee that each combination of the refactored base system and the using system will display the same semantic behavior in the future.

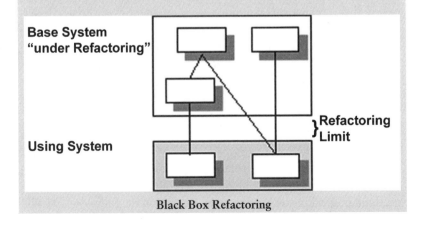

Black Box Refactoring

The complexity of identifying possible effects on a using system during the refactoring process is caused by the fact that object-oriented systems in principle allow two orthogonal ways of base system usage and specialization:

1. Call of those methods that are accessible via the interface of a class; also called *Black Box Usage*.
2. Specialization of a class through inheritance; also known as *White Box Usage*.

In the first-mentioned case, a refactoring in the base system can be executed with relatively few problems, because the internal structure is to a large degree encapsulated and changes are thus transparent. Only changes to the public interface of a class are critical, such as e.g. the removal or addition of a method. However, the use of refactoring tags enables proactive communication of these modifications and even – as described in Section 6.4 – mostly automated adaptation in the using system.

The second case, however, has yet another aspect that must be considered when refactoring the base system: changes in the system structure can have additional semantic effects on the using system, because the latter is implemented based on a specific syntactical structure. Inheritance causes the structure of the code basis to lie open and thus forms the basis for developing the using system. As a consequence, changes to this structure can affect the conditions present at implementation and therefore directly affect the program's semantics. Modifications of the program's semantics cannot be completely handled with refactoring tags alone, because refactoring tags are only meant to deal with changes of a class's interface. The complete, implicit interaction of base system and using system is not covered by the capabilities of refactoring tags.

Thus it is necessary to establish some additional procedures to ensure that a refactoring will not alter the semantics of the whole system: to this end, information for changes to the public interface of a class must be checked – not only in regard to its callers, but also in the context of the inheritance hierarchy, while keeping the using system in mind. Possible conflict situations have already been addressed in Section 6.3. It should not go unmentioned though that conflicts in the inheritance hierarchy cannot be sufficiently solved by 'mechanically' changing all references, because such an action may create significant semantic conflicts.

In effect, not only the isolated migration efforts in the base system must be considered, but moreover their impact as well as the required migration steps in the using system. In the following, we will discuss this problem and illustrate it using two examples. We will examine how far usage and specialization must be distinguished in the refactoring process, and whether a semantic conflict analysis is required or not.

Semantic Conflict Scenarios through Black Box Refactoring

The difficulties encountered in Black Box Refactoring can be demonstrated with a simple example. In our example, the base system implements an accounting system that generates invoices when one or more products are purchased. One component of the accounting system is the discount module: this module allows calculation of a certain discount based on a product price. In our example, the discount functionality is implemented as follows:

```
public class DiscountOffer {
  int individualDiscount;
  public DiscountOffer() {
    individualDiscount = this.initialDiscount();
  }
  public int initialDiscount() {
    return 0;
  }
  public void setDiscountUser(Customer customer) {
    this.individualDiscount =
      this.initialDiscount() + 0;
  }
  public int getDiscount(int price, Customer customer) {
    this.setDiscountUser(customer);
    return price * individualDiscount / 100;
  }
  public int getDiscount(int price) {
    return price * individualDiscount / 100;
  }
}
```

The customer discount is composed of an initial discount granted to all buyers, whether they are registered customers or not. This percentage is determined by the method `initialDiscount()`. Persons who are already registered customers can be given an additional discount. This percentage must be determined with the method `setDiscountUser(Customer)`. Within the generic functionality of the base system, both values are set to 0%.

This base system is distributed to various users, who can define different specifications for the generic discount function provided by the base system, depending on the kind of discount offer they wish to create. The concrete discount offer is implemented with the aid of the inheritance mechanism in the using system.

A company wishes to give all its buyers an additional discount of 5% t as part of their summer discount offer. Regular customers (who are already registered) are not supposed to get this extra discount. Accordingly, only the initial discount must be adapted and set to 5%. This requirement will be implemented in the using system:

```java
public class SummerDiscountOffer extends DiscountOffer {
  public int initialDiscount() {
    return 5;
  }
}
```

A test of the using system shows that the requirement is met as desired. The call summerDiscountOffer.getDiscount(100) returns the result that a discount of 5 Euro has been given based on a price of 100 Euro.

Independent from the tests, the developers of the base system continue to work on the accounting system's implementation. To prepare the implementation and usage of the class DiscountOffer for extensions, they move the predefined values into two new instance variables: initialDiscount and customerDiscount. They apply the *Inline Method* refactoring in the constructor to achieve a more efficient and clearly-structured implementation. Since the public interface shall not deviate from that of the earlier version, the method initialDiscount() is kept and adapted to the new structure. For better legibility, only changes to the class DiscountOffer are listed below:

```java
public class DiscountOffer {
  ...
  int initialDiscount = 0;
  int customerDiscount = 0;
  public DiscountOffer() {
    individualDiscount = initialDiscount;
      //Inline Method
  }
  public int initialDiscount() {
    return initialDiscount;
  }
  public void setDiscountUser(Customer customer) {
    this.individualDiscount =
      initialDiscount + customerDiscount;
  }
}
```

The behavior of the class DiscountOffer in the base system is identical to the class's behavior in the previous version, i.e. all tests return the same results as before. The new version of the base system is now ready for distribution.

The first step of integration with the system that implements the summer discount offer initially appears to be successful, since no syntactical errors occur and the whole system can be compiled without problems. Nevertheless, the program semantics have changed, so that the requirement is no longer met correctly. The call `summerDiscountOffer.getDiscount(100)` now generates the result that no discount will be given.

The reason for that error is that – due to the Inline Method refactoring – the specialization of the method `initialDiscount()` is no longer considered in the system, thus leading to a faulty initialization of instances of the class `SummerDiscountOffer` and generating the incorrect program behavior.

This altered behavior is caused by the fact that the call graph has been changed during refactoring: the method `initialDiscount()` which was originally called in the constructor, is no longer called on. Therefore, the specialization in the class `SummerDiscountOffer` is disregarded. This conflict will only be recognized when the base system and the using system are analyzed together. As part of the refactoring process on the base system level, this change poses no problem.

Even the application of refactoring tags will not help in this case: the public interface of the class `DiscountOffer` has stayed the same. In effect, no refactoring tags are defined and thus no changes are triggered in the using system.

This example clearly demonstrates that an exclusively proactive approach for describing the impact of a refactoring in the base system is neither sufficient for the using systems, nor will an analysis and test of the base system alone suffice. Only a comprehensive function test of the whole system will bring certainty that an integration of basic and using system was truly successful. But even this approach will only be partially helpful for error analysis: in order to analyze the cause of the system's semantic misbehavior, comprehensive knowledge of the entire system is required. For that reason, integration of an automated, semantic analysis in the refactoring process is advisable to offer programmers additional support during development of a distributed system.

Gray Areas in Black Box Refactoring

Besides direct changes to the call graphs, especially so-called 'Big Refactorings' will lead to constellations that literally provoke semantic conflicts. The combination of different changes that are made in the course of a refactoring will often lead into 'gray areas' that can not be resolved in the base system and that will only become visible in combination with the using system.

Particularly modifications that are meant to prepare the ground for extending the base system are often dangerous. To illustrate such a situation, we will now return to our accounting system example. Based on the now familiar implementation, first a new discount offer for the coming Christmas season is implemented in the user system, granting a 5% discount to all buyers as well as an extra 5% to regular customers:

```
public class ChristmasDiscountOffer
  extends DiscountOffer {
  public ChristmasDiscountOffer() {
    individualDiscount = initialDiscount = 5;
  }
  public void setDiscountUser(Customer customer) {
    customerDiscount = 5;
    super.setDiscountUser(customer);
  }
}
```

In the base system a method getDiscount(price, customer) already exists to calculate a customer's discount in a single step. For a price of 100 Euro a customer will accordingly receive a discount of 10 Euro.

The introduction of the class *Person* as superclass of *Customer* shall prepare the base system for future extensions. This plan is also reflected in the implementation of the class DiscountOffer: the interface for the method getDiscount(price, customer) is altered and the parameter of the type *Customer* is changed to a parameter of the superclass's *Person* type. No change takes place for the callers, since the generalization of a parameter for using this method is transparent.

```
public class Person { … }
public class Customer extends Person { … }
public class DiscountOffer {
  ...
  public void setDiscountUser(Person person) {
    this.individualDiscount =
      initialDiscount + customerDiscount;
  }
  public int getDiscount(int price, Person person) {
    this.setDiscountUser(person);
    return price * individualDiscount / 100;
  }
}
```

This change is in itself uncritical, but in connection with the user system it results in a changed discount calculation because the specialization for `setDiscountUser(customer)` from the class `Christmas-DiscountOffer` will no longer be called on. Thus customers will receive the wrong discount amount of 5% instead of the offered 10%.

This example clarifies that gray areas which cannot always be eliminated inherently exist in refactoring processes. The application of refactoring tags can help in this case: the *Past* tag is implemented for the method `set DiscountUser(Person)` here. Unfortunately, this approach also has a disadvantage. All callers of this method must execute an extra type cast of the object *Customer* after *Person*. This contradicts the original idea of utilizing the options object-orientation has to offer and keeping modifications of the base system transparent for all callers through generalization of this method, while also creating as little as possible (ideally no) demand for migration within the using systems.

Support of the Black Box Refactoring through Semantic Conflict Analysis

Both examples underline that distributed development in Black Box Refactoring harbors the danger of creating semantic conflicts that stem from the combination of base system and using system. These conflicts can hardly be avoided by documenting the changes alone.

Here we must differentiate between two scenarios: in the first scenario, we are dealing with changes of a class's interface that have to be communicated to the using system. This can be done via refactoring tags. Changes to certain categories of classes, their effects on the using system as well as possible measures for avoiding or removing conflicts have been discussed in detail in Section 6.5. In this respect, this scenario is clearly structured and can be handled.

Things are different for the second scenario, where changes occur in the inheritance interface itself: the using system must be informed of these changes. The number of potentially possible conflicts exceeds that of those possible in the public interface: adding to them are the effects of changes to the internal structure and the implementation of the base system itself. For example, changes to the call graph can lead to errors in the combination of base system and using system. The same is true for generalizations or specializations on the class and method level that are not entirely alleviated by classic documentation concepts for a class's interface. Their effects will vary strongly, depending on which specializations are implemented in the using systems.

Since the number of possible effects of changes in the inheritance interface is fairly large – even for simple refactorings – a reactive innocuousness check is required besides a documentation of the changes: on the one hand, this can be achieved by running an as comprehensive function test as possible of the using system; on the other hand, a semantic error analysis for certain error classes following the integration of the modified base system will ensure that the system's behavior has remained semantically unaffected.

Semantic Error Analysis in the Refactoring Context

In order to recognize the semantic conflict situations discussed here, information about inheritance structures as well as the call graph is required – information also needed by refactoring tools to enable a mostly automated execution of refactorings. One peculiarity of semantic error analysis is that changes between the status quo prior to a refactoring and the status quo after a refactoring do matter. Without this differentiation, it is not possible to identify the conflict situation depicted here.

This prerequisite proves critical, particularly for the execution of a refactoring in a base system without direct relationships to possible using systems: the data needed for recognizing the conflict must be obtained from both systems. Therefore, the call graph of the system plays a pivotal role that goes beyond the scope of the actual refactoring. In our first example, the conflict originated from the fact that a call was removed from the base system and thus a specialization from the using system was no longer observed.

Yet another obstacle must be taken into account: it does not suffice to consider the current combination of the system consisting of the refactored base system and the using system. Moreover, the condition created by their combination must be compared for the base system as well as for the using system before and after refactoring. These prerequisites make it clear that recognition of a conflict based on a concrete misbehavior can only take place on the using system's side. In addition, both variants of the base system must be available to allow a comparison.

Stepping over the system boundary between basic and using system has yet another consequence: the release and thus integration of the base system is not restricted to a single, atomic refactoring. To enable an efficient development cycle on the one hand and a rewarding integration scenario on the other, a new version of the base system must contain a series of changes. Here, we can distinguish between an exclusive refactoring, exclusive continuous development and a blend of the two. All variations have in common that modifications of the source code will bring about a large number of changes in the program structure.

This distinction hardly matters for semantic conflict analysis, because occurrences of the described conflict situations are thinkable for all variations. However, evaluations showed that the number of possible semantic conflicts in a refactoring cycle is particularly high, because in a refactoring cycle most work takes place in existing classes and methods which already supply their functionality to using systems. The realization of new functionalities will rather lead to the implementation of new classes and methods that are not yet in use – a fact that reduces the danger of semantic conflicts. This confirms that semantic conflict analysis, especially for large refactorings, is an indispensable means of support for controlling and limiting the number of a refactoring's possible consequences.

Further evaluations prove that a separation between pure refactoring cycles on the one hand and development cycles on the other makes sense when developing a universal base system with a series of possible clients. The integration of base and using system can be treated in different ways in the base system, depending on the type of change: suitable integration steps (depending on the type of change), for example the execution of a semantic conflict analysis exclusively in the course of the refactoring cycle, can lower the risk of running headfirst into an unrecognized misbehavior of the whole system without losing the option of quickly integrating new functionalities.

Tool-Based Recognition of Semantic Conflicts

Changes in the call graph of the base system can hardly be monitored manually. Especially when the execution of a complete refactoring or development cycle is examined, it is impossible to document all changes in the form of additional tags. This is also the case for necessary evaluations that must be carried out in the using system during integration of the refactored base system.

Therefore, it is necessary to automatically record the data, for example by extracting the relevant data from the source code and transferring it to a suitable meta model or by using the existing meta information offered by a refactoring tool. In the next step, the actual states before and after a refactoring must be evaluated to identify possible conflict situations.

This procedure can be realized algorithmically as follows:

1. Determination of the potential for conflicts as the amount of all changes of the base system before and after refactoring or, respectively, the development cycle.
2. Analysis of the dependencies between the potential for conflicts and the using system.
3. Identification of concrete conflicts based on the identified dependencies while applying adequate rules for conflict recognition.

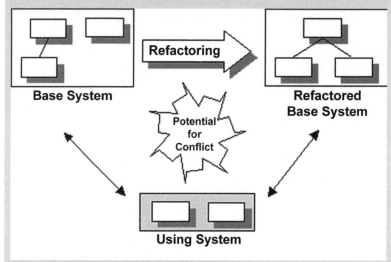

Potential for Conflicts through a Refactoring of the Base System

In this context, the definition of a rule depends on the specific error scenario. For our first example that does disregard method specialization, a suitable rule looks like this:

1. Determine the potential for conflicts consisting of all method calls that have been removed from inside the modified basic module.
2. Find all methods that have been overwritten by the basic module in the using system and therefore have been specialized.
3. Identify the potential for conflicts as the amount of all methods found in step 2 that are also part of the potential for conflicts determined in step 1.

Analogously, rules for the recognition of further conflicts can be created and integrated in the recognition algorithm. Here, most rules operate based on a straightforward number of basic operations and structural information provided by the software system. If these are available, the definition of new recognition rules is in most cases feasible with calculable effort.

This principle of conflict recognition is realized in combination with additional semantic analyses in JaMB, the Java Migration Browser. JaMB is a tool for the detection of semantic conflicts that occur during the further development and migration of object-oriented systems. It obtains its required information directly from the Java byte code and stores it in a suitable meta model. More information about JaMB can be found in Pipka and Mezini (2000).

Another approach to recognizing conflicts and making them transparent during the development process is the backward compatibility tester. Here, the interfaces of the contained classes are analyzed and incompatible changes are pointed out. However, this analysis is exclusively syntax-based. More information about this tool can be found on IBM's Alphaworks website
(http://www.alphaworks.ibm.com).

6.10　Another Approach: 'Catch Up and Replay'

Another approach to support API refactorings is presented by Johannes Henkel and Amer Diwan in their work 'CatchUp! Capturing and Replaying Refactorings to Support API Evolution'. They follow the idea of recording refactorings that are made to APIs. In their case, this is done automatically whenever the developer uses the automatic refactoring support of the IDE and this way changes the API. To adjust clients of the API, they replay those scripts on the client code using automation. Developers do not need to change the client code manually.

Since this degree of automation is extremely useful for refactoring published APIs, this approach is limited to those changes that are done via the automatic refactorings of the IDE. Otherwise the script recorder has no chance to pick up those refactorings. You can find more information on this approach at http://www-plan.cs.colorado.edu/diwan/icse2005.pdf

References and Further Reading

Bloch, J. 2001. *Effective Java*. Addison-Wesley. Bloch argues that inheritance must be planned. If inheritance from a class has not explicitly been provided for, it should rather be prevented (for example through setting the class to final). In this book you will find – besides a number of very useful tips for Java programming – an instruction for realizing typesafe and expandable enumeration types (typesafe enums) in Java.

Fowler, M. 1999. *Refactoring: Improving the Design of Existing Code*. Addison-Wesley. Not only does Fowler describe basic refactorings here, he also introduces the distinction between public and published interfaces.

Gamma, E. & Beck, K. 2003. *Contributing to Eclipse – Principles, Patterns, Plug-ins*. Addison-Wesley, Eclipse Series. In this standard work about plugin development with Eclipse the authors depict very diverse mechanisms realized in the Eclipse framework. Among them are patterns that simplify evolution between subsystems, such as, for example, the Adaptable mechanism.

Gosling, J., Joy, B. & G. Steele, G. 1997. *The Java Language Specification*. Addison-Wesley. A language specification for Java.

Havenstein, A. 2003. *Werkzeuge für die Migrationsunterstützung von Anwendungen auf neue Rahmenwerksversionen*. Diploma thesis, Software Engineering Group, Dept. of Informatics, University of Hamburg, Germany. Here, tools for the handling of refactoring tags as well as implementation methods for these tools are presented. Also discusses how much help converters can provide for migration.

Havenstein, A. & Roock, S. 2002. *Refactoring tags for automatic refactoring of framework*. In *Proceedings of Extreme Programming Conference 2002*, Villasimius, Cagliari, Italy. This article is the first one to introduce the concept of refactoring tags.

JavaSoft, 2000. *How and When to Deprecate APIs*.
Part of the Java2 Documentation. Describes work with the deprecated tag.

Lippert, M., Roock, S. Wolf, H. & Züllighoven, H. 2001. JWAM and XP – using XP for framework development. In Succi, G. & Marchesi, M. (eds). 2001 *Extreme Programming Examined*. Addison-Wesley. Conference publication of the XP-2000 Conference, pp. 103–117. Illustrates various experiences in the use of XP techniques (such as refactoring) for frameworks.

Meyer, B. 1992. *Eiffel: The Language*. Prentice-Hall. Meyer introduces the reader to the language Eiffel, which offers an option for marking classes and methods as deprecated with the keyword *obsolete*. Just like with using the *deprecated* tag in Java, the compiler will generate warnings for obsolete elements.

Pipka, J.U. & Mezini M. 2000 Weiterentwicklung objektorientierter Softwaresysteme: Risiken und deren Vermeidung. In: Informatik *2000*, Springer-Verlag. This work provides an overview of important migration conflicts in literature and practice, which are further scrutinized using Java. The focus is on conflict scenarios that can emerge during the integration of more complex subsystem versions. To support the integration process, a tool-based solution for the recognition of such conflicts is introduced as an example: the Java Migration Browser JaMB.

Rivières, J. des. 2001. Evolving Java-based APIs. http://www-eclipse.org/eclipse/development/java-api-evolution.html. Depicts possible API changes and their compatibilities. The focus is only on binary compatibility, not on source code compatibility though.

Roock, S. 2001. : eXtreme frameworking – how to aim applications at evolving frameworks. In Succi, G. & Marchesi, M. (eds). 2001. *Extreme Programming Examined*. Addison-Wesley. Conference publication of the XP-2000 Conference, pp. 71–82. Analyses of problems related to API changes and some ideas for solutions.

Szyperski, C. 1997. *Component Software*. Addison-Wesley. Standard work about components that also offers insights on some of the aspects discussed here.

7
Tool-Based Detection and Avoidance of Architecture Smells

By Walter Bischofberger and Henning Wolf

Architecture smells are difficult to detect 'manually,' since to this end information from the entire source code must be collected and condensed. As we already pointed out in Chapter 3, IDEs cannot be used for architecture analyses because they visualize relations between classes and packages. For an analysis of architectural aspects, developers must work on the levels of class, package and subsystem relations and not on the method call level.

    In this chapter, we will demonstrate how architecture smells can be found with tool support and how large refactorings can be closely monitored. Our tool of choice will be *Sotograph*, a product of Software-Tomography GmbH. We decided to focus on a commercially available tool because as far as we know there are currently no other tools in existence that support both architecture analysis and visualization for object-oriented systems in a similarly comprehensive manner.

Introduction

7.1 Specifications of an Analysis Tool

Chapter 3 discusses how architecture smells can be found on different abstraction levels (class, package, subsystem and architecture). In consequence, tools for the detection of architecture smells must be able to handle these or related abstraction levels. Depending on the abstraction mechanisms offered by the supported programming language, more or less high-level abstraction levels must be user-definable.

Levels of Abstraction

    Based on the abstraction levels at the developers' disposal, the following analyses can be executed:

Types of Analyses

- *Architecture analysis*, i.e. an analysis of how well the source code observes the restrictions specified in the architecture model (who is allowed to use whom, and who is allowed to inherit from whom), and where these restrictions are not observed.

▦ *Cycle analysis*, to analyze the cyclic relations between artefacts. More precisely, this means the search for classes, packages and subsystem groups that are strongly coupled in cyclic relations.

▦ *Metrics-based analysis*, in order to identify potential architectural problems using metrics.

Interpretation of Analysis Results

All three analysis types deliver distinct indications of a multitude of problems that will range from those that can be neglected to those that are quite serious. To assess the seriousness of a problem as efficiently as possible, it is important that the tool provides explanations, or at least the basic data of its analysis. In this context, visualization – for example with class diagrams or package graphs – is a major issue. Particularly since architectural problems, after all, become manifest in unexpected and unwanted cooperation of artefact groups, graphs can make it much easier to understand such cooperation structures.

It is very laborious to analyze a version of a software system in detail. In most cases, the members of a project team who possess the required knowledge to conduct such an analysis will be highly in demand. This is another reason why it is unrealistic to continuously monitor a software system's quality without adequate tool support, even though continuous monitoring would be the most useful approach in such a situation.

Continuous Monitoring

Tools that are suited for the continuous monitoring of large software systems will only issue information that has changed since the last analysis was conducted and will also filter it based on its relevance. A metrics tool, for instance, will only show those metrics values that were already bad a week ago and have gotten either worse or better since. An architecture tester will merely display new architecture violations. In an ideal case, the weekly time exposure for interpreting the obtained data can be reduced to under half an hour.

Ad hoc Analyses

In big projects, frequently questions will come up that cannot be answered with the aid of predefined analyses. Therefore, a tool for large-scale software analysis should offer users an easy-to-learn mechanism to enable them to formulate new metrics and ad hoc queries.

Support of the Refactoring Process

Depending on the kind of restructuring that is needed, the execution of a large refactoring can take place over a rather long period. Without careful organizing it will soon become difficult to determine what parts of the refactoring have already been carried out, and to what extent the architecture's status quo already approximates the targeted architecture. The latter question can be answered precisely with the right tool. Furthermore, a tool can provide a lot of useful information about a refactoring's present stage if it has monitored the development of a software system over a longer period. For example, it can point out what classes have been modified in which subsystems, and which methods of these classes have been newly created, deleted or changed.

Typically, modern software systems consist of distributed systems which are tied into different processes on various machines and managed at runtime by application servers, for instance.

Analysis of Distributed Systems

If one considers only the static relations of such a system exclusively from a language point of view, one will see a quantity of isolated parts, e.g. Enterprise Java Beans or .Net components. Apparently these are not cooperating, because they don't use each other directly, but solely communicate via the application server. Architectural analyses of such systems will only make sense if the tool for the analysis of distributed systems can handle various interprocess communication mechanisms and component models. Then distributed systems, including their relations beyond processes, can be analyzed and visualized as a whole.

7.2   Architecture Analysis with Sotograph

In this chapter, we will elaborate on how to use the *Sotograph* as a tool for analysis and scrutinize its role as an analyzing software system, that is, we will apply Sotograph to versions 0.90, 0.95 and 0.96 of Sotograph's source code. We will use relatively old versions because from version 0.96 onward Sotograph has been used to further its own development. Thus the newer versions will deliver less interesting results for architecture testing.

The underlying concept of the Sotograph is derived from computerized tomography as it is applied in medicine, i.e. it extracts – just like a computer tomograph – as much information as possible about the system it examines, before it commences actual analysis. For software systems, its analyses comprise byte and source code, which will yield information about references, artefacts on the method level, fields, classes, packages and relations between these elements. Sotograph stores this information in a relational database and then proceeds to make available a number of closely integrated tools in order to analyze and visualize the gathered information. At present, Sotograph possesses analyzers for Java, C++ and C.

The Underlying Concept

In addition, Sotograph can manage information that encompasses a series of a software system's versions in a database, thus enabling analysis of a system's changes over time.

Moreover, information about the (desired) architecture model can be fed into Sotograph's database. This extra information will serve as a basis for analyzing the system's architecture.

Abstraction Support With classes, files, packages, subsystems and tier architectures, Sotograph supports five abstraction levels on which analyses can be conducted. Whereas in object-oriented languages classes are surveyed on the lowest abstraction level, for procedural languages – such as C – it is important to have the abstraction level 'file' at hand. Moreover, files (and directories) constitute the entities that physically structure the code (e.g. several classes in one file).

For systems implemented in Java, the packages defined in the source code are used directly as an abstraction level. Since only very few programming languages offer an abstraction level that is equivalent to the Java package, Sotograph will aggregate all files located in the same directory in a package of the same name as the directory for these languages.

Packages can be combined to form subsystems using a subsystem description language. For each subsystem, it can be defined where its explicit API is located (if applicable). For example, a subsystem should only be used via certain interfaces that are placed either in a subpackage 'interface' or directly in the subsystem's root directory. Other references from outside this subsystem constitute an architecture violation. The subsystems form the abstraction level on which the system's architecture can be reviewed. For small and medium-sized software systems, one subsystem model will normally suffice. For large software systems, often several subsystem models are needed for the modeling of architectural levels that are relevant for analyses.

Building on one subsystem model each, tier architectures can be specified. These tier architectures serve the purpose of limiting the amount of relations that are permissible between subsystems.

Identifiable Architecture Smells Architecture testing with Sotograph allows identification of the following architecture smells:

- Subsystem-API bypassed (Section 3.5.5).
- Upward references between layers (Section 3.6.2).
- Strict layering violated (Section 3.5.3).
- Relations between product-specific subsystems of product line architecture (briefly mentioned in Section 3.5.5).

Figure 7-1 exemplifies these architecture smells in a 3-tier architecture.

Definition of a Subsystem Model Before we can begin with the actual architecture analysis, we must first define at least one subsystem model and one architecture model.

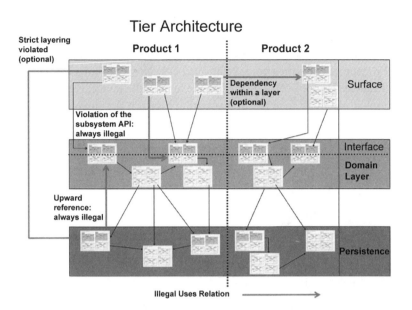

Fig. 7-1
Architecture
Violations

Sotograph defines subsystem models with a simple subsystem description language. Basically, there are two ways of describing a subsystem:

1. There are rules that specify how package trees will be aggregated in subsystems. The following rule, for instance, leads to the generation of one subsystem for each of the three package trees:

```
RuleBasedSubsystem Public {
    InterfacePath "";
    Packages "com.sotogra.'(util|guiutil|plugins)'";
}
```

   ▦ Using a regular expression, the packages statement defines the root packages of the package trees that are combined into subsystems.

   ▦ The name of a generated subsystem will be derived from the rule's name and the name of the package tree's root package, e.g. *Public.util*.

   ▦ The interface path statement defines the path from the package tree's root to the package that contains the subsystem's API classes. In our example this is the root package.

2. Through counting the packages contained in it. This sort of definition is mainly used in generated subsystem models or in such exceptional cases where a subsystem cannot be defined by rules.

Once a subsystem model has been defined and set as an effective subsystem layer, the subsystems defined in this layer can be employed analogously to classes, files or packages in all tools offered by Sotograph. For instance, all inheritance relations between subsystems can be visualized (see Figure 7-2). The thicker the lines in the image, the greater the number of inheritance relations existing between the subsystems.

Fig. 7-2
A Section of a
Subsystem Graph

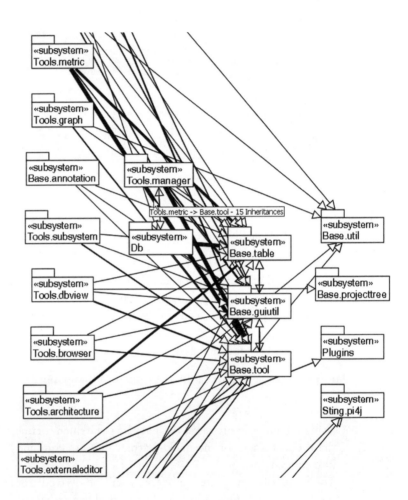

Definition of an
Architecture Model

Sotograph defines tier architectures with a simple architecture description language. In this language, one

- defines the underlying subsystem model;
- assigns subsystems or packages to single layers;
- defines if the subsystems or packages of a layer are allowed to use each other mutually, and whether the layer model is subject to strict interpretation or not.

For comprehensive software systems, developers will often define several architecture models that focus on various aspects as well as separate architectures for large or complex structured subsystems.

The following is an excerpt from Sotograph's architecture model description:

```
ArchitectureModel Overview {
  Uses Default; // used subsystem model
  ArchitectureLayer Manager {
    // layer may use all deeper layers
    InterLayerUsage = True;
    // the layer's subsystems may
    // mutually use each other
    IntraLayerUsage = True;
    // subsystems contained in the layer
    Subsystem Tools.manager;
    Subsystem Access;
  }
  ArchitectureLayer ToolsAndServices {
    InterLayerUsage = True;
    // the layer's subsystems may
    // not mutually use each other
    IntraLayerUsage = False;
    // selection of subsystems belonging to the layer
    // with a regular expression
    Subsystems "Tools.([^m]|met).*";
  }
  ArchitectureLayer ToolInfrastructure {
    InterLayerUsage = True;
    IntraLayerUsage = True;
    Subsystem Base.annotation;
    Subsystem Base.dbupdate;
    Subsystem Base.migration;
  }
  ArchitectureLayer Frameworks {
```

Once an architecture model has been defined and evaluated, the illegal relations that were found can be examined. First, we will take a look at the list of illegal relations between subsystems (see Figure 7-3). The table shows the number of architectural deviations between subsystem pairs, sorted based on architecture smells. The last three columns contain the values for Sotograph versions 0.95 and 0.96 as well as changes that occurred between these versions.[1]

Analysis of Architecture Violations

---

[1] One prominent feature of tables displayed in Sotograph is that they often contain Id columns. Based on these Id columns, commands can be given, evaluations started and graphs generated. This feature allows programmers to use the same generic visualization infrastructure for the results of preconfigured and user-specific evaluations.

Fig. 7-3
Overview:
Architecture

subRefin...	subRefing	subRefe...	subRefed	errorKind	v1	v2	⌃ diff
65965	Default.Db	65962	Default.Base.table	UPWARD	829	788	-41
65965	Default.Db	65959	Default.Base.guiutil	UPWARD	364	359	-5
65966	Default.Tools.architecture	65976	Default.Tools.subsystem	INTERFACE	30	28	-2
65958	Default.Base.annotation	65959	Default.Base.guiutil	INTERFACE	39	39	0
65959	Default.Base.guiutil	65972	Default.Tools.manager	UPWARD	11	11	0
65961	Default.Base.projecttree	65969	Default.Tools.dbview	UPWARD	1	1	0
65962	Default.Base.table	65959	Default.Base.guiutil	INTERFACE	8	8	0
65963	Default.Base.tool	65969	Default.Tools.dbview	UPWARD	2	2	0
65963	Default.Base.tool	65971	Default.Tools.graph	UPWARD	15	15	0
65963	Default.Base.tool	65975	Default.Tools.result	UPWARD	8	8	0
65963	Default.Base.tool	65976	Default.Tools.subsystem	INTERFACE	2	2	0
65964	Default.Base.util	65959	Default.Base.guiutil	UPWARD	19	19	0
65965	Default.Db	65958	Default.Base.annotation	UPWARD	123	123	0
65965	Default.Db	65964	Default.Base.util	INTERFACE	7	7	0
65965	Default.Db	65972	Default.Tools.manager	UPWARD	26	26	0
65965	Default.Db	65976	Default.Tools.subsystem	INTERFACE	6	6	0
65965	Default.Db	65977	Default.Tools.trend	UPWARD	28	28	0
65973	Default.Tools.metric	65977	Default.Tools.trend	INTRA	139	139	0
65975	Default.Tools.result	65972	Default.Tools.manager	UPWARD	3	3	0
65976	Default.Tools.subsystem	65964	Default.Base.util	INTERFACE	42	42	0
65964	Default.Base.util	65963	Default.Base.tool	UPWARD	0	2	2
65974	Default.Tools.query	65964	Default.Base.util	INTERFACE	94	96	2
65964	Default.Base.util	65972	Default.Tools.manager	UPWARD	56	60	4
65966	Default.Tools.architecture	65964	Default.Base.util	INTERFACE	38	42	4
65963	Default.Base.tool	65959	Default.Base.guiutil	INTERFACE	31	36	5
65966	Default.Tools.architecture	65977	Default.Tools.trend	INTRA	74	80	6
65965	Default.Db	65963	Default.Base.tool	UPWARD	738	802	64

Exceptions of Trend Architecture Model Sotograph for v1 = 0.95 and v2 = 0.96 — Filter — Help

If you analyze a system for the very first time, it is recommended that you get an idea of how badly the system is afflicted by architecture violations. This will be accomplished by marking the illegally referenced subsystems in a subsystem graph (see Figure 7-4). Here, you can see clearly that about onethird of all subsystems of Sotograph are used in a manner that is not permitted. At first sight, this might come as something of a shock. However, our practical experiences have proven that this result ranks rather low on the scale of software systems that were developed without architecture testing.

In the next step of your architecture analysis, we will take a close look at the list of architectural deviations to identify the sources of the detected problems (again, see Figure 7-3). Usually we will encounter quite a variety of problems that can easily be solved by moving classes into another package or by moving packages into another subsystem. In most cases, more than enough architecture smells will remain that can only be cured with more complex refactorings.

Architecture testing should always take place parallel to other project-related work. Therefore, it is important that the ongoing monitoring process is not too time-consuming – at least not after the first comprehensive analysis. Thanks to Sotograph's Trend support this demand is also realistic. The table's last column (see Figure 7-3) displays those changes that took place between the last two selected versions of the lsystem. In the context of a continuous monitoring it will

Fig. 7-4
A Marked Subsystem Graph

do to scrutinize the new ones as well as the eliminated architecture violations. Double-click on a table row to zoom in on the package level first, the level of basic references next, and the source code last. Figure 7-5 lists all basic references for illegal relations between the packages *architecture* and *jflex* of the subsystems *Tools.architecture* and *Base.util*. You will immediately recognize those illegal relations that were already present in version 0.95 as well as the four illegal relations that have crept into the system in version 0.96.

7.3   Architecture Analysis Based on Cycles

Sotograph allows the identification of cyclic relations between classes, files, packages and subsystems. The related architecture smells and their negative effects are depicted in Sections 3.1.3, 3.3.2 and 3.5.2.

Fig. 7-5
Architecture Violation on the Package Level

Trend architecture exceptions between package architecture and jflex for v1 = 0.95 and v2 = 0.96

refingId	refingSymbol	refedId	refedSymbol	referenceType	locality	changes
189622	me_parseArchitectureModel()	189206	cl_SyntaxErrorException	TYPEACCESS	LOCAL	NEW
189622	me_parseArchitectureModel()	189206	cl_SyntaxErrorException	TYPEACCESS	LOCAL	NEW
189622	me_parseArchitectureModel()	189212	me_getLine()	CALL	LOCAL	NEW
189622	me_parseArchitectureModel()	189213	me_getColumn()	CALL	LOCAL	NEW
189622	me_parseArchitectureModel()	189206	cl_SyntaxErrorException	TYPEACCESS	LOCAL	SAME
189622	me_parseArchitectureModel()	189206	cl_SyntaxErrorException	TYPEACCESS	LOCAL	SAME
189622	me_parseArchitectureModel()	189206	cl_SyntaxErrorException	TYPEACCESS	LOCAL	SAME
189622	me_parseArchitectureModel()	189206	cl_SyntaxErrorException	TYPEACCESS	LOCAL	SAME
189622	me_parseArchitectureModel()	189206	cl_SyntaxErrorException	TYPEACCESS	LOCAL	SAME
189622	me_parseArchitectureModel()	189206	cl_SyntaxErrorException	TYPEACCESS	LOCAL	SAME
189622	me_parseArchitectureModel()	189206	cl_SyntaxErrorException	TYPEACCESS	LOCAL	SAME
189622	me_parseArchitectureModel()	189206	cl_SyntaxErrorException	TYPEACCESS	LOCAL	SAME
189622	me_parseArchitectureModel()	189206	cl_SyntaxErrorException	TYPEACCESS	LOCAL	SAME
189622	me_parseArchitectureModel()	189206	cl_SyntaxErrorException	CATCH	LOCAL	SAME
189622	me_parseArchitectureModel()	189212	me_getLine()	CALL	LOCAL	SAME
189622	me_parseArchitectureModel()	189212	me_getLine()	CALL	LOCAL	SAME
189622	me_parseArchitectureModel()	189213	me_getColumn()	CALL	LOCAL	SAME
189622	me_parseArchitectureModel()	189213	me_getColumn()	CALL	LOCAL	SAME
189622	me_parseArchitectureModel()	189213	me_getColumn()	CALL	LOCAL	SAME

One fundamental problem of cycle analysis is combinatorial explosions. Most of the commercial systems we have analyzed until now are so closely coupled that thousands of cycles will be detected. Thus Sotograph will search all cycles of length 2 in a first step, then eliminate those for further searching, and scan for continuously longer cycles. This procedure enables interpretation of the cycle analysis results within a reasonable time frame without losing relevant information.

At the beginning of any cycle-based architecture analysis, the most sensible approach is to search for package cycles across subsystem boundaries. Figure 7-6 shows the results of that query. One line represents a relation in a cycle, and all lines of the same *cycle* Id represent the entire cycle.

Fig. 7-6
Analysis of Cycles on the Package Level

Package Cycles - Restricted to Focus: No , Locality All

pckgFr...	package from name	pckgTold	package to name	cycle	refs
279	tool	280	util	0	215
280	util	279	tool	0	2
300	manager	280	util	1	264
280	util	300	manager	1	60
272	guiutil	280	util	2	184
280	util	272	guiutil	2	19
339	registry	280	util	3	19
280	util	339	registry	3	3
300	manager	265	server	4	2
265	server	300	manager	4	8
277	table	279	tool	5	174
279	tool	277	table	5	663

The first two lines point at a cyclic relation between the *tool* and *util* packages. Since only two references exist from *util* to *tool*, but 215 references in the other direction, it is safe to assume that the references from *util* to *tool* should be eliminated. For further analyses, you can zoom in on the basic references level with a double-click. A second double-click will display the corresponding source code. This view works well if you start to break up cycles. Since Sotograph will break down long cycles into short ones during analysis to avoid combinatorial explosions, you must make a survey of where critical amassments of cycles are present.

For this purpose, you must sort the table, listing the detected cycles by package name. When this is done, you will recognize at a glance which packages are involved in what number for many cycles. The tangle surrounding such critical packages can best be viewed in a graph. Figure 7-7 shows the graph that contains all packages which maintain cyclic relations with the package *tool*. This graph exemplifies very well how software systems start to 'lump' due to their constantly growing number of cycles in the course of their evolution. It is pretty obvious that it will take new developers quite an effort to familiarize themselves with such a chaotic dependency graph.

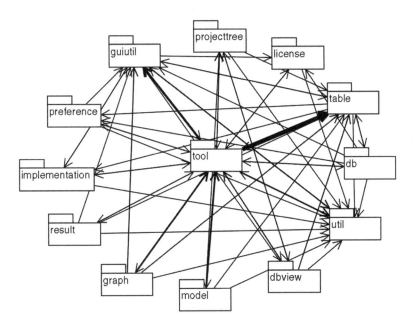

Fig. 7-7
Packages in Relation to the "tool" Package

In practice, it is not always wise to eliminate all cyclic relations from a software system. On the one hand, it can be advantageous to have two classes using each other on the class level. On the other hand, it often takes too much effort to eliminate all unwanted cycles in systems that were not developed with the aid of cycle analyses from the very beginning. This is why support of a cycle analysis is indispensable: it helps to distinguish existing cycles from newly introduced ones. This kind of information is provided by Sotograph's metrics tool.

7.4   Metrics-Based Architecture Analysis

The central problem of any type of metrics-based software analysis is the huge amount of metrics values that will be generated even for medium-sized software systems. All this information must be examined and interpreted.

The fundamental prerequisite for an efficient metrics-based first analysis is sophisticated tool support. Here are examples of what such tool support can do:

- Fast elimination of metrics results for parts of the system that have already been recognized as being irrelevant or basically problematic.
- Explanation of a metrics value. Without an explanation, one has to search the reason for each suspicious metrics value in the source code and the IDE.
- Visualization of metrics values. Particularly for high numbers of couplings the graph is best suited for determining what a certain value means.

For a regular analysis that proceeds parallel to other project work, it is first and foremost important that developers review only 'relevant' values. In our experience, these will normally be metrics values that were bad before and have now become worse, or metrics values which were bad but have improved.

Figure 7-8 shows a part of the Trend metrics tool of Sotograph with its 'Problems Worse' filter activated. Metrics underlaid with dark shading contain values that have not been filtered out. The selected PckgCyclicRefPckg metrics calculates the number of packages with which a single package maintains a cyclic relation. In this example, we can see that the package *base.tool* that already caught our attention in the cycle analysis described in the previous section has been cyclically coupled with a new package between releases 0.95 and 0.96.

In this case, it would be interesting to learn if the number of packages which have cyclic relations with *base.tool* increases constantly. This information can best be obtained from the diagram in Figure 7-9. This diagram proves that the increase occurred already between releases 0.90 and 0.95 – another indication that the package *base.tool*

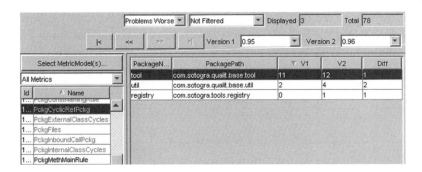

Fig. 7-8
*A Section of the Trend
Metrics Tool*

and the packages closely coupled with it should be examined much more closely in the future, prior to any changes and expansions. In this way we can prevent new problems being introduced to the system, and eventually establish a more orderly system.

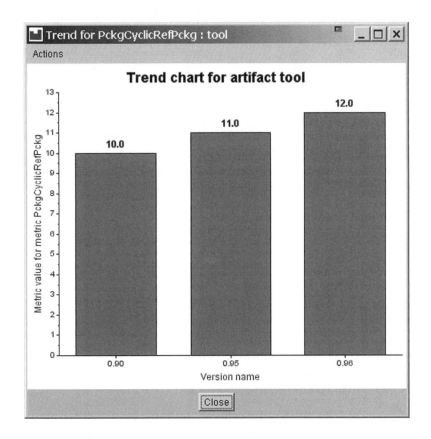

Fig. 7-9
Trend Chart

After the diagram window has been closed, it makes sense to carefully analyze what exactly has changed in *base.tool*'s vicinity. A double-click on the metrics value will take us to the explanation in Figure 7-10.

Here we can see that a cyclic relation with package *base.util* has been newly inserted. The package *base.util* could now be highlighted in the last generated package graph, or one could look at the relations between *base.tool* and *base.util* in detail.

Fig. 7-10
Explanation of Cycle Metrics

sourceId	targetId	Identifyer	Scope	△ Chan...
279	280	util	com.sotogra.qualit.base.util	NEW
279	267	db	com.sotogra.qualit.base.db	SAME
279	272	guiutil	com.sotogra.qualit.base.guiutil	SAME
279	273	implementation	com.sotogra.qualit.base.guiutil.imple...	SAME
279	275	preference	com.sotogra.qualit.base.preference	SAME
279	276	projecttree	com.sotogra.qualit.base.projecttree	SAME
279	277	table	com.sotogra.qualit.base.table	SAME
279	293	dbview	com.sotogra.qualit.tools.dbview	SAME
279	295	graph	com.sotogra.qualit.tools.graph	SAME
279	312	result	com.sotogra.qualit.tools.result	SAME
279	314	model	com.sotogra.qualit.tools.subsystem...	SAME
279	331	license	com.sotogra.tools.license	SAME

After the cycles have been analyzed, one can proceed to survey the critical values of other metrics. The procedure is quite similar to that used for the PckgCyclicRefPckg metrics.

Other Smells that Can Be Detected with Metrics

Basically, the following architecture smells can be detected automatically with metrics or specific analysis queries:

- Unused artefacts (Section 3.4.1).
- Too small artefacts (Section 3.4.3, 3.5.3).
- Too big artefacts (Section 3.4.4).
- Tree-like dependency graphs between classes (Section 3.2.2).
- Type queries (Section 3.3.1).
- List-like inheritance hierarchy (Section 3.3.2).
- Too deep inheritance hierarchy (Section 3.3.6).
- Packages too deep or unbalanced (Section 3.4.5).
- Packages not clearly named (Section 3.4.6).
- Too many subsystems (Section 3.5.4).
- Subsystem API too big (Section 3.5.6).

In contrast to the results yielded by architecture-based and cycle-based analysis, the values calculated for these metrics will only point at potential problems, each of which must be examined in detail. Artefacts that are recognized as not being in use are not necessarily unused. For instance, it is possible that objects created via reflection at runtime and used polymorphically are not recognized as being in use. For many metrics the main question concerns the upper and lower boundaries: at which point does a metrics value begin to indicate a problem, e.g. at which point does a class or a package become too big?

To usefully apply metrics in projects, it is in our experience recommended to let the team decide which metrics are beneficial for this specific project and thus should be pursued further in the course of the project. Then, project-specific, commonly accepted upper and lower boundaries must be defined for the selected metrics. The calculation of, e.g., too small and too big artefacts only makes sense if the team manages to agree on upper and lower boundaries. Otherwise, the determination of such metrics values will lead to futile discussions, or the metrics will simply be ignored.

7.5   Support for the Preparation of Large Refactorings

As the name already indicates, large refactorings can have a noticeable effect on large parts of a software system. Therefore, it is all the more important to understand which code sections will be affected in what manner before beginning with a refactoring. Especially where restructurings of libraries are concerned, this sort of information can hardly be obtained with the tools that are available today. Sotograph can make it much easier to understand software systems in general, as well as the effects of changes specifically. This is demonstrated here using an analysis of the internal API of Sotograph's tool framework. For lack of space, we will focus exclusively on the inheritance interface. The call interface can be analyzed analogously.

Before the actual analysis of the interface is carried out, we have to get an idea of how broadly the framework will be used. In our example, we are dealing with the subsystem *Base.tool*. Here, we can let the *Crossreferencer* identify all classes that use *Base.tool* and have them displayed in a subsystem graph. Likewise, it is possible to generate a graph that shows which classes inherit from classes in *Base.tool*. Figure 7-11 depicts two sections of each of the two graphs. Right away it will become clear that changes of *Base.tool* can affect significant parts of the system. It is remarkable that most subsystems do not merely use *Base.tool*, but also inherit from it. However, it is not surprising that the central tool framework is widely used for the implementation of software analysis tools.

In the next step, we are going to call up a display of the inheritance hierarchy of the subsystem *Base.tool* classes. In this graph, we will then highlight the classes which were overwritten outside the subsystem and insert the overwritten methods, as depicted in Figure 7-12.

Fig. 7-11
Marked Subsystem
Graph 1

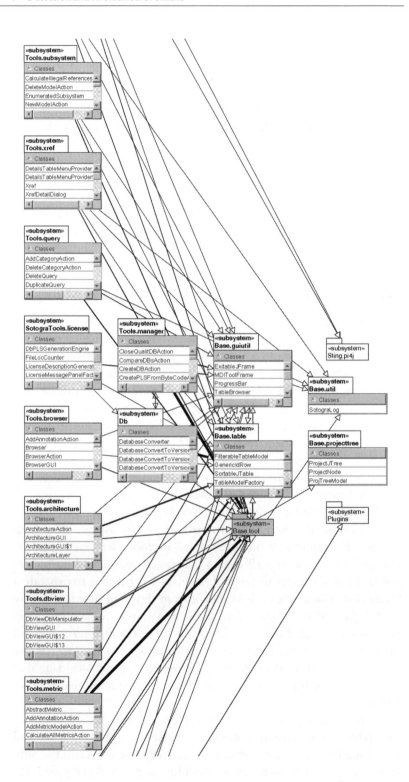

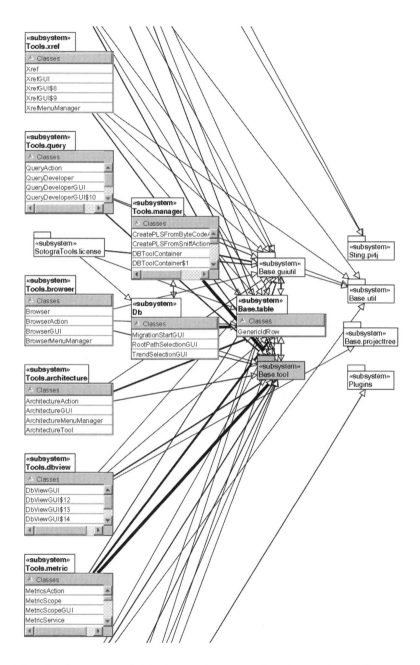

Fig. 7-11 (cont.)
Marked Subsystem
Graph 2

The disadvantage of this form of presentation is that no difference between often and rarely overwritten classes and methods is visible.

In this way Sotograph also offers the option of identifying all those classes and methods of a subsystem or package which are typically overwritten, i.e. those that are overwritten by most of N most important clients. Figure 7-13 depicts the resulting graph, which shows far

Fig. 7-12
Marked Inheritance
Hierarchy

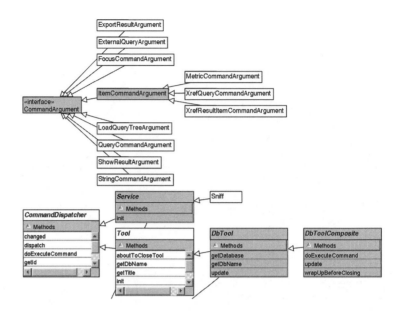

more clearly than the previous image what changes should be avoided if one does not wish to provoke severe side-effects. It also proves clearly that – in spite of generous use of the tool framework – only few methods are overwritten by a relevant part of the clients, at least in the section of the graph displayed here.

Fig. 7-13
Marked Hierarchy,
Based on Frequency

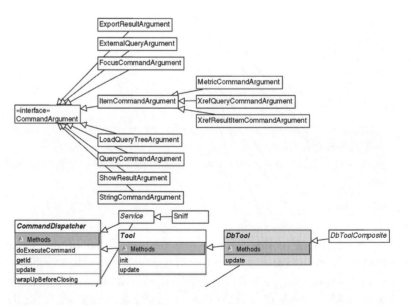

Based on such graphs, a rough assessment of the effects of a refactoring on a part of the tool framework can be made. Prior to the actual refactoring, one should proceed further to get an in-depth impression of the analysis done with Sotograph and examine various aspects in greater detail.

7.6 Support of the Refactoring Process

A fundamental problem of large refactorings is that often clients of the restructured code are also affected by changes. This will have quite an impact on much-used libraries, whose users are no longer in touch with the developers, and for which the developers are unable to directly adapt the customer code in the course of their refactoring. In this case, it is pivotal that the users learn what has changed in between the different versions of the respective library.

Sotograph possesses a variety of query options which help developers to find out which artefacts were generated, deleted or modified between two versions. The overview for *Base.tool* will result in the following figures on the class and method levels for differences between versions 0.90 and 0.96:

New classes	3
Deleted classes	0
Modified classes	49
New methods	21
New public methods + public methods with changed signature	11
Deleted methods	0
Modified methods	88
Modified public methods without changed signatures (new + modified)	69

The data on which these figures are based can then be visualized. Figure 7-14 pictures all new public methods and all public methods with changed signatures in the inheritance hierarchy's context. All modified classes are marked.

7.7 Conclusion

This chapter shows that a tool such as Sotograph allows continuous monitoring of a software system's architectural quality during development without much effort. Thus it is feasible to cure many architecture smells before they become so firmly rooted in the system that they can only be eradicated with very sophisticated refactorings.

Fig. 7-14
Changed Classes,
Marked

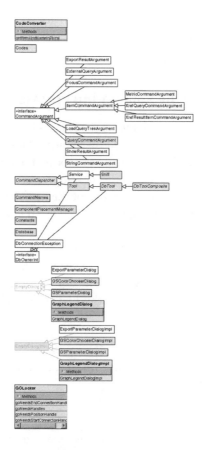

For several years now, the Sotograph has been in for professional analyses of large software systems. Apart from a few exceptions, a high number of architecture violations and cycles were found in the examined systems. These analyses clearly proved that architectural decay in most cases begins with the first code lines and not later on, in the maintenance phase. This also held true for the implementation of Sotograph itself, as this chapter showed.

Furthermore, it is an interesting experience that architecture analyses and large refactorings contribute to enabling economic maintenance of such projects which have been declared not maintainable, and this with only a few manmonths of work. Of course, these experiences are only transferable to projects that concern software systems of a decent technical quality.

In this chapter, the Sotograph was used as a vehicle for illustrating the technological possibilities of architecture analysis as well as for supporting the preparation and execution of large refactorings. Further information about Sotograph can be found at www.software-tomography.com.

8
Conclusion

Object-oriented programming has been around for a couple of decades. In its early days, it was quite difficult for this approach to become established. Lack of tool support as well as performance concerns often led to the continued use of 'classic' programming languages such as Cobol or C, in spite of the propagated superiority of object-oriented concepts.

Object Orientation for Large Projects

Over the years, object-orientation succeeded in entering the world of commercial software development; venturing there from small, not business-critical systems. Today, object-oriented programming languages offer – besides exclusively object-oriented concepts – everything that makes them perfect for application in extremely comprehensive projects:

- A standardized programming language.
- Platform independence.
- Performance.
- Support from popular manufacturers.
- Libraries and frameworks for all significant technologies, such as databases, network communication, etc.
- Powerful tools plus highly integrated development environments.
- Products for application with high transaction rates, transaction monitors and application servers.
- Developers with the necessary know-how.

Moreover, a substantial part of the available tools and libraries is open source software. Now, we can finally roll up our sleeves and get to work on switching the no longer maintainable systems from the good old days of Cobol and C to the seemingly superior object-oriented technologies.

But wait a second here! The already existing object-oriented systems should serve as a warning: a considerable number of these

Object-Oriented Legacy Systems

object-oriented systems fall in the category of legacy software, which is difficult to maintain. These systems quite clearly prove that not much will be gained with object-oriented programming languages and technologies alone. The newly won flexibility will not automatically result in easy-maintenance systems. If this flexibility is wrongly applied, it can even make system maintenance harder than it would have been using classic, non-object-oriented technologies.

Recognizing & Solving Architecture Problems

We hope that this book will contribute to making object-oriented systems easier to maintain. We don't pursue the goal of delivering a perfect system design at as early a stage as possible – we think this approach is illusional anyway, particularly for large systems. Instead, we hope that the contents of this book will help to point at ways for recognizing and solving architecture problems in systems with the aid of various refactoring techniques.

Architecture Smells

Architecture smells indicate where architectural issues might be present. Especially the 'lumping' problem drastically reduces the maintainability of large systems. While we are still smiling mildly at programs written in Basic, which – thanks to the *goto* statement – happily and frequently turn into spaghetti code, similarly critical spaghetti structures are not rarely present in more complex systems these days. This phenomenon will not occur on a single method's or statement's level, but on higher ones, such as classes, packages and subsystems. Here, clearly defined structures are often lost. Since recently though, adequate tools – like, for example, Sotograph – are available that can identify these smells in a system.

Whereas finding potential architecture smells with the aid of available tools is mostly a rather menial task, evaluating smells requires a lot of architecture *experience*. Whether there really is a problem or not depends strongly on the system context.

Refactoring Plans

Minor structural weaknesses can be eliminated in the course of our everyday development work. We use small refactorings, preferably aided by a suitable IDE, to keep the structure clean and easily changeable. However, should architectural problems that call for more comprehensive code restructurings arise, creativity is needed more than anything else. In such situations, we must look for ways to solve the architecture problem on the one hand and modify the system in small steps on the otherhand. We can create refactoring plans that will guide us in solving the problem. These plans must constantly be adapted to reflect the refactoring's progress. During a large refactoring, we will always learn something new that will lead us to further adapt our plan.

Database Refactorings

Large refactorings are rarely limited exclusively to the program code. Most commercial systems work with (relational) databases. Therefore, data structures too must often be modified in the course of a refactoring. Problems will arise because relational databases hardly offer any options for concealment: the effects of changes to the data model can hardly be restricted to merely one partition. In addition, not only must the data structures of an already running system be altered, but the existing persistent data must migrate to the new data schema.

In the course of this book, we came a step closer to our goal of improving database structures in the course of an evolutionary development process. We also gained and discussed some expert knowledge that shows how evolutionary changes to an object-oriented system can affect the database connection, and how this task too can be solved using an evolutionary approach.

Subsystems are important instruments for structuring large systems: *API Refactorings* they hide their internal realization behind a published interface (published API). Other subsystems access this subsystem exclusively over the API. When architecture problems exist on the subsystem level or even in layers, the subsystems' interfaces usually must be adapted as well.

This poses special challenges for refactoring. After all, the subsystems have entered into *contracts* with each other via the interfaces that govern their collaboration. These contracts cannot be changed by one side alone: the client subsystems must migrate to the altered interface. With a few simple tricks and tools, the developers of the subsystem to be changed can make life (that is: migration) much easier for the developers of the using subsystems. The techniques discussed here can also be applied for restructuring frameworks, for example, without provoking a high migration demand for the applications.

Agile methods negate the validity of large architecture designs (*Big* *The Architect's Role* *Upfront Design*). Consequently, this also implies some criticism of those who create such big architecture designs: the software architects. We do not believe that agile methods do away with the need for software architects. Of course, systems developed with agile methods do have a software architecture too, and of course this architecture must meet present requirements. In an agile project, the architecture can develop in the course of the project period, but in a more complex project somebody must monitor this development and alert others to emerging problems, i.e. architecture smells. Problems on the architecture level cannot efficiently be found by simply reading the code. Here, we clearly see the task of software architects in agile projects: they should not merely define the architecture, but first and foremost provide their architectural experience as a service to other team members.

The discussion about large refactorings certainly won't end with this *Outlook* book. The concepts and procedures presented here are derived from our project experiences. Their application in further projects will create new incentives for future discussion in the field of large refactorings.

Glossary

Acceptance Tests

Tests assuming the user's perspective that describe the system's acceptance criteria. Ideally, as large a number of these tests as possible shall be automatically executable. Of course there are limitations to this approach, particularly where the system's ergonomics is concerned. See Chapter 4.

Architecture Smell

An *architecture smell* is a smell that indicates a problem in the software architecture. Whether such a problem does exist or not must be verified through detailed testing. See also *Code Smell*. See Chapter 3.

Automated Refactoring

Automated refactorings are refactorings which are supported by an IDE and therefore can be executed automatically. The IDE guarantees that the system's behavior will remain unchanged. In consequence, automated refactorings are also always *safe refactorings*. Moreover, automated refactorings can be carried out in a very short time, regardless of the system's size.

Basic Refactoring

Refactorings that are primarily based on elementary, object-oriented constructs. Most refactorings introduced in Fowler (1999) are *basic refactorings*.

Code Smell

A *code smell* is a smell that indicates a problem in the code. Whether such a problem does exist or not must be verified with detailed testing. See also *Architecture Smell*. See Chapter 3.

Detailed Refactoring Plan

The *detailed refactoring plan* specifies details of a refactoring plan. It breaks down single refactoring steps into basic refactorings wherever this is feasible and analyzes the remaining modifications in detail. See Chapter 4.

Function Test

In the context of this book, the term *function test* is used synonymously with *acceptance test*.

Large Refactoring

Refactorings are considered *large refactorings* if the following criteria are met: they last longer than a day; they alter significant parts of the system; and they become visible to all developers involved in the project even while the refactoring is being executed. See Chapter 4.

Manual Refactoring

Manual refactorings are not supported by the IDE, which means that developers have to conduct them manually. They are the opposite of *automated refactorings*.

Merciless Refactoring

Merciless refactoring reflects a particular attitude and practice in software development: developers will not wait with refactorings until a system structure has degenerated. Instead, even minor flaws will be eradicated at once. See Chapter 2.

Merge

Merging is the incorporation of parallel changes to one and the same class. One can only partly automate this process with *merge tools*. See Chapter 4.

Merge Tool

Merge tools support the merging of two simultaneously altered versions of a class. They serve to point out differences between both classes and thus enable developers to either manually incorporate changes to one class in the other one or to let the merge tool automatically integrate these changes. However, automatic *merging* is not safe. It is possible that merging results in a non-compilable class. See Chapter 4.

Public Interface

The public interface of a class. The public interface includes all public methods and attributes. We must distinguish between *public* and *published API*. See Chapter 3.

Published API

The *published interface* of a component, which allows us to use the components' services. See Chapters 3 and 6.

Refactoring

Refactoring means changing the internal structure of a software in such a manner as to make it more understandable and changeable without affecting its visible behavior at runtime. See Chapter 2.

Refactoring Plan

A *refactoring plan* sketchily lists the single steps required in the course of a large refactoring. The plan is discussed by all members of a team. It should fit onto a flip chart and be posted publicly, i.e. clearly visible to all those involved in the project. The large refactoring's progress will be visualized on the refactoring plan (by checking off the single steps). The refactoring plan is further specified by the *detailed refactoring plan*. See Chapter 4.

Safe Refactoring

Safe refactorings are refactorings that can be executed without risking changes to the system's behavior or creating errors. If, for example, a tried step-by-step instruction for a refactoring is available (such as the *Mechanics* in Fowler, 1999), the refactoring can be carried out with no risk of creating new errors.

Save Point

A *save point* is one stage of a large refactoring at which the system structure is definitely better than prior to refactoring or, respectively, better than before the previous save point. See Chapter 4.

Smell

A *smell* hints at a potential problem in the system. See Chapter 3.

Unit Test

A *unit test* tests the components on which a system is based. In non-object-oriented imperative programming, single procedures and functions are tested. In object-oriented systems, classes and sets of classes are tested.

There are open source tools available that allow developing and running unit tests for almost every programming language. See Chapter 2.

Unsafe Refactoring

Refactorings for which no tried step-by-step instructions are available that would allow their safe, incremental execution. One example of an *unsafe refactoring* is the renaming of a class.

Index